200_ . THE URGENCIES OF ARCHI-TECTURAL THEORY

T0327161

A SYMPOSIUM CONVENED BY MARK WIGLEY

EDITED BY JAMES GRAHAM

GSAPP BOOKS, 2015

The GSAPP Transcripts
series is a curated record
of the major events that
take place at the Columbia
University Graduate School
of Architecture, Planning
and Preservation. Embrac-
ing the simple idea that
publication is the act of
making something public,
these books form a channel
through which the discourse
internal to the school
enters the public arena
of architectural media
and ideas, in the form of
edited talks and symposia.
In each case, the original
lectures and discussions at
the core of these books are
augmented with supplemen-
tary material, additional
imagery, and critical commentary, expanding their
debates and provocations
beyond the confines of the
lecture hall.

Rem Koolhaas
Preservation Is Overtaking Us
with a supplement by
Jorge Otero-Pailos (2014)

Yvonne Farrell
and Shelley McNamara
Dialogue and Translation:
Grafton Architects
with an essay by
Kenneth Frampton (2014)

2000+: The Urgencies of
Architectural Theory
ed. James Graham (2015)

Group Efforts: Changing
Public Space
ed. Gavin Browning, with an
essay by Mabel Wilson (2015)

Angelo Bucci
The Dissolution of Buildings
with an essay by
Kenneth Frampton (2015)

INTRODUCTION
James Graham

On April 18, 2014, sixteen historians, theorists, and practitioners of architecture gathered in Wood Auditorium at Columbia University's Graduate School of Architecture, Planning and Preservation (GSAPP). Their aim was to discuss the stakes of contemporary architectural theory as it has evolved since its supposed heyday in the late twentieth century. Marking the end of Mark Wigley's tenure as dean of GSAPP, the daylong symposium was in many ways a gathering of friends (new and old) with a shared interest in the theoretical problems and possibilities currently confronting an architectural discourse that relishes its connections to other fields, continually interrogates its own fundamental disciplinarity, and sees itself as a register of broader intellectual histories. This book is a document of those conversations.

The conference was convened by Wigley under the title of "2000+," a temporal hinge that swings both ways. This is not a return to futures past, but a look at the futurities latent within the disciplinary history of architecture—or, as Wigley puts it, the idea that "theory is the act of framing a discourse around a possible future." The immediate   → **p. 268** reference is a February 1967 issue of *Architectural Design* guest edited by John McHale, "scholar-artist" and "father of Pop," in Reyner Banham's memorable estimation, and a founder of the London-based Independent Group. At a moment of anxiety over the global spread of capitalism, the quality of urban life, and the future of the planet's inhabitability, this originary *2000+* posited a potential reconciliation between design and the technosocial milieu of the human environment. (McHale's atmospheric urgencies feel no less pressing today. To the chagrin of the reader encountering his text a half-century later, the science on carbon emissions was clear even in 1967—"no small argument in favor of banning *with* the bomb the comparably lethal uses of coal and other fossil fuels.")

Despite the specificity and visual richness of McHale's collected eco-futures, the editorial mission of *2000+* was not a project in prognostication but in *ways of looking forward*—the dispositions, to borrow a term advanced by Keller Easterling,

through which we understand theoretical → **p. 89**
urgency, rather than the concepts and concerns
themselves. The "2000" of McHale's title was subordinated to the "+," in that the forward trajectory might be more important than the temporal destination. By belatedly reclaiming this millenarian signpost, the most immediate suggestion of Wigley's title seems to be that a "futures-orientation," as McHale called it, might be intimately tied to a backward glance.

Those of us coming of architectural age in the early 2000s were generally taught that it was an era defined by a sense of "afterness"—after theory, as it were, postcritical, even post-post-modern in "our post-9/11 world." That vision of architectural discourse is now historical in its own right, but one of its continuing aftereffects is that "theory" in its many guises remains an underarticulated part of contemporary pedagogy and practice. As far as the historiography of theory's more self-conscious manifestations goes, the year 2000 also marked the last issue of *Assemblage*, a journal that did much to explicate and extend architecture's embrace of continental philosophy across the long 1990s, and which listed Mark Wigley on its editorial board for much of its run. It's telling that this particular A-word hardly appears here. While K. Michael Hays and Alicia Kennedy insisted at the time that "the end of *Assemblage* has nothing to do with the end of theory" (in an editorial dryly subtitled "The End of 'the end of'"), that didn't stop many theorists—and theorists they were—from deploying the journal's demise as a tidy punctuation mark that concluded architecture's so-called "theoretical turn." Thanks in large part to the journal's self-conscious commissioning of a celebratory issue that took its own finality as its main subject—its broad array of tributes and testimonials arranged alphabetically, it might be noted—this moment of closure generated an extensive bibliography across the early 2000s, a discursive "afterness" that began not after but within *Assemblage* 41 itself.

But what seemed for a few years like a moment of closure might instead have marked a subtler turn in how we think about architectural theory, one resistant to institutional organs like *Assemblage*. A recurring refrain among the contributors to this volume is that theory isn't simply constituted by a network of universities, thinkers, and journals, as significant of a role as media practices do play in producing discourse. Spyros Papapetros explores how concepts—in this case, the concept *ornament*, as teased out in Wigley's diverse writings on the subject—offer a kind of connecting → **p. 165** medium between the more confined ideas of authors, books, buildings, and epistemological systems. Theory is anything but immaterial, and can be located in all manner of disciplinary formations. Bernard Tschumi, in locating theory within seemingly untheoretical → **p. 221** moments of building like the tectonics of the envelope, argues that "theory is the opposite of 'common sense.'" In this way one might see theory embedded in any practice (of design or of scholarship) that follows Theodor Adorno's call, in his well-known "The Essay as Form," to militate against "the orthodoxy of thought."

A common misapprehension of architectural theory has been that it positions the architectural thinker at a remove from the realities of life. On the contrary, several of this book's contributors regard theory a conscious architectural being-in-the-world, to borrow a Heideggerian → **p. 301** phrase used here by Eyal Weizman. And there are plenty of urgent matters for us to confront. Mabel Wilson's work with the group Who Builds Your Architecture? points to the field's widespread failure to take responsibility for the labor that goes into making buildings—the ongo- → **p. 283** ing human rights catastrophe of the 2022 Qatar World Cup being the most drastic. Weizman's Forensic Architecture project dedicates itself → **p. 239** to understanding buildings as a kind of witness and creating the forums in which "facts" (of history, politics, human life) are constructed. Pelin Tan asks us to consider the possibilities of "transversal materialism," which might allow a more nuanced method of interpreting the effects of architectural objects—a proposition that she → **p. 216** explores by looking at the subjectivities produced in refugee camps. Architectural theory has always been a search for disciplinary blind spots, those matters of concern that fall squarely within our field's purview but are too often overlooked.

During his time as the dean of Columbia University's Graduate School of Architecture, Planning and Preservation, Wigley was known to remark that a building that rises to the level of discourse is one that produces a moment of hesitation. Not prevarication, not doubt, certainly not mystification or obscurity—hesitation. One could say as much for theory. Wigley himself here describes theory as a "flash" in which the world being constructed with the assistance of architecture is made visible, not as a revelation → p. 272, 274 but as a gap between subject and world. For Catherine Ingraham, one of critical theory's contributions to architecture is found in the act of Derridean deferral, where "every inquiry begets a hundred further inquiries and each veil pulled back reveals yet another → p. 61 world," a fruitful kind of temporizing that similarly looks for openings rather than closure. Mark Cousins considers Lewis Carroll's White Rabbit—the spirit animal of architects, forever → p. 48 fretting about being late—as an embodiment of architecture's persistent temporal neuroses. Felicity Scott, following on Etienne Balibar, proposes the vital function of "taking time," noting how urgencies themselves paradoxically "both mark the contemporaneity → p. 194 of, and serve as potential traps for, theory." At the moments of the most pressing need for thought, she argues, the role of the university is to create the space to reflect on the intersections of architecture and politics—not a replacement of action, but a supplement to it.

The writing of history is one such space. The texts contained here are not about recuperating the past, nor simply *understanding* the past for the edification of the present (a familiar, if banal, justification of history curricula in professional schools of architecture). The urgency of today's historian, these texts suggest, is to consider the concepts, media, and construction of facticity by which "the past" is constituted, and the ends to which that past is deployed. We are returned to the Parthenon in Lucia Allais's text, in which → p. 23 she explores how buildings participate in the construction of both memory and a body politic. We revisit the ninth century Buddhist temple of Borobudur with Mark Jarzombek—"a *modern* → p. 136 building," he insists, that demands we rethink our description of such architectural artifacts as "pre-Modern" and thus of concern only to preservationists and "pre-1750" historians. We are also urged to render visible those moments of architectural technology that have all too often fallen outside of the historian's purview, whether in Beatriz Colomina's meditation on architecture and sleep → p. 119 or in John Harwood's look at walls, wires, and the technics of mass media (even today in "our only apparently wireless world"). → p. 97

Finally, in the self-reflexive mode that is theory's most significant influence on any discipline, several of the essays here remind us that to see theory as circumscribed by symposia and books like these would overlook theory's real efficacy. Arindam Dutta cautions us that "theory is always contingent upon a situation," and that if we limit our understanding of theory to its most familiar → p. 76 instantiations, "we are not only actively obfuscating the various sites and vectors in which theory operates in a university, we are also obfuscating what universities do." And in her consideration of plaster casts as an architectural mass medium, Mari Lending makes note of Sylvia Lavin's diagnosis (in the closing months of 1999, for the millennially minded) of a "will to anthology." This is a → p. 147 tendency of collectors and organizers, whether of plaster casts or of discourse itself, exhibited by a spate of primers on architecture theory published across the 1990s—the two most notable of which were published by this very institution, Columbia University GSAPP's Office of Publications, then known as the Columbia Books on Architecture. Anthologies, for Lavin as for many others, are a museifying medium, historicizing and thus "completing" theoretical projects that were meant to be open and ongoing.

In that spirit, this book should be taken as a counter-anthology—not a lay of the land, not a compendium of essential texts, but a collective effort at articulating some of the eminently individual stakes of architectural thought. It is arranged alphabetically, as was the symposium that preceded it (with one exception brought on by the vagaries of PowerPoint, preserved in print form as a reminder that even purportedly non-schematic schema exist to be upended). As a nod to the day's collegiality, these sixteen essays are accompanied by edited transcripts of the conversations that followed each panel. That collegiality should itself be seen as an important act of theory. Ingraham at one point lamented that it was impossible for the entire audience to join the dinner afterward—that → **p. 57** the work of theory has always been to expand the number of voices at the table and to vigilantly combat its own perceived exclusivity. This book, then, might be seen as an inadequate invitation, not to read these authors but to think with them, to contest them and converse with them, and—when the time comes to look back and wonder what 2015 was about, anyway—to see *them* historically in turn.

Event poster designed by
MTWTF, 2014 →

2000+: THE URGENCIES OF ARCHITECTURAL THEORY—10AM, FRIDAY, APRIL 18, 2014—WOOD AUDITORIUM, AVERY HALL

LUCIA ALLAIS (Princeton University School of Architecture)

BEATRIZ COLOMINA (Princeton University School of Architecture)

MARK COUSINS (Architectural Association)

CATHERINE INGRAHAM (Pratt Institute)

MARK JARZOMBEK (MIT HTC)

MARI LENDING (Oslo Centre for Architectural Studies)

SPYROS PAPAPETROS

FELICITY SCOTT (Columbia University GSAPP)

PELIN TAN (Mardin Artuklu Üniversitesi)

BERNARD TSCHUMI (Columbia University GSAPP)

EYAL WEIZMAN (Goldsmiths, University of London)

MARK WIGLEY

MABEL WILSON (Columbia University GSAPP)

ARINDAM DUTTA (MIT HTC)

JOHN HARWOOD (Oberlin College)

COLUMBIA UNIVERSITY GRADUATE SCHOOL OF ARCHITECTURE, PLANNING, AND PRESERVATION—ARCH.COLUMBIA.EDU

JUST IN TIME: HENRI BERGSON AND THE INTELLECTUAL WORK OF CONSERVATION ON THE ACROPOLIS
Lucia Allais

Whenever an architectural urgency is declared, I am reminded of "The Architectural Cult of Synchronization," an article Mark Wigley published in 1999 to call for a new theory of temporality in architecture. Wigley's essay contained a threefold critique of the ways architectural time had been conceptualized in the twentieth century: By the avant-garde (with its obsession with newness and nowness), by historiographic grand priests (with their "eternal present"), and by computer-age prophets (with their fixation on dematerialization).[1] With characteristic understatement, Wigley dismissed them all, but especially the last, through a simple "perhaps." Did "buildings no longer hold memory," as millennial fear-mongers warned? "Perhaps," replied Wigley, "but the point has been made for a very long time now."[2] If this essay was not received as a scathing disciplinary indictment, however, it was because Wigley crafted all of its parts into a single compelling story, illustrating one of his more famous methodological pronouncements: that to do theory is to tell stories.*

Despite this unassuming stance, however, Wigley's article was incredibly timely. It prefigured a decade of scholarship reassessing the significance of the Independent Group.[4] It captured the renewed relevance of Alois Riegl's "Modern Cult of Monuments" essay from almost a century earlier, which has now been widely reread, its evocative title subjected to ever more clever variations.[5] And it also took a fresh look at the Parthenon: A building once admitted into modernist architectural discourse only via Le Corbusier's photographs and Eisenstein's films, it had, Wigley revealed, also been recast in plastic by John McHale. Since 1999, the relative urgency of each element in Wigley's polemic has been reconfigured: Projects have proliferated around the Parthenon and turned the Acropolis into an increasingly frenetic construction site. Conversely, a less rushed consideration of the effects of the digital redefinition of "memory" onto architecture is now ongoing. And somewhat unexpectedly, practices of architectural conservation once

*"I think it is useful to consider architectural theory as a kind of storytelling. It seems to me that that's what architectural theorists do, they tell stories about architecture."[3]

Lewis Hyde, photograph of the northern colonnade of the Parthenon, 2006

considered retrograde have become the newest reference point for contemporary architects who want to rethink the relationship of building and time.

Today I would also like to tell a story about temporality on the Acropolis. In Wigleyan fashion, this story will be but an alibi to ask what gets designated as "architectural theory" and where it gets located in history—in buildings and texts, but also in boardrooms and diagrams, in new designs and in preserved buildings. Theory, in my story, is of two kinds. On the one hand there are two competing theories of time (Bergsonism and Einstein's theory of special relativity); and on the other hand there is theory as the practice of scholars and thinkers—more specifically, the scholars and thinkers, including Henri Bergson and Albert Einstein themselves, who gathered in Geneva in the 1920s and 1930s under the resolutely vague banner of "international intellectual cooperation." I am interested in the architectural politics of passivity that was produced between these two theoretical registers, and I want to contrast it against more recent, willful, and familiar importations of Bergsonian thought into architectural discourse.

Bergson, you might recall, was a frequently dropped name in American architectural theory in the 1990s. Mostly, he appeared as a supporting actor to Gilles Deleuze, whose own *Bergsonism* was a key reference for digital architects seeking to transform architectural thinking and making.[6] Especially useful was the way Bergson's alternative theory of time also offered a redefinition of the terms, such as "body" and "image," by which architectural experience was understood. Bergson himself had settled on time as the crux of his philosophical system to undermine the Cartesian division between mind and body, proposing instead a theory of "duration" wherein human bodies and inert matter are philosophically indistinct, both ruled by "the undeniable fact of material succession."[7] Two diagrams from *Matter and Memory* were frequently reproduced.[8] Whereas "associationist" theories bisected the act of cognition by drawing an arbitrary distinction between past and future

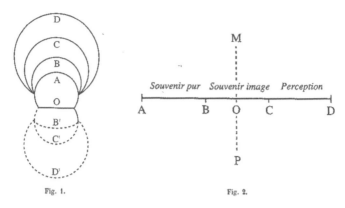

Fig. 1. Fig. 2.

Henri Bergson, "Fig. 1" and "Fig. 2" from _Matière et Memoire_ showing the "intellectual work" of "reflective perception" represented as "a circuit" (left) and "thought" represented as a "continuous line"

(along axis M–P), Bergson posited a cognitive continuum.[9] Past memories, current images, and future perceptions belonged along a single range of becoming (along axis A–D). And rather than assuming that perception was instantaneous (occurring in plane O, labeled "the present"), Bergson deepened its temporal span by describing the circuits (drawn as arcs) through which present experience reached back to past memories, and also looped forward with the "virtual" lines (drawn as dotted arcs) of the future action.

Attracted by this graphic mirroring and its attendant language of virtuality, digital architects tended to map this distinction of real and virtual onto either side of a computer screen. More generally, statements like "matter is...in great part the work of memory" gave Bergsonian philosophy a radical feel, apparently reversing the usual hierarchy between architecture and its representation, between "image" and "reality."[10] And more broadly still, the revolutionary potential that Deleuze read into Bergson's philosophy seemed particularly exciting for spatially minded philosophers because Bergson joined into one cognitive process the continuity with the past usually associated with historicism and monumentality, and the forward-looking projection usually associated with modernism and the avant-garde, apparently superceding both.*

In the field of architectural conservation, Bergson's name has a slightly different purchase, also derived from the virulent attack against the historical method that he delivered through his concept of "memory."* Bergson usually appears in conservation textbooks as part of a philosophical soup of post-Nietzschean "theories and concepts" that supposedly contributed to the emergence

*Elizabeth Grosz has argued eloquently for a project to "re-spatialize" both philosophy and architecture by reading Bergson *against himself*, in order, among other things, to confront architecture's continued deployment of "virtuality" by and for a gendered, disembodied, digital self. Significantly she begins with a critique of the way "architecture has tended to face time and temporality through the questions posed by history and through its response to the ravages of that history, its orientation towards monumentality."[11]

of a modern, anti-historicist turn in conservation in the twentieth century.[12] Here, by far the most frequently cited aspect of Bergson's work lies outside the text: It is his presidency of the League of Nations' Commission for Intellectual Cooperation (CIC), the institutional sponsor for the first-ever international conference devoted to architectural "conservation," the 1931 Athens Conference.[13]

The idea that some buildings belong to a timeless collective and therefore warrant a special politics of

*Throughout this text I have used *conservation* in deference to the League of Nations' own adoption of this term in 1931 and its continued use in internationalist discourse—instead of "preservation," which in the American context is more familiar and has a slightly more architectonic (as opposed to art-historical, museographic, or ecological) connotation. This is an imperfect but expedient solution for an essay in which I do not address the history of these semantic distinctions.

conservation was of course not new in 1931. But the Athens Conference produced the first diplomatic statement that there exists an international mandate for this politics, declaring in its "Conclusions" that monuments are the "property of mankind" and trusting the care of this property to the "community of states, which are wardens of civilization."[14] Mentioning Bergson's presence at the helm of the committee that sponsored this famous

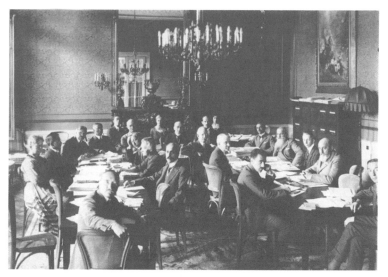

First meeting of the Comité de Coopération intellectuelle (CIC) at the League of Nations, in Geneva, May 1922, with Henri Bergson presiding and Gilbert Murray seated on his right

Athens Conference, then, has the effect of elevating conservation as branch of architecture: It ensures that the story of its appearance in international organization is a story not of debasement or bureaucratization, but of becoming philosophical. The stakes of this claim are high, allowing conservation to continue to be seen as the theoretical, idea-driven practice that it was when William Morris authored his SPAB Manifesto in 1877.[15] Similarly, the "Conclusions" of the Athens Conference have been retroactively called a "Charter," in part to compete with the much more famous CIAM-authored *Athens Charter* of 1933.

What, then, are we to make of the oft-cited historical detail that Bergson, a philosopher at the height of his fame as a theorist of temporality, was at the origins of the genre of cultural diplomacy that eventually ushered architectural conservation into the international order? To be sure, we could find an affinity between Bergson's well-known philosophical preference for time over space in the League of Nations' institutional mandate and cultural agenda, which were always articulated in temporal rather than spatial terms. The League of Nations was invented in 1919 not to resolve specific geopolitical issues but rather to regularize the rhythm of international relations. Two things were new about this so-called new diplomacy—its regularity and its publicity.[16] In contrast to the old diplomatic system, with its secret envoys and bilateral pacts, the new diplomacy would place nation-states in what one historian has called "a permanent state of conference."[17] We can think of the Athens Conference as an attempt to apply the rhythm of the new diplomacy to monumental objects. Just as the League would regularize state relations, so the Conference proposed to regularize monument maintenance.[18] And in the Athens Conference's famous "Conclusions," we can detect this push for regularization in a language of witnessing. Monuments were to be protected because they were "concrete testimonies of all ages of civilization," and which would in turn help to coalesce a political constituency. "The general public" was to be educated "with a view to associating [the public] in the protection of the testimonies of any civilization."[19] The political mission of an international architectural monument, then, was to produce a kind of temporal suspension, becoming a site of perpetual witnessing in which an international public could be born.

But to trace a more specific connection between Bergson and this architectural delegation of international authority means navigating the history of an intricate and evolving bureaucratic structure that begins when Bergson was first appointed in 1922. There was not one single committee devoted to monuments protection at the League; rather, they were subject to overlapping agendas and committees, all acting under the common umbrella of Intellectual Cooperation. This group was heterogeneous—it included philosophers like Bergson, scientists Einstein and Marie Curie, art historians Henri Focillon and Josef Strzygowski, writers Karel Capek and Paul Valéry, among many others—and its channels of cooperation were also diverse. Just to trace the link between the League and the Athens Conference, we have to go through the CIC itself, an Institute in Paris, an Arts and

Letters Sub- (later Permanent) Committee, a Museums Office, and finally a Monuments group, which was to be formed in the wake of the Athens Conference, but actually never met.[20]

What all of these groups had in common, however, was that they conceived of themselves in frankly organicist terms as an international "mind" that could direct the League's diplomatic "body." To convince themselves they were not just a mandarin

The CIC on an outing in Thoiry, France, July 25, 1930; Albert Einstein is seated third from left, Gilbert Murray is fourth

elite, these intellectuals regularly compared their "intellectual labor" to that of the industrial workers of the International Labor Office.[21] They also talked constantly about their own bodies. Bergson's body became an especially admired political instrument during a particularly fractious period in 1925, when his "moral authority" became essential to the survival of the group. One art historian reported that Bergson "came to Geneva to preside for days on end over the commission's work" despite having been beset by "a mysterious illness" that left him "afflicted by fevers that reached above forty, and tortured by throbbing pains throughout his limbs." According to this witness, it was "a spectacle worthy of an ancient philosopher," with Bergson "lying prone and congested on a bed, eyes glowing with fever but showing no signs of suffering."[22] It was as if, in a rather literal application of Bergson's theory of material duration, the expenditure of his bodily pain was a measure of the difficult labor of birthing a new cultural diplomacy.

Yet by 1931 Bergson had long stepped down as the head of the CIC, so even if we believed this organicist myth no connection exists between his body and the Athens Conference. Might we then see a more diffuse theoretical influence at play? For example, might we see an analogy between the predictive nature of Bergson's theory of intellection and the equally anticipatory powers the CIC claimed for itself when devising its program? As president, in 1922 Bergson commissioned a draft "International Convention for the Regulation of Archaeological Excavations" that, with much hubris, would have required archaeologists to divine what possible objects might lie underground by asking them to start by creating "a list of such archeological treasures that have *yet to be brought to light*."[23] Here, the cognitive processes posited by Bergson as internal to the mind aligned with the regulatory mindset of a fact-finding group. This alignment is all the more problematic in that Bergson was a harsh critic of such scientific prediction, for instance as he found it to be motivating the entire field of evolutionary biology.[24]

If we pursue the question of whether Bergson would have allowed us to speak in this manner of an analogy between his philosophy and the bureaucratic processes of world governance, once again we arrive at a discussion of temporality—not in the sense that we are led to speculate philosophically about time, but rather that we encounter a philosophical discussion that took place in the mid-1920s, in a number of public venues, between Bergson and Einstein on the nature of time.[25] This notorious feud is remembered for having established a lasting opposition between "the philosopher's time and the scientist's time" and has recently reemerged in the field of Science Studies with such relevance that Bruno Latour—in what can certainly be taken as a performative turn in theory—has reenacted it with various interlocutors.[26]

Nowhere are the motivations behind Bergson's commitment to intellectual cooperation more evident than in this debate with Einstein. The feud revolved around Einstein's so-called twin paradox, a thought experiment in which twins carrying clocks travel at different speeds and return with clocks marking different times, despite having been away the same duration. Einstein used the experiment as proof of his theory of special relativity; Bergson claimed on the contrary that time may be understood as relative only through mental willfulness. Note that the original disagreement was not about the relativity of time, but rather about who was better poised to theorize it. What was at stake, to put it another way, was the distinction between clocks and subjects as bearers of universal standards, a distinction that Bergson had already made in the context of the CIC's cultural diplomacy. There was a difference, Bergson insisted, between agreement achieved by technical commissions that dealt with "things" (such "hygiene or the railroad") and agreement as reached between "persons" (such as delegates on the committee).[27] Einstein believed that intellectual cooperation should model itself on scientific internationalism, a movement that had since the late nineteenth century sponsored the sharing of scientific information, the standardization of units, and so forth.[28] Bergson, on the other hand, felt that philosophers were especially well-suited to pacify international tensions and that the CIC should therefore facilitate a kind of meta-political conversation.[29]

If we want to trace the intellectual origins of conservation at the League, then, we cannot fixate on Bergson alone. Instead we have to see architectural conservation becoming a focus of international diplomatic activity in part through a committee that debated—but never resolved—the question of whether agreement should be achieved through "things" or "people." It is my argument, here and in the larger work from which I am drawing, that this 1920s debate around timekeeping technologies was reconfigured at the 1931 Athens Conference in an international debate about architectural objects with timekeeping properties.[30] The Athens Conference gathered over a hundred speakers from a wide variety of fields: architects, planners, archaeologists, curators, scientists and politicians, who met in Athens over the course of four days and then set off on a ten-day cruise. Here I focus only on one small episode, which occurred on the last day of the formal event.

Nikolaos Balanos giving a presentation at the Athens Conference on October 25, 1931

The last session of the Athens Conference took place on the Acropolis and was led by the architect in charge of the site, Nikolaos Balanos, who gave a tour of the work he had completed over the course of his career, including the restoration of the Erechtheum, and the lifting back up of the Parthenon's north colonnade. Balanos then described his proposal for the Parthenon's south side, and invited the conference's experts to pronounce their opinion on this project. The "Conclusions" record that they unanimously endorsed Balanos's project of performing "no restoration beyond anastylosis," defining *anastylosis* as the "reinstatement of any original fragments that may be recovered" and the use of "recognizable new materials" to support these fragments.[31] In ancient Greek, the term ἀναστήλωσις means "the erection of a temple"; its modern return to mean "re-erection" appears to have been native to the Athenian archaeological scene and can be tied to Balanos's appointment to the Acropolis by an international committee of archaeologists in the wake of an earthquake in 1894.[32]

But *anastylosis*, this apparently stabilizing term, was in fact fraught with difficulties. The unpublished transcripts of the conversation reveal that every aspect of Balanos's method was challenged.[33] He had to admit, for instance, that some column drums he found on the northern grounds might have been moved from south to north. The deliberations also foregrounded the constructive nature of his technique, and in fact, modern materials rather than ancient artifacts dominated the discussion. What kind of continuity could be designed between the new and the old? Balanos indicated that he had originally intended to use marble to replace missing drums, as he had done at the Erechtheum. But since the new marble would never match the old, for the Parthenon Balanos had switched to constructing new pieces out of a combination of stone and cement stained to look like marble. He had also fastened old and new drums with iron connectors, in the same I-shaped slots where the ancient Greeks had used metal.

Objections to these methods abounded. Some pointed out that new iron would corrode, expand, and cause the ancient marble to crack. Others rehearsed the hydrometric dangers of abutting stone against concrete. A variety of alternative solutions were discussed—lead, bronze, or stainless iron; a different concrete; another marble. But Balanos was deaf to these objections and referred to his system as a kind of cladding that could

Nikolaos Balanos, the northern colonnade photographed during restoration; 11th stone drum removed from the fourth column (top) and new concrete drum core (bottom)

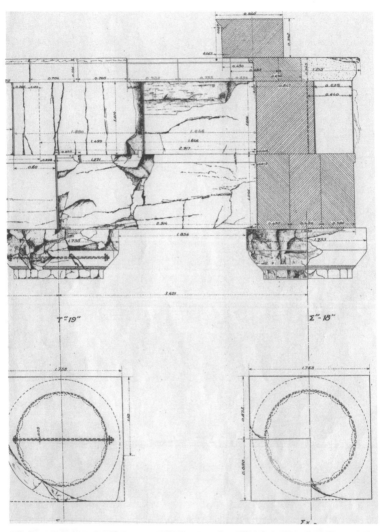

Nikolaos Balanos, detail from entablature and capitol (interior elevation) of the northern colonnade of the Parthenon

be replaced.[34] Time has proven Balanos tragically wrong, so to speak, and his restoration caused exactly the kind of damage the conference predicted. The new iron ties corroded and cracked the stone. He had also been cavalier with the ancient pieces, cutting away at old fragments to fit them against new ones like puzzle pieces, and the clean diagonal lines with which Balanos regularized the edges eventually gave cracks a pattern along which to propagate.[35]

Why, then, despite having essentially predicted these problems, did the conference endorse Balanos's work? Certainly, the opportunity to elevate *anastylosis* into an international archaeological norm was too attractive for this meeting of internationalists to pass up. By codifying a technical standard, the conference engaged in the kind of scientific internationalism that Einstein promoted to create shared norms. But a careful review of the language of the "Conclusions" shows that this endorsement was only made in the "special case" of the Parthenon.[36] The Parthenon became an example at the same time as it became an exception. In this sense, the Athens Conference approved not only a *technique* for temporal stabilization but also a specific *project* belonging in a temporal arc of international activity at the Acropolis.

The project to re-erect the southern colonnade of the Parthenon dated to 1928, and it is crucial to note Balanos proposed to treat the south differently than the north. Whereas on the northern side enough original drums had been found to rebuild each column in its entire height, up to the architrave, on the south only a few drums had survived, and strict anastylosis would only allow partial columns to stand. This difference between the treatment of the two façades had already been extensively debated among the international cultural circles of the American and German Archaeological Institutes, and the presence of the League's delegates in Athens had been timed so that the *new* diplomacy could also weigh in.

The Athens delegates, in other words, were only the latest in a string of international visitors brought to "witness" the ongoing Parthenon project, and they arrived *just in time*

Lucia Allais

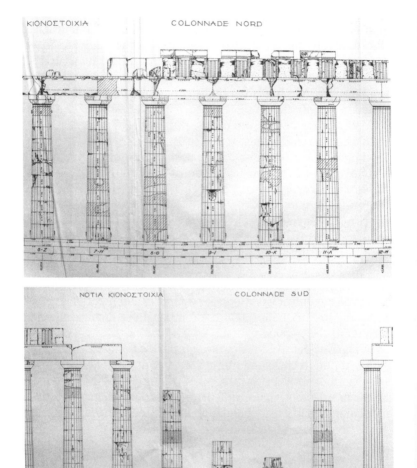

Nikolaos Balanos, details from elevations of the Parthenon anastylosis; northern colonnade (top) and southern colonnade (bottom)

to certify and authorize the latest developments. Indeed, a few months before the Conference met, Bergson's successor as CIC president, the British classicist Gilbert Murray, had already visited the Acropolis and approvingly written to Balanos and his American backers. There was "a case for having raised the North and leaving the South down," Murray wrote, but after visiting the site he ultimately felt that "the imaginative assistance to be got" from restoring the south side would "be worth a great deal."[37]

Imaginative assistance: This, then, was to be the intellectual work facilitated by Balanos's restored Parthenon. That Murray proposed to use monuments to "assist" an international public in constructing a mental "image" is less banal of a statement than you might think. Consider the alternative, that one side of the monument would be given "an image" and the other not. Instead, Murray argued that if one side of the monument could be redesigned to project an image of constructive completion, the other side could be designed to reflect destruction or incompletion. Balanos and his donors had also made this distinction, talking about these two colonnades as bearing two kinds of memories. To quote from one of Balanos's supporters, the American newspaperman John Hudson Finley, "There will thus remain...on the one side a memory of the Parthenon *as the world has known it* for two hundred years and on the other the *longer memory*."[38] The reference, here, was to two epochs of the monument's history—before and after the explosion of gunpowder that had toppled so many of its columns in 1687. But these two memories were not referred to as separate, discrete, or sequential; rather, they had what can only be described as overlapping durations.

Again, it may seem unsurprising to conclude that international cultural officials designated the Parthenon as an object that could "hold memories." Commemoration is after all one of the main functions of monumental architecture. But this memory-making capacity takes on new meaning in light of the peculiar temporal dynamic of the new cultural diplomacy. Certainly this talk of designing memories was consistent with a Bergsonian ontology, in which the world is itself composed of images, and memory is a specific kind of image that jumps between past, present, and future. Memory was the concept through which Bergson redefined the role of the body in the act of cognition. "The task of the body," Bergson wrote, is "not to store up recollections" but rather "to select, in order to bring back to distinct consciousness, the *useful memory*, that which may complete and illuminate the present situation...with a view to ultimate action."[39] This language could easily have been used to describe the goal of international intervention at the Acropolis—not only to authorize certain techniques, as Einstein would have it, but also to help "select the memory" that would be most "useful" in promoting international "action," as Bergson might. Here, in these unguarded judgments, produced and transmitted behind the scenes of an international conference and confirmed in its official pronouncements, we find one of the most influential theorizations of the Parthenon of the twentieth century. Wielding a Bergsonian lexicon and moved by an Einsteinian cause, cultural diplomats helped redesign this architectural object on the cusp of its entrance into the official international imaginary.

The politics of this international memory selection was conservative, in that it relied on the architecture to do the acting, and valued continuity over radical breaks. Again, I don't mean that the monument was made to project an *image* of historical continuity. *Anastylosis* as a technique partakes in a modernist aesthetics of collage and discontinuity. Rather, and more complicatedly, the monument was redesigned to exist in a continuum that could absorb temporal differences. Recall that the task of the conference was to coalesce an international public: Here all of the intellectual "labor" of creating this public was delegated to the architectural object, in the hope that generations of visitors might glean a positive political message from its ability to convey overlapping memories.

As we revisit our assumptions about architectural theory and its political charge, then, we might also become attuned to the more reactionary valences of Bergson's philosophy, especially when its eloquent abstraction is embraced with techno-scientific zeal.* We might see that the lines and planes and axes through which Bergson was fond of representing "the present" are not always unassuming abstractions, that they do not always correspond innocently to the plane of a façade, to the threshold of a computer screen, or to a path leading us through a felicitous experience of "the now." Rather, they stand also for a temporal suspension that produces a spatial exception, and in which we too often locate ourselves, safely, as we wait for architecture to act on our behalf.

*Max Horkheimer already voiced a suspicion of Bergsonian philosophy on these grounds in 1934. "Bergson developed his metaphysics at the same time as a positivistic theory of science," he wrote. "The extent to which both support and condition each other is testimony to their close relationship." More recently Orit Halpern has argued that Bergsonian temporality was predictive not only in itself but also of later developments in cybernetics, showing how Bergson "contributed to the very possibility of technicizing perception," by providing both an "affective kernel" and a memory of "older disciplinary sciences" in Norbert Wiener's work, and thereby helping to produce the "devolution inward" that lies at the core of the postwar computational paradigm.[40]

Delegates of the Athens Conference seated on the steps of the Parthenon, October 25, 1931

41

1   Mark Wigley, "The Architectural Cult of Synchronization," in *Journal of Architecture*, vol. 4, no. 4 (1999), 409–35.

2   Wigley, "The Architectural Cult of Synchronization," 9.

3   Mark Wigley, "Story-Time," in *Assemblage* 27, Tulane Papers: The Politics of Contemporary Architectural Discourse (August 1995): 80–94.

4   This reassessment was spearheaded by a special issue of *October* in which Wigley's own text reappeared; see *October* 94, The Independent Group (Autumn 2000).

5   Alois Riegl, "The Modern Cult of Monuments: Its Character and Development" [1903], trans. Kurt W. Forster and Diane Ghirardo, in *Oppositions* 25 (Fall 1982), 30–51. Later interpretations include Thordis Arrhenius, "The Cult of Age in Mass Society," in *Future Anterior*, vol. 1, no. 1 (Spring 2004), 74–80 and Mario Carpo, "The Postmodern Cult of Monuments," in *Future Anterior*, vol. 4, no. 2 (Winter 2007), 51–60.

6   Gilles Deleuze, *Bergsonism* [1966], trans. Hugh Tomlinson and Barbara Habberjam (New York: Zone Books, 1988). One characteristic appearance of both Deleuze and Bergson can be found in *ANY* 19-20: The Virtual House (1997), which included a translation of Deleuze's "The Actual and the Virtual" and Erik Oger's "Mirrors, Ghosts and Open Zones: Virtuality in Bergson's Philosophy."

7   Henri Bergson, *Creative Evolution* [1897], trans. Arthur Mitchell (Mineola, NY: Dover, 1998), 10–11.

8   Henri Bergson, *Matter and Memory* [1911], trans. Nancy Margaret Paul and W. Scott Palmer (New York: Zone Books, 1998).

9   Under this term Bergson included Cartesian and Kantian idealisms, but also phenomenology and assorted materialisms. Bergson, *Matter and Memory*, 182.

10   The original quote is in Bergson, *Matter and Memory*, 182. See Sanford Kwinter's *Architecture of Time: Toward a Theory of the Event in Modernist Culture* (Cambridge, MA: MIT Press, 2002), where several chapters are epigraphed with Bergsonian statements of this nature.

11   Elizabeth Grosz, "The Future of Space: Toward an Architecture of Invention," *Architecture from the Outside* (Cambridge, MA: MIT Press, 2001), 111; originally published in *Anyhow*, ed. Cynthia Davidson (Cambridge, MA: MIT Press, 1999), and "Embodying Space: an Interview," in *Architecture from the Outside*, 3–30; originally published in *Aedon*, vol. 4, no. 1 (1996), 47–64.

12   See "Theories and Concepts," in Jukka Jokilehto, *A History of Architectural Conservation* (Oxford: Butterworth-Heinemann, 1999), 213–44; and John H. Stubbs and Emily G. Makkas, *Architectural Conservation* (New York: Wiley, 2011), 55.

13   See for instance Jokilehto's account of the Athens meetings in *A History of Architectural Conservation*, 284.

14   "Conclusions de la Conférence," published as an appendix in Office International des Musées, *La Conservation des Monuments d'Art et d'Histoire* [henceforth *CMAH*] (Paris: OIM, 1933), 405 (French), 450 (English).

15   William Morris, "Society for the Protection of Ancient Buildings: Manifesto" [1877], republished in *From William Morris: Building Conservation and the Arts and Crafts Cult of Authenticity 1877-1939*, ed. Chris Miele, *Studies in British Art* 14 (Yale University Press, 2005), 337–40.

16   See Cornelia Novari, "The New Diplomacy and the New State," in *Internationalism and the State in the Twentieth Century* (London: Routledge, 2000), 252–69.

17   Harold Nicolson, *The Old Diplomacy and the New* (London: Davies Memorial Institute of International Studies, 1961).

18   "Conclusions de la Conférence," 451–52.

19   "Conclusions de la Conférence," 405 (French), 450 (English).

20   Jean-Jacques Renoliet offers a history of intellectual cooperation in *L'Unesco oubliée* (Paris: Sorbonne, 1999); see also Jan Kolasa, *International Intellectual Cooperation* (Wroclaw: Travaux de la Société des Sciences et des Lettres, 1962).

21   The CIC gained a reputation as inextricably elitist and politically powerless as soon as it was created, an assessment largely borne out by historians. See for instance T.V. Sathyamurthy, "Changing Concepts of Intellectual Cooperation," in *International Review of Education*, vol. 9, no. 4 (1963–64), 386–95.

22   George Oprescu, "Bergson-Oprescu: Correspondence Inédite," in *Romanian Journal of Sociology* (January–December 1991), 117.

23   Emphasis mine. "Résolution by the Chairman on the subject of Archaeological Research" (August 4, 1922), in Committee for Intellectual Cooperation, "Minutes of the First Session, Geneva, August 1–5, 1922," IICI Archives/UNESCO Archives, 30.

24   Bergson articulated this critique of "radical mechanism" via Laplace in *Creative Evolution*, 38.

25   Jimena Canales provides and extensive analysis of this debate and its stakes in *The Physicist and the Philosopher* (Princeton: Princeton University Press, 2015). See also Jimena Canales, "Einstein, Bergson, and the Experiment that Failed" *MLN* 120 (2005), 1,168–91 and "Of Twins and Time" in "Neutrality in twentieth-century Europe," edited by Rebecka Lettevall, Geert Somsen and Sven Widmalm (New York: Routledge, 2012), 243–71.

26   Two instances are "Three Days of Making Time: Revisiting the Debate Between Bergson and Einstein" (Institut für Raumexperimente, February 9–11, 2011), www.raumexperimente.net/cat/conversation; and "Le débat Bergson/Einstein" (Centre Pompidou, June 21, 2010), www.centrepompidou.fr/cpv/resource/caj8oKR/rj7A79j.

27   Henri Bergson, letter to Oscar Halecki (1924), (SdN registry, 1924, Coop Int., 13c/33877/33877/IX), IICI Archives/UNESCO Archives.

28   On scientific internationalism, see Jean-Jacques Salomon, "The Internationale of Science," in *Science Studies*, vol. 1, no. 1 (January 1971), 23–42; Brigitte Schroeder-Gudehus, "Probing the Master-Narrative of Scientific Internationalism," in *Neutrality in Twentieth-Century Europe* (London: Routledge, 2012), 19–44. On Einstein's pacifism after World War I, see Otto Nathan and Heinx Norden, *Einstein on Peace* (New York: Simon & Schuster, 1960), 58–89.

29   On Bergson's political life see Philippe Soulez, "Les philosophes dans la mêlée," in *Vingtième Siècle* 10 (Apr–Jun 1986), 122–24 and *Bergson Politique* (Paris: PUF, 1989).

30   The Athens Conference is the subject of a more extensive analysis in my forthcoming book, from which this text is adapted.

31   "Compte rendu des délibérations de la Conférence d'Athènes au sujet de l'Anastylose des monuments de l'Acropole," *CMAH*, 452–53. "Proceedings of the Conference on the Anastylosis of the Acropolitan Monuments," *CMAH*. "VI. The Technique of Conservation," in "Conclusions de la Conférence," 450.

32   "ναστήλ-ωσις, εως, *setting up of a monument*, Ptol. Heph. ap. Phot. *Bibl.* p. 147B." Henry George Liddell and Robert Scott, *A Greek–English Lexicon* (1940), revised and accessed online in the Perseus Digital Library, Tufts University. Balanos claimed to have coined the neologism in 1925, in *Les monuments de l'Acropole: relèvement et conservation* (Paris: Massin et Lévy, 1935), 7, fn. 1–2.

33   *Conférence Internationale d'Experts pour l'étude des Problèmes relatifs à la protection et la conservation des monuments d'art et d'histoire: Procès-Verbaux*, LoN Archives/OIM.4.1932, 6.

34 *Conférence Internationale d'Experts.* Here I provide only an abbreviated discussion of the Athens Conference debate. A more in-depth description, with appropriate citations and references, appears in the book-length study.

35 For a devastating critique of Balanos's methods and its effects, see Richard Economakis, *Acropolis Restoration: The CCAM Interventions* (London: Academy, 1994), 323–26.

36 The conference "refrained from expressing their general opinion" on his methods. "Proceedings of the Conference on the Anastylosis of the Acropolitan monuments," *CMAH*, 453.

37 Murray was cited in a Letter from Walter Lippman to John Hudson Finley (April 19, 1931), Finley Papers, New York Public Library.

38 Letter from Finley to Raymond Fosdick (September 13, 1933), Finley Papers, New York Public Library.

39 Bergson, *Matter and Memory*, 182.

40 See Max Horkheimer, "Bergson's Metaphysics of Time" [1934], trans. Peter Thomas and Stewart Mertin, in *Radical Philosophy* 131 (May–June 2005), 9–19; Orit Halpern, "Dreams for Our Perceptual Present: Temporality, Storage, and Interactivity in Cybernetics," in *Configurations*, vol. 13, no. 2 (Spring 2005), 283–319.

THE ARCHITECT AND THE RABBIT
Mark Cousins

The urgencies of theory? The title certainly wasn't there to help the contributor. It's like a certain class of titles of books or conferences—it's not that it doesn't have a "plain" meaning; it's that it seems to have only a plain meaning. One wants to lean over and whisper in someone's ear, "But what is it really about?" Does theory have an urgency and does it come in the plural? About this point I put the question to one side and returned to marking papers.

Later, months later, the editor called to ask where the paper was. I started lying too quickly by saying it would have been delivered had it not been for illness, preparing new courses, etc., but that now he could have it very soon. He seemed quite sanguine perhaps because, although he hadn't gotten the essay, he had deliberately caught me in an obligation to reply to him. But he also probably realized it would still take him more time to get it out of me. We began an irregular correspondence in which I would give him a brief digest of illness, bereavements, all of which had conspired to make me...late.* The urgencies of theory were becoming more *real* if no more intelligible. The essay would simply have to perform this lateness to the point where lateness ends. After all, it would be about something that is a portion of every architect, the experience of fear, of being late. I use the term *lateness* bluntly. I do not mean *belatedness*, nor architecture in late capitalism, nor death and the late architect. It's just about being late. Like the rabbit.

*Of course, these were also lies. They hid the fact, or rather, didn't hide the fact, that I just returned to something else, or more precisely, I returned to something else I wasn't doing.

"Oh dear! O dear! I shall be too late," says the rabbit, and again, when turning a corner. "O my ears and whiskers, how late it is getting." He appears again exclaiming, "Oh the Duchess, the Duchess. Oh! Won't she be savage if I've kept her waiting?" The combination of being late, of feeling guilt, and expecting punishment are established briefly by Lewis Carroll and can obviously be extended to the architect. The rabbit doesn't need a watch to tell him the time, but to repeat to him that he is late.

But the watch ticks an ambivalence. He is late, so he must hurry. But beneath this there is a more dreadful possibility: He is already too late, he has already missed the event that has yet to happen—let us call it the deadline—he has already missed the lifeline that is withdrawn by the passing of the deadline. The rabbit (and the architect) move between the two levels of being late, driven by the exhausting hope that hurrying can make them catch up. But it seems that the rabbit's lateness is established by not only being late for the duchess, but by the rabbit's more basic relation to time. The rabbit isn't really inside measured time. The rabbit is behind time itself, trying to catch up with time itself that continuously vanishes like the back of a missed train. It is not so much that a train has been missed. It is the whole world. The attempt to catch up with time itself is no simple adventure. After all, it is not a question of the rabbit having a bad reputation for timekeeping. "Oh that rabbit. That rabbit's always late." Nor does anyone say, "Oh Rabbit's finally here. Let's get started." The rabbit is not just late for meetings. He is late for time. He passes the deadline without ever meeting it. He is marooned in time's own past. *I am late, I was late, I will be late* is how the rabbit conjugates time.

The rabbit and the architect share a relation to time that doesn't seem to be recognized by philosophy. Certainly there is no text with a title like "Being (Late) and Time." My remarks flow from the same observations you will have made. The rabbit's response to being and fearing being late is to hurry even if it is not quite clear what hurrying is. In economic terms, "hurrying" is the increase in what can be done within a limit, usually of time. Most "hurrying" involves the modification of the limit, an extension or postponement of the limit. The most obvious forms would be working faster or working longer, the intensification of work or the extension of work. Both would increase the time available while still respecting the limit. Put like this it can seem like a rational solution, adjusting the rate and length of work to the scarce resource of time. But it already nurtures the fantasy that this formula means that one is already late before starting and that the solution is an emergency, an exception in the normal world of organizing time. In this sense, architects come to regard their relation to time as exceptional, in which the "always already" sense of being late becomes a source of guilt.

We see architectural students systematically trained to catch the fever of urgency, of always catching up, of getting down to it. It reaches its apotheosis in the fact that on campuses across the world the architecture school is open all night. Architectural students are convinced that this is no more than is demanded by their reality. Without this concession they surely could not complete their assignment. But by working in this way they stir up the guilt. On this count, working through the night on a frequent basis is a badge of commitment and working off of that guilt. Across the planet, in different cities, in different time zones, in the flickering global sequence of lighting conditions that have replaced day and night, the architectural school is open. Surely other schools might have claimed that their disciplines were just as urgent; they close shop at the end of the working day. Architecture has become the discipline that never sleeps. Architects have designed very few beds though they have designed many daybeds and *chaises longues*. Obviously, they are for people who haven't slept at night.

See Mark Wigley's account of architecture students at night → p. 277

See Beatriz Colomina's discussion of architects and beds → p. 120

This has all been concerned with the architect's relation to time. Note that that is the architect's relation to time, not the relation of architecture to time that is an entirely different matter. The former complex involves elements of the fear of time but a fear that, where the architect is concerned, there is not enough. It involves the fear of a deadline and the use of time both to meet it and to delay it. Hurrying and postponing have become twinned. Fulfillment and its deferment have gotten inside each other. This complex can be regarded as a symptom. It exploits individual traits of nearly everyone since everyone is nearly the rabbit. But it has molded them into the web of design. It is a symptom that exploits common human psychical life, but that is then fitted into the practice of architectural design. The neurotic potential lies in the architectural student, but the manifest symptoms belong to the order of a practice. Around time, there is architectural misery. In which case we might think that the question would be, how can this symptom be cured? But before threatening anyone with a cure, we should ask what the symptom, considered globally, is doing. It might be that whatever discomfort the symptom causes, it plays a positive role in the practice itself. Freud had something of this in mind when he joked that one should be wary of psychoanalyzing a surgeon, for one might cure him of his sadism.

We normally assume a plasticity of psychical life and relate the peculiar characteristics of individual neurosis to the determining "history" of the individual. But we still recognize typical neurotic formations—obsessionality, perversity, hysteria, etc. Perhaps above that there is a layer of "professional" neurosis. Starting with the sadism of Freud's surgeon, we have all met hysterical actors, obsessional train-spotters, perverse bankers, etc. In a sense the neurotic character of the individual "matches" the very specific tasks that characterize the particular practice. Probably this is widely noticed. But even more significant here is when a practice enables the individual to displace his or her symptoms into another realm, so freeing the individual from the weight of neurotic pain in being exploited by the demands of the particular practice. I think the architect, and certainly the architectural student, fall into this category. All their problems of time can be seen as a displacement, almost translation, of their problem with space. This would create the following picture. Architectural practice needs to exploit the spatial unconscious life of the architect. This would be too chaotic and painful, too mad, if it were direct and unmediated. Yet the architect is able, at least in part, to export, to displace spatial symptoms onto a temporal one. The anguish and misery of the architect's temporal life is the conflicts of his or her spatial life fought out on another terrain. It is even a defense mechanism to preserve their positive neurotic spatialities.

In effect, we should see whether the formation of the architect's time complex has a spatial analogy. The rabbit fears he doesn't have enough time to get to where he should be at a certain time. At the very same time we can detect that the architectural student uses this attempt to also undermine it by creating more time (all night) as a further opportunity for procrastination. The origins of procrastination lie, paradoxically, in the conviction that "I need to wait to start until I have only exactly enough time to finish it, *so I don't have to think about it, just do it*." There are two levels of "lateness" here: The first and conventional signification is that the rabbit hurries, in effect to produce more time. The rabbit has a problem of too little time. The architectural student thinks that this is true for him or her also. But hidden, lurks the opposite: Design is so painful to think out that I will wait to start until I have no more time to think, just to do it unthinkingly. The architect, it seems, has too little time and too much time all at the same time. If we read this as a displacement from space to time, then we produce the formula that the architect has both too little space and too much.

We should see whether the hypothesis of the displacement from space to time has any plausibility. We can see that the rabbit's sense of being late is a kind of pressure. When we are late we can't really think of anything else; the time that is left to us is the only thing that matters. We are distracted and we complain that we cannot attend to anything. This pressure, or as some people call it, stress, is thought to result from having to attend to at least two things at once. It is widely associated with "work" or even "being at work," a fantasy in which different voices call to us, demanding the fulfillment of different tasks and leading to a painful conflict of mind in which it is difficult to do anything. This is a common opinion despite the fact that what we call work is not very difficult, not noticeably hurried. But if you tell someone that they look rested and relaxed they will never say, "Yes, I've been spending a lot of time at the office." But to the architectural student, his or her wishes for the success of the design is accompanied by the sense that the very surface of the design, what was a blank sheet of paper that mirrored an empty site, is already linked with constraints, anything that enters the space of design from the brief to the invisible but spatial regulations. The blank sheet of paper, the representation of space, is already strewn with the invisible structures of the starting point. There is not enough space, and the space that is there is not space enough. That is why, at least initially, students are indulged by setting as few constraints as possible. In the rest of their education they can be seen to be the unchallenged prince or princess of the projects. Their portfolio belongs to them and no one suggests that it belongs to architecture. But already the shadows are falling on this scene of narcissism.

This space, the space of design, is also too big. From antiquity, architecture has been burdened with a division of the object into a whole and parts. Design is enjoined to keep both in mind and to continuously adjust each to the other. This might be intelligible from the point of view of a completed design or a building itself. But it is very difficult to understand in terms of design itself. Is it an injunction to keep your eyes on both poles of the design at once? This suggests that the distinction between part and whole does not create an amiable couple that meshes together. The part and the whole belong to violently opposed registers, to that part of the subject that designs from the "inside," that is from the past, and another part of the subject that designs from the "outside," that is, the whole. It takes a certain violence on the part of the architect to engineer a "fit" so that the "outside" is reduced to the scale of the parts. A consequence is that there is more space left over as a necessity of design. Perhaps we currently pay so much lip service to the idea of the site as a compensation that supplements architecture with a simpler, more rustic sense of the inside and the outside.

But where and with what do we design? Despite claims to the contrary, it seems very unlikely that we design with our minds, if the mind is considered as self-consciousness. It seems to be subjective but escapes any clear attribution as a subject. Something happens in design that cannot be reconstructed as a sum of the mind's decisions. This does not explain anything except why it does not satisfy the architect's narcissism. The architects have no clear mandate to describe the actual process of design as their presentation of the project in lectures often demonstrates. In a sense they can feel excluded, as if the space and what happened there remains for them a confused state in which the design happened almost behind their back. The rewards of narcissism come later and from a different source. The space was too big to occupy.

CONCLUSION

The argument so far has, I fear, a number of powerful defects. The first is that it reads, even to me, as being thoroughly implausible. Am I really saying that the easily admitted phenomenon of the problem of time, with its economy of deadlines and lateness, is a displacement of spatial problems that do not show up in professional life? More than a displacement, a kind of projective screen in which those spatial problems appear in the writing of time but that can be read in spatial terms. Yes, I suppose I am. In the end I'm not really writing of architecture but of the architect's relation to design. Of the architect's own space/time.

James Graham, you have been
so patient, so long suffering, so
infinitely polite, I thank you.

HOSPITALITY
Catherine Ingraham

As usual, Dean Wigley has given us the difficult task of doing everything and then undoing it in the next second. The fact that my name disrupts the alphabetical order of the day (a serendipitous development, thanks to some technological contingencies) perhaps gives me a certain power: I can say something from this position and then quickly move to my later-in-the-alphabet proper position and unsay it. You never do not say something, even if you are unsaying it. This rear-rangement of the alphabet also allows me to reflect on Lucia's exemplary piece of scholarly work, expertly researched and delivered—I want to honor that. See Lucia Allais's text ← p. 22–45 The only part I would quibble with is the strange role that theory seemed to play, which Lucia—indeed, all of us—now feel compelled to explain or excuse. I want to paraphrase something that Hal Foster said recently (perhaps he was quoting from Rosalind Krauss's work; it was a *Fêteschrift* for her). Some of us, he said, read for methodology first. We look for the theoretical structures that compose themselves as methodologies inside and around the work. We check on the persuasiveness of those structures. In other words, theory is not subject-specific.

Commitment to an intellectual point of view, and the research it entails, always gives us a theoretical background against which to push, if we choose to. The greatest prevaricator of them all, Jacques Derrida, never failed to ingeniously frame the background against which or in accord with which the critique was working. We have a choice, of course, of how much to make of this background, how much to foreground it. Derrida's belief was that one can never turn the page on philosophy, never turn the page on anything, not logocentrism, nor antiquity, modernity, or the eighteenth century. His hyper-awareness of method reinforced this belief. Given all that, it really is something to be able to bind ideas together in a lucid form, in the midst of the many drag anchors that condition scholarly and creative work. The theoretical bond established between ideas is not a separate preparatory or underlying body of work. It *is* the work.

So theory obviously is not one thing and does not belong to one era. In architecture, we have, nevertheless, assigned it a particular historical moment in the latter part of the twentieth century. I recall in the 1980s—when I was at The Charnley House, a research center in Chicago that was subsidized by the SOM Foundation—that John Whiteman, the director, once called up the stairs to me (I was working on the top floor). He asked me to identify myself for a symposium poster. "What should we call you?" And I responded: "You should call me an architectural theorist."

That was a new title. But it didn't refer to a new idea. It meant something fairly specific, but it's obvious that Vitruvius, Colin Rowe, Reyner Banham, Claude Nicolas Ledoux, Aldo Rossi, Bernard Tschumi, and innumerable other historians and architects have been and still are theorists—architectural theorists. At that moment, however, the use of the word *theory* pointed to a specific kind of training that resulted in a form of discourse, which I will say more about in a minute. Crudely, one of structuralism's first moves was to shift the emphasis, vis-à-vis structural anthropology, from diachronic events—historical relationships traditionally governed by chronology—to synchronic, contemporaneous events governed by proximity and adjacency. Such shifts are difficult to sustain and, in fact, this shift cannot be seen as a standing or hard distinction. Time is a force as well as an invention. This shift was, instead, a hypothesis about different forms of inquiry. History in particular, in its traditional ordering of a dynamic and elusive past, was thus put on guard.

Theory in architecture, during the time period in question, signified an unusually coalesced project to draw out, in architectural terms, a series of ontological and metaphysical dilemmas. But at almost any time you could choose, architecture has tried to contend with meanings and beginnings, although the specific orientation and philosophical basis of these discussions changes constantly. I suppose this "Urgencies" conference might be meant to either resurrect the spirit of common pursuit that characterized this era, or perhaps to put this era formally to rest, so new things can emerge or even to bootstrap between different eras in order to, among other things, remember and recharge.

Maybe I should start, like Norbert Weiner in *Cybernetics*, with the dinner parties. My training was in critical theory during its heyday at Johns Hopkins University—Jacques Derrida, Samuel Weber, Carol Jacobs, Michael Fried, and many others were at Hopkins then. I like Mark's idea of making this a friendly day—I don't like the fact that everybody here can't come to dinner, although I understand the logistical problems with that. One of the most persistent laments about theoretical discourse was its perceived exclusivity. The debates happening in architecture during that time spread through many disciplines, but there is a tendency in new intellectual work, if it succeeds in capturing people's attention, to develop something like an insider trading attitude toward knowledge, which mystifies it. That exclusivity was a big problem for theoretical discussions. More people and less mystification should have been at the table.

Although post-structural discourse reached a definite limit in both architectural practice and the imagination—suffering from intellectual gridlock—it shaped an entire continent of new work in our field. It was an unusual moment when things began to pinwheel around themselves: Theory theorized itself, architecture architected itself, and history historicized itself. It was exhausting after a while—the doubling back, what we now call "the turn"—but, like all moments when we reflect on automatic or entrenched ideas, we learned things that we really needed to know.

I find it interesting that many of those who were most interested in post-structural philosophy in architecture had some training not only in philosophy, history, and/or critical theory, as the case may be, but were also avidly interested in psychoanalysis (which is now cognitive therapy, but that is a different story). Many, including myself, saw psychoanalysis as a powerful apparatus, often metaphoric, through which relations to objects were elucidated. It was highly appropriate, I thought, that Mark Cousins, a critic and psychoanalyst, both opened and so brilliantly closed The Specter of Derrida conference in 2012 in Belgrade. Belgrade was amazing because it seemed to be at a place almost exactly twenty years earlier than where we are now in the United States. Everyone still smoked cigarettes and wanted to have long involved discussions about linguistics and architectural meaning. We, those of us who reconvened there around the "state of theory" so to speak—Mark Wigley, myself, Bernard Tschumi, Jeff Kipnis, and many others—kept thinking, and saying, "Oh my god, I can't believe architects in Belgrade are still interested in this stuff." And yet that conference was also a gathering of friends in the end. It was not a nostalgic event because the subject matter was so alive to those in Belgrade. It reminded people that theory is still a live discourse, not only for those who live in Belgrade, but for all of us. Alive, although different now.

I mention the psychoanalytic in order to remind people about depth structures. This is to say that deconstruction was not about visible destruction per se. The aesthetic requirement that architectural structures be seen to clash or decay in order to qualify as "deconstructive" always had an oddity to it. Frozen and stylized portraits of dynamic and entropic activity are inevitably cartoonish, yet sometimes powerful, architectural acts. But deconstructive architecture, seeking the dissolution of received ideas, mostly modernist in character, did not follow surrealism, which found a distinct vocabulary for its resistance to modernism—the excessively sharp composition of dreamscapes. Architects experimented with diagonal, asymmetrical, folded, and unstable structures, each of which had a psychological profile, so to speak. The problem of the dynamic and the entropic is still with us. Its theoretical enunciation has changed over the past ten or twelve years from first-order systems theory (cybernetics) to second-order systems theory (complexity, emergence), from old phenomenology (sociology) to new phenomenologies (cognitive science). The difficulty of acting within a Derridean form of analysis—from within its own history and concerns—became, for a time, architecture's number one problem. Architecture began to refuse Derrida's project almost immediately—even before it knew how it wanted to proceed—even to the point, very early on, of ridiculing Derrida's inability to grasp architecture. Although I think we should cease characterizing architecture as that profession which is profoundly misunderstood (our victim complex), there is an ongoing truth to it. Peter Eisenman frequently remarked on Derrida's conventionality when it came to architecture—for example, Derrida's remarks that it would be nice to have benches in Parc de la Villette, and why didn't the architects provide them? Benches here would refer to a banal foregone humanist gesture that Derrida, Peter imagined, would not be caught dead advocating. Peter's version of deconstruction (in both built and discursive forms) was exceptionally influential because he never lost sight of the defense of architecture—a habit we all have internalized. Peter has been, in some sense, a persuasive spokesman for architecture's unconscious for much of his career. Catching Derrida at his own game was both an inside joke and a warning to architects not to be taken for fools when it came to philosophy.

The "Deconstructivist Architecture" exhibition at MoMA in 1988—however mixed up—was a moment of reclamation, and redefinition, of our own discipline as it began to digest and negotiate a set of ideas that, like most other ideas in architecture, required translation into what we used to call, as editors of *Assemblage*, "the strictly architectural." The autonomous language promised to our discipline and practice (by the modernists, among others)—and which we had nurtured like a sacred flame in and through modernity—had also produced a form of self-flattery that acted as an inoculation against every such arrival from outside. We are a discipline and practice that feels itself to be vulnerable to every lance and knife thrown at artistic and intellectual practices that claim accountability to reality (a concept which, since I began working on the subject of property, I no longer bracket with quotation marks). We feel the need, accordingly, to protect the architectural domain from any attempt to expand or involve itself with other disciplines and practices, although the entire momentum and energy of the discipline has been historically constituted around the hybridization and naturalization of ideas that come in, as with all energy in any system, from the larger outside. Our protective impulse has been good in that we have evolved survival tactics that have preserved the system: "If you won't let me design the whole city, thank you at least for this parking lot project; if the building is being designed by that large development firm over there, thank you at least for letting me do the cladding," and so forth. But this impulse has been bad, at least periodically, because it makes us small and narrow.

I think this narrowness has placed us in serious danger of disappearing as serious players in culture. There are now only a few critics, a couple of theorists, a handful of architects currently building who are willing to take architecture to a more engaged place. It is no accident that we still rely heavily on patronage and have been completely left out of the discussions that we originally sponsored and formulated: The building of credible public space, for example, the future design of the city, technological and infrastructural innovation that is consequential, the re-composition of a model of environment, and so forth. There are, however, glimmers of deep experimentation in parametric architecture, and we have reached a point in that learning curve when, perhaps, the process can begin to look both further out and closer in than has so far been the case.

Architecture, as with many sciences, is generally embarrassed by philosophical questions and wishes no one would ask them. Yet these are the questions that motivate any enterprise. Study of synaptic junctures in the operation of the brain would never be funded or pursued if they did not lead to studies of the mind. In other words, we spend enormous amounts of time and money researching new building techniques and materials. But none of this matters if we have no framework for making those materials and techniques act significantly in one way rather than another. As has often been said (by John Ruskin, among others), there is no other need for architecture than for its excess of symbolic engagement. Builders and developers can do everything except for that. They don't have the training to build architecture, and training is everything.

The hyper-productivity of Derrida's method of inquiry is that every inquiry begets a hundred further inquiries and each veil pulled back reveals yet another world. It was precisely this work that architecture found compelling but impossible, as implied earlier, because it took too much time. The amount of time it took to enact a Derridean analysis had to be weighed against the time an architect might have to develop an architectural idea, which was always a project, built or unbuilt. Deconstruction was powerful as a theoretical method of inquiry because it refused to close—it fought its own systematicity. Its purpose was to place systems in question, not become one itself. An unrelenting rigor was required to patiently peel back the logic of structures, not in order to dismiss them but to view them in a different way. Such tactics, in architecture, promised to reveal the forms and structures of designing and planning, historical practices, languages, forces, and systems. This was also its arrogance, as many have noted. But it is undeniable that Derrida's work was immensely creative. And it was, I believe, the first generation of a contemporary, enunciated, new intellectual dimension to architecture. The second generation is still in gestation. We went, as many know, from the process studios, famous at Columbia University, to the paperless studios in which Greg Lynn and Hani Rashid, among others also at Columbia, pressured the computer to deliver its architectural future on the fifth floor of Avery Hall. We went from way too much discussion to that peculiar silence induced by computation. But our excommunication of theory did not settle matters really. We went away for a while to work on our computers and then we came back, not to the same moment but to some of the same questions, some of the same desires, some of the same forces.

The prevarication and delay (*temporizing*, as Derrida called it) that constitutes meaning in a Derridean schema repaid the labor and patience involved in the analysis. Derrida's provocations—often loosely coupled with Deleuze's deeply probative analysis of material worlds—were a heyday for tectonic metaphors. Architecture, it seemed, was underneath everything and everywhere consequential. We were, as we have so often wished to be, the *ur*-discipline. Buildings, in architecture, are almost always a matter of settling, in a semi-fixed way (as Colin Rowe most famously asserted) disputes between the ideal and contingent. At a certain moment, more analysis is the last thing that can be afforded. The pathos of this (to use Rowe's word) is that we always fail to do what we thought was going to be possible and the complex narrative of creation becomes the impoverished, yet poetic, narrative of lament. Architecture as an *ur*-discipline is fragile, in other words, yet capable of virtuoso action.

In my own work over the years, I have often registered (as a direct result of my training) some aspect of Derrida's thinking on whatever subject I am working on—on animals, for example, or on law and justice, or art. The ecstasy of the late twentieth century, for those of us involved in it, was caused by a tremendous tension between language and the hardness of things. This was not a contest between language and visual artistry, but the immersion of the confidence of vision in the shifting domain of words. We also found form only in enigma—enigmatic diagrams that became floor plans somehow, and then were extruded into buildings. The plan is no longer at the center of architectural design, at least not per se, but we have continued to pursue the enigmatic form in iterative patterning and parametric design although our hope is that these forms are going to be capable of intelligence. The shift from the process studio to the digital studio, at least so far, was thus not a complete break. However, the almost eighteen years that have passed since the paperless studios—which was our learning curve—have dovetailed with amazing new developments in other fields that began in the late twentieth century: the ascendency of biological, genetic, and neurological research; breakthroughs in immunological medicine; and the evolution of systems theory. John Holland, a scientist who studied complex adaptive systems at the Santa Fe Institute, likens systems theory to a vaccine, which "levers the immune system into learning about the disease, saving the costly... procedure of learning about the disease *on line*." He writes:

Without theory we make endless forays into uncharted badlands. With theory, we can separate fundamental characteristics from fascinating idiosyncrasies and incidental features. Theory supplies landmarks and guideposts and we begin to know what to observe and where to act.

It is very evident when a discipline—architecture in our case—is not feeling hospitable, when it does not want to talk about other disciplines or, in truth, even its own discipline. Language, Homi Bhabha said, *is* hospitality. The character of post-structural debates should not be confused with the politics of intellectual life, which is notoriously small-minded. Some recent discussions display a parsimonious closure of architecture to the hospitality of discussion—a fatal loss of energy and knowledge—and this is signaled by a kind of desperation at not having, for every theory, an architectural style immediately at hand. What one would hope for is a willingness to risk certain dissolutions or at least an opening of our self-made borders in order to participate in the incredible, even earth-shattering, rethinking of forces that directly concern us—dramatic environmental changes, institutional restructurings in which our discipline is in every way implicated, fascinating research in science, relations of material and intellectual work. This entails, as always, a theory of architecture guided by parameters that give us insight into our own work and discipline and, at the same time, are deeply in the world.

Perhaps I have spent too much time complaining about architecture's resistance to theory. But I have asked myself on occasion if I ever really wanted architecture to become "genuinely Derridean," whatever that might have meant. The very reason I entered architecture was to make my academic training in critical theory confront structures that were not easily digestible as a semantic construct. Yet one's disciplinary training is very powerful; there is never a total escape. I feel a more accurate answer to this question would be that my grasp of post-structural theory did not coalesce until I had to put it to work in the field of architecture. The question "What does this or that theoretical concept have to do with architecture?" was the galvanizing and wholly skeptical question from which architectural theory slowly emerged as a method for me. Architecture's resistance to theory becomes then a necessary part of its attraction to theory.

Derrida was in some sense a painful presence then, and is a painful presence now. He was celebrated and vilified. His belief in the diagnostics of language—what is said and what is left unsaid—was immensely fruitful, but also capable of profound disturbance. He himself was a calm man who wrote in the mornings in his bathrobe, and nothing lay outside his interest. At stake, however, was not a language game, neither mine nor Derrida's nor anyone else's. What was at stake was freedom. We should see theory, Derrida argued, as holding on to our freedom in relation to received ideas wherever they may occur. *Freedom* is a tricky word and it doesn't mean the same thing it might once have meant. In the name of freedom, terrible things, terrible architectures for example, have been done. Yet I still think freedom and constraint are meaningful ideas, worthy of architecture's attention. We are not obliged to question everything, only to have the freedom to question, and we are not obliged to be disciplined by constraint, only to recognize its powers and creative potentials. Both of these positions are harder to sustain than they appear. It is not a matter of simply willing it.

Conversation

MARK WIGLEY: Mark, you've argued before that you'd rather start with the word "drawing" instead of "theory." Why is that? What might give drawing precedence?

MARK COUSINS: One of the dumb things that happened when "the digital" arrived was you got these self-proclaimed defenders of drawing, or at least a lot of rather conservative people saying, "We're losing drawing." These same people would then go on to describe the functions of drawing in such a broad way that if you lost them all, I mean, the place just couldn't function. Drawing remained fundamental even in the moment of its supposed demise.

No one wants to use the term "representation" any longer, but that gap leaves a space within architectural education for what you might call "graphic signification." That would permit a genuine commerce between our physical understandings of letters and writing in a way that joins it to a history of drawing.

MARK JARZOMBEK: Lucia, could you speak a bit more about the relations between preservation and the public, in the sense that these preserved buildings act as a sort of architecture memory? In preservation, the public is often seen as something outside the building, and it gets produced in a particular way.

LUCIA ALLAIS: There is an assumption that, as soon as you speak of historic buildings, architecture's public grows—that conservation is what happens when the public gets involved in buildings. And so I was trying to tell a story

where that enlargement occurred through a very
calibrated project by a very rarified group
of individuals using very specific technological
metaphors, and building those metaphors into
the stones of the Parthenon, so that it might
take on a memorial abstraction for the rest of
the world—for "the public." I don't think
that's any different today. It seems to me that
the notion that architecture needs no translation—which is the alibi used by institutions
like UNESCO that want to "build a public"
through architectural conservation—is still
constructed using very specific, highly rarefied
architectural technologies.

The other point that I wanted to make regards
the assumption that "this will kill that," as
Victor Hugo put it—that architecture needs
a public because without it buildings will be
dematerialized, or will be killed by other
media. My point here is that the public is not
a monolithic thing. Any "public" is made out
of the same substances (technologies, media)
as everything else.

JARZOMBEK: I also have a question for Catherine, about the Derridean or post-Derridean
world you mapped out. How might that translate
into pedagogy, instead of historical work?

CATHERINE INGRAHAM: I agree with what Mark
Cousins was saying earlier, about how different things get taught in different eras. It's
like the overcrowded mind problem in neurosci-
ence. You need everyone to learn the alphabet
but there isn't room in the structure of the
DNA for an alphabet gene because the alphabet

belongs to an ever-changing phenomenon, language. There's an underlying, usually fairly conservative, curriculum, and then there are the various sorts of mechanisms that allow some change. When you're a faculty member who's been teaching through a number of different phases, it starts to get interesting. Certain things move to the center of pedagogical focus, and other things move to the edge. But, that is why pedagogy has to be supplemented by scholarly or practical work. You don't just develop in the classroom, and the curriculum doesn't just flow out of you as a result of that development. You need a parallel development in order to both exceed and precede pedagogical organizations.

I thought that what Mark said about how theory can actually save practice from going through every possible experiment in order to discover how certain things can be done was an excellent point. A certain kind of theoretical management can be extremely helpful. But I don't think that is the main job of theory in architecture.

COUSINS: At the Architectural Association, funnily enough, at least one aspect of this theoretical management seems to happen almost overnight—the space of the library is far too small for the books we have, so at any given time you only have access to those books that the library staff thinks will be needed for the next term. I can remember very vividly one term when every bookshelf was groaning with Derrida, or someone on Derrida, or someone against Derrida. And you came back after the summer holiday, and goddammit, they've all been replaced with books which seem to be covered in pictures of fish. [Laughter] I said, "What's this new thing all about?" And someone said, "Complexity." Charles Jencks had put on a conference on complexity. They were all interested in some institute for... [Pause]

AUDIENCE: Fish? [Laughter]

COUSINS: No, it's for very complicated things. It's somewhere in the Southwest.

AUDIENCE: Santa Fe.

COUSINS: That's it, the Santa Fe Institute of Complicated Stuff. [Laughter]

THE POLITICAL ECONOMY OF THEORY
Arindam Dutta

Prior to the "liberalization" of the Indian economy in the early 1990s, criteria as to what constituted "culture" depended on a loose contract between state institutions and a select smattering of artists and cultural practitioners close to these institutions. Both state and artist were generally liberal—even vanguardist—in outlook; together they were responsible for whatever grants, appointments, favors, or awards stood for institutional recognition. The occasional disagreement or controversy over censorship or political nepotism kept up the impression, broadly speaking, of a state oriented toward modernization and modernism, and therefore one whose agendas civil society could, or should, actively support. For instance, in the Hindi film industry, there were two awards, one state-patronized, the other commercial—reflecting India's "mixed economy" model—both of them instituted, oddly enough, in 1954.

The state hosted the National Film Awards, juried by mostly auteurish filmmakers and intellectuals, thus casting the Indian state somewhat in the Malrauxian mold; from the commercial side, there were the Filmfare awards, sponsored by the *Times of India* Group, more echoing popular taste and financial success in the market. For some forty years, one could argue these two formats produced a kind of presumed cohabitation, if not complicity, holding up a mirror to the ideology of the mixed economy model and the happy complementarity between liberal state and protected market, officialdom and commerce. On their part, the National Awards tended to reward particularly grim, badly lit but soul-searching art-house cinema, offering up something like a national conscience in its explorations of class disjunctions, gender, caste, and so on. At the Filmfare Awards, sappy, melodramatic performances were prized above self-consciousness about formal style. Between these two formats, Indian moviegoers could sense something like the dialectic of modernity in operation, on the one hand a radical modernity (somewhat ironically) promulgated by the state, and a conservative modernity representing the complacent interface between a protected market and an equally coddled civil society.

That dialectic held well until the mid-1990s, when television broadcasting was first deregulated in India. Within a few years, the market was flooded with new entrants—including Rupert Murdoch's Hong Kong–based Star TV. With all that added airtime, competition over audience attention became much more pressing than in the old days, when people were more or less forced to accept whatever fare was on offer when they tuned in to India's single state-owned channel, Doordarshan. Generating new content was key, and soon all the newly launched private television channels were falling back on a newly-created film and celeb industry to fill up airtime and attract eyeballs. The new television companies had noted that each time one of the film award ceremonies was held, television viewership went up significantly. So they figured, what if, rather than waiting all year for the one prestigious event, there were several of these events throughout the year, each one sponsored by a different television network? Think, instead of just the Oscars and the Golden Globes, an NBC film awards, a CBS film awards, an ABC version, a Sci-Fi channel version, and so on. What they further surmised was that audiences didn't particularly care who the prizes went to, what they were more interested in were the performances—dances and comic skits, etc., by sundry film stars and starlets—interspersing the award announcements.

Today, every media organization thus hosts its own version of film and television awards, which are more performances than they are awards. Award shows actually pay certain actors to show up and perform at the awards, and whoever shows up gets an award. Unlike, say, the Oscars, where the songs and dances provide digressive relief amongst the suspense and implied critical judgments on view, in today's film award shows in India, songs and dances are what are on show: it is the awards that are offered as digressive relief, outcomes that in the end nobody cares about. Even more important, media conglomerates who had stakes both in film and television figured out that these faux awards presented something like a marketing opportunity; so, in effect, many of these ceremonies were occasions for corporations to give awards to their own products. The Filmfare and the National Film awards still exist, but who cares nowadays what a select bunch of apparatchiks or hoity-toity film critics might think? The rubric of judgment had inexorably moved from being ensconced within a so-called "competent" circle of critics who held the reins of official approbation to one of market attraction or persuasion.

It is tempting to compare this surge in "awards" to the recent global surge in "competitions" in architecture. Although this is not new, today fewer and fewer competitions today refer to any actual site where anything has the prospect of being built: More and more of them are about generating "ideas" about this or that fanciful future, where this or that firm or industry uses the competition as a market venue to effectively generate ad copy whose intention is to garner media attention. An energy company hosts a competition to design sustainable cities; a car company hosts a competition to imagine the future of mobility. The trick here is to generate responses that appear to come from society at large rather than one initiated by industry: Through the invocation of genius, a private intervention can be posed as a form of public judgment. in question. The media feeds will read: "Here is what the world's smartest architects are thinking of in terms of the future of mobility." The sponsoring industry will be noted in passing, enough to stick in the brain, but innocuously enough since the report will be in the "culture" section.*

Alternatively, real estate developers will use this attention to secure clientele and finances for a project that will inevitably veer away from the vague program stated in the competition brief.

In the United States and Europe, for the more or less struggling offices that flock to these competitions to generate the flood of ad images for free

* Architects appear to be quite aware of this sham economy. Take, for instance, the following commentary in the *Architect's Newspaper*: "...the evidence is building and the case becoming clearer: The competition industry in the U.S. is having equally as bad or worse effects on the conception of architecture than we already know it has on the business of architecture. The old argument that competitions drive architectural innovation is no longer credible. Developers, cultural institutions, and government agencies have mastered the use of design competitions as publicity campaigns. Their claims of

73

or for next to nothing, these "prizes" or "honorable mentions" are crucial to supporting not so much the promise of actual building commissions but rather adjunct or junior careers in academia where other "objective" forms of validation are lacking. Sooner or later, these "ideas," winning or otherwise, will find their way into appointment or promotion portfolios. What was ad copy in the first instance has now become academic materiel, sitting alongside math formulas, scientific papers, art history monographs, and literary critiques, awaiting valuation and accreditation on the desks of university administrators. Today, these "ideas" are, in the eyes of the university, architectural knowledge.

searching for the best ideas is just an alibi that unfortunately continues to seduce too many of our best talents. These drawn-out exercises also make very little practical sense when it should be easy enough for clients to choose between architects...by picking up a few monographs or even just looking at their websites. The real justifications are simple. Developers and institutions gain fantastic and relatively affordable publicity from the mad traveling circus of design competitions. By helping them attract financing and donors, we encourage the proliferation of these sham exercises where enormous projects are fully rendered without contracts, necessary approvals, or even clear programs."[1]

Think of the Ordos 100 project, curated by the artist Ai Weiwei (with the requisite "dissident" credentials) and Jacques Herzog and Pierre de Meuron, in effect an effort by local real estate developers and land barons to use the "creative clout" generated by an international cadre of designer participants to effect a brazen land grab. If Ordos 100 is today a ghost town, its reality, in fact, lives on in the portfolios of dozens of architects in prestigious architecture schools for whom this validation—i.e., recognition by the celestial judgments of Ai Weiwei et al.—stands in as criteria for professional accomplishment. In future years, were we to look at the archives of American institutions, you would see these buildings appended in portfolios as evidence of competence, as attesting to various promotions or appointments to professorships, chairs of departments, and so on. I hope you see where I'm going here: The "economy" of academic judgment is not very different from hack television shows that portend to hand out awards on histrionic excellence.

Site model for the Ordos 100 competition, with individual houses from the selected architects, 2008

How do we evaluate Ordos 100, then, this Chinese encyclopedia of disparate strange objects whose secret code lies in the tricks surrounding the expropriation of land? As bogus real estate speculation riding on the coattails of international artistic reputations to bring name-recognition to its backers? As yet one more node in a global circuitry of roving curatorships, as a sign of a curatorial opportunism, if not desperation, to secure one more site of curation and therefore bring a kind of facticity to the act of curation as a crucial cog in the wheel of "creative economies" and real estate speculation? As the architects'—a self-anointed avant-garde in the most conventional role, chasing employment benefits—continued incomprehension of reality even at the very cultural moment that they all profess to be embracing reality ("the West is over, and along with it, modernity... Asia is where it's at...")? Or is this in fact the new reality or new normal for a self-proclaimed architectural avant-garde, in which a mix of curatorial networking and academic buzz promulgates largely paper careers that on the other hand inveigh against paper architecture per se, in the name of embracing "practice" (or should we say the post-theoretical)? Which is to say, the utopia of anti-utopianism?

Which brings me to the question of our conference today, the "urgencies" of theory. I don't know what theory is. I would only say this: If there are theories, they are to be found not only in the books of a Badiou or Derrida. Theory is embedded in the most mundane of statements, whether this be marketing ads, journalistic reports, weather forecasts, stock options, legal settlements, wedding vows, mowing the lawn, you name it. That is to say, in the context of institutions such as universities, theory does not reside only in those sound perturbations or marks of ink that we call words, spewed by that category of epistemic bureaucrats that we call professors. Theory is inherent in the acquisition of land, committee deliberations, investment, recruitment and fundraising patterns, hiring patterns, salary and benefits packages, the making of buildings, apportioning of spaces, and so on and so forth, the totality of which we call a university.

Theory is always contingent upon a situation. To the extent that we believe that conferences such as these—or the people in these conferences—determine what theory is, we are not only actively obfuscating the various sites and vectors in which theory operates in a university, in fact we are also obfuscating what universities do, what they are about. Universities are not centers of knowledge production any more than a corporate board meeting or a farmer's field in Bangladesh are centers of knowledge production; what they are, in fact, are gambles for institutional validation. What we identify as "theory" within universities reflects a certain dispensation of governments and the division of various kinds of competencies with regard to various kinds of knowledge, a dispensation owed to the long legacy of German idealism in the history of modern nation-state formation, but now in headlong retreat.

To say that the university is defined by the quest for knowledge is to suggest that the price of money is determined by the value of gold. Let me restate this, just to be clear: To speak disapprovingly today of the "neoliberalization" of the university, to pine for the "golden days" of the "liberal" university, is as kooky an idea as the wish to revert to the gold standard as a defense against present-day capitalism. To See panel discussion → p. 114 speak of knowledge production in the university in the Kantian idiom of disinterestedness, at best this amounts to explaining one fiction by recourse to another, of some resplendent "ground" upon which knowledge becomes transparent to itself. The humanist image of rational dueling has long served as a billboard for the university; academic culture has thrived on the idea that the university's primary mission is to catalog and test the modes of judgment—"method"—by which compacts about knowledge or ethics can be determined.

Other than being flagrantly misleading—the university's institutional power equally lends it to dogma, sinecurism, political manipulation, surrogate factionalism, exploitation, nepotism, concept-peddling, hobby-horsing, cabalism, not to rule out continuing feudal and neofeudal paternalism—burnishing this lapsarian, historical image of the "modern" university today may well amount to putting on ahistorical blinders in that it appears incapable of gauging the terms of its own present. In the old, modern, exhortation, signaled by the founding of the University of Berlin in 1810, knowledge legitimation more or less drew from the upside-down validity conferred on philosophy by Kant in *The Conflict of the Faculties*: The further one retreated from interest or the "subjective" senses, the better the acuity of the dispassionate system to be designed and deployed in confronting phenomena. Lyotard's "Report on Knowledge" of 1979 had pointed to the already compromised stakes in the establishment of that system in terms of an innate conflict between the conception of the university as the house of knowledge (Wissenschaft) and as the house for training or practice, "in some ways reminiscent of the split introduced by the Kantian critique between knowing or willing."[2] The postmodern university, in that sense, is defined by the exacerbation of the brief placed on the pragmatic outcomes of science and knowledge; its "symbolic capital" is being detranscendentalized into more mundane forms of extraction.

And yet, to view the contemporary shift solely in terms of the Kantian move—from a rubric of truth to a rubric of practice—belies the myriad ways in which forms of knowledge and the powers of the "imagination" are instituted, operationalized, and consumed in the world, and the ways in which the domain of the university is being gerrymandered to conform to these imperatives. No longer does the university retain a legitimate claim to disinterest, nor do the votaries of various interests couch themselves in merely utilitarian or pragmatic propositions. Far from being an ivory tower, the contemporary university is the epitome of the hybridized ways in which interest and disinterest, epistemic legitimacy and paradigm-breaking, work together in the contemporary marketization of knowledge.

Just as gold appears as an objective determinant covering over the social contracts that determine monetary value, knowledge production might also be seen as a thing whose work is to mask the contemporary university's burgeoning briefs and claims to influence. To quote Michel Foucault, "We have to produce truth in the same way, really, that we have to produce wealth, and we have to produce the truth in order to produce wealth."[3]

It might be interesting to produce a taxonomy of the university's many identities today:

— The university as short-term fiscal stimulus: Governments see universities as a site to build up knowledge assets in a global economy, in partnership with a host of private actors, as a way of conveying competitiveness in the techno-workforce markets. This is different from the logic of *long-term* stimuli—the "fate of future generations" and the "advance of humanity," etc.—that has been the university's traditional rhetorical brief.

— The university as tax haven: Contributions to university bodies offer corporates and wealthy donors an avenue for managing asset portfolios.

— The university as investor: Private universities hold large financial portfolios, which, along with employment retirement portfolios, comprise large stakes in the financial markets, as insistent as any others on greater and greater returns to fund their growth.

— The university as real estate agent: In many cases, universities benefit from older gifts or grants in land as well as current exemptions on their land acquisition to rent or lease land assets on preferential terms to corporate bodies or affiliated real estate companies. (Cambridge University's Trinity College is the third largest landowner in the United Kingdom; Cooper Union subsists on rents from major real estate holdings in New York City, including the Chrysler Building.)

— The university as advertising billboard: The humanist aura of the university affords multiple players a venue to burnish their market credentials by funding research initiatives or bursary programs or building projects. Energy companies sponsor the discourse on sustainability; defense industries sponsor programs in the study of peace and conflict, and so on.

— The university as incubator for new biocommodities: These commodities range from devices aimed at the management of pleasure (apps, games, etc.) to managerial techniques to security hardware to philosophical concepts to the engineered components of what Donna Haraway has called "Life® Itself."[4]

— The university as labor (sub)contractor: A vast pool of scientific labor, in the form of graduate students and postdocs, is made available by the disciplining modalities—the incentive to work toward a degree, a job, etc.—of the university as a pliable workforce. The professor's right to fail the student makes her into the best subcontractor for industry's effort to employ technoscientific labor.

— The university as a consulting firm composed of "experts" (as opposed to a professoriate): For contemporary capital, the figure of the professor often represents an intractable and inefficient body through which to relate knowledge and efficient decision-making. From thickening the layers of administration, to empowering students by recasting them as consumer clientele, to introducing new measures to test pedagogical efficacy, professors are less and less the front for knowledge evaluation. New EdX-type initiatives seek today to parcelize education into transmissible packets of facts and testable insights, crowdsourcing the points of learning, and doing away with the physical corpus of the teacher.

— The university as a captive market for biofinance: As tuition fees and bursaries are raised and at the same time desubsidized, students are expected to turn to private lenders to fund their education. At the macroeconomic level, correspondingly, the situation may be little different from the mortgage market in real estate that tethered the expectations of the last financial boom (and bust); financial players are entering the educational loan market with expectations that growth from higher levels of higher education warrants the higher amounts and number of loans. In the U.S., Sallie Mae is following in the footsteps of Freddie Mac and Fannie Mae; in many cases, the two are linked as parents refinance their home mortgages at lower rates to fund their children's education. On the one hand, this flood of cheap credit inevitably entails the further exploitation of education as a privatized profitmaking sector; on the other hand, the imperatives of investment-driven growth are turning universities into giant health care-education-real estate complexes, the new front for what we may term *biocapitalism*.

— The university as training mechanism for "soft power" and "people skills" (managerialism in place of the humanities): The financial premium therefore put on students to choose fields that will repay this outlay best and fastest will in itself have a tremendous impact on the future of the disciplines. At the very least, one can foresee a retrenchment in the post-WWII subsidization of the humanities, since more and more "research" in the university will rely on private and corporate funding and tie-ups for their subsistence. Already, this reliance is first and foremost on university budget-writers: A corporate-sponsored doctoral student in science and technology costs one-fifth of the outlay required for a student in the humanities. Among elite institutions, one can thus foresee the humanities as reverting to an old-style, Whiggish, "aristocratic egalitarianism"; non-elite institutions will talk up the humanities as necessary for communication skills, creativity, and "people skills." "Soft power" will be the new mantra, in place of the old, idealist emphasis on "imagination."*

* Countries across the world have redefined industrial and educational policies to accommodate these large, multibillion-dollar complexes that capitalize, or hope to capitalize, on these knowledge industries. Whether it be the "reforms" undertaken by the Blair-Cameron governments in the UK, the Bologna Process to establish a European Higher Education Area, or new policy initiatives by the UPA 1+2 governments in India, or Projects 211 and 985 undertaken by the Chinese government, these research-industrial complexes are seen as critical in economic competition between nations or regions. China overtook the US in 2013 in number of patents filed, a development that has set alarm bells ringing within the Obama administration, as will, no doubt, the day when the former surpasses the latter in number of doctoral degrees granted.

Does the above list look like what Ian Bogost has termed a "Latourian Litany"? Perhaps. But the brunt of the argument here goes against the faith that nonetheless resides in all of Latour's writing: A "parliament" can be assembled where heterogeneous phrase regimens can confront each other with equanimity, conforming to some given agreement as to how to voice, or settle, disputes.

As for the humanities, which is to say the fields most likely to harken to the "golden days" of the university, and the fields most likely to sigh at the "decline of theory," simply think of how much money it takes to train the average doctoral student in the humanities in institutions such as ours (MIT, Columbia, etc.): a half-millon dollars per capita. We forget that the effort to shore up the humanities in the postwar era was also an ideological decision, no less "neoliberal" than the neoliberalism that we now declaim as a newly arrived antagonist that is now putting humanists out of jobs. In that sense, subsidies to universities were in keeping with a series of other equally unequal or uneven subsidies in other areas (agriculture, industry, pension funds, and so on) that governments today find themselves more and more unable to honor, or repay.[5] Why "unequal"? you may ask. Then consider this: The average French cow earns $800 a year, an income that is higher than 1.2 billion of the world's poor. The cow's "salary," so to speak, therefore, must be seen as only one component in an entire chain of similar such salaries—including the paid-up philosophes at the Collège de France or the École des hautes études, who are charged by the French state to regurgitate the matter of the socius and generate "theory"/milk. When we think Althusser, Derrida, Badiou, Latour, we don't think paid-up cows. It's just that in modernity, a modernity that university professors never tire of espousing, the clericalism of the professoriate is perhaps the last to be defrocked.

In Mark Wigley's dissertation book and articles published in the 1990s, he brilliantly argued that this architectonic of the disinterested foundations of theory—as set out in the Kantian idiom—in fact amounted to something like a material supplement or mnemotechnical supplement in the form of the architecture of the library, tethering the vocation of the previously itinerant university to a supposed material core (that is, a building). This was a centering action by architecture even as architecture, as a discipline, itself became sort of invisible or pushed to the margins, since it belonged neither to the "verifiable" discourses of the sciences, nor purely to the "imaginative" territories of the arts.

Should we reconsider that supplement of humanism today, given that now all the vital architectural development of universities appears to occur at their peripheries, and that on the other hand, instead of knowledge production, universities are now declaring "design" as their core mission? We are experiencing, in both intellectual and material terms, an inversion of what Wigley had deduced in the high era of humanism. At MIT and Columbia alike, the buildings at the core are allowed to deteriorate. The elevator in my building hasn't been changed for fifty years; you can think of Avery as somewhat suffering the same fate. The periphery of the university, on the other hand, is full of shiny new speculation, branded buildings, new Ordos 100s, that promise new and imminent epistemological revolutions every day, more and more fights undertaken to save the world, protect humanity, ensure peace within and between societies. The unchecked liquidity that central banks are injecting into the global financial markets today finds its way into a surfeit

Fumihiko Maki and Associates, MIT Media Lab Building, Cambridge, Massachusetts, 2010

of "projects" for whose ad copy the "truth-criterions" spawned by universities are a natural ally. (Daniel Defoe had noticed a similar link between a sham "projecting spirit" and inflation at the turn of the eighteenth century, after the Bank of England had begun to infuse large amounts of liquidity into European markets, quite like today's US Fed.)[6] From the standpoint of the university, what is most important to grasp here is the manner in which funds routed to labs escape a disciplinary embrace. Indeed, such is their calling card: to break down disciplines in the pursuit of what they construe as "innovation." To the extent that universities use labs as proxies to maximize their amenability to these multiple kinds of patronage, one can garner the extent to which the older model of humanism is now in peril. Each funding pitch claims to redesign a world. The result has been a complete disintegration of whatever went in the name of disciplinary thinking, in the direction of a relentless entrepreneurialism that now infects administrations, faculty, and students alike. Everybody aspires to a lab of one's own. It's like Virginia Woolf in the era of venture capital, in which one seeks not the subsidized freedom, the aunt's bequest, to write as one ought, but rather a launchpad to pitch for funds that will tide you over till you pitch for the next tranche of funds. So this may be a question for today: How will architects cope with this new profusion of claims to design from fields other than architecture?

It is now quite conventional to state that architect's claims to validity in practice do not rely on truth criterions. I am thinking of Jesse Reiser's sharp claim in *The Atlas of Novel Tectonics* that "bad science" could be the inspiration for good architecture just as well as bad. This is simply to say—in fact going back to old Kant—that there is no inherent reciprocity between verifiability and design: In the Kantian idiom, design comprises a negotiation between purposiveness and the "purposiveness-without-purpose" that is the aesthetic.[7] But Reiser's epistemic insouciance—putting it that way sounds better than "advice not to learn anything properly"—itself risks being outdated if one considers that the truth criterion was in the first place the outcome of an economic or ideological arrangement, which is to say a pattern of apportioning subsidies, or in what amounts to the same thing, a way of appointing committees and settling the boundaries between disciplines.

We could say that the pivotal science of the twentieth century, and the prime promulgator of the truth criterion, was the field of physics, whose aura was further bolstered by the sense that its representational models presented a phenomenology of nature as such. In the older ideology of funding, the era of Big Science, physics was logos, and logos was, in a manner of speaking, physics. Today's pivotal disciplinary science, by contrast, biotech, even if it delves even more deeply into the phenomenality of nature, cites no such impetus toward methodological reduction or methodological reconciliation. Biotech is, strictly speaking, not so much a discipline as an ongoing and ever-changing, if not transparent, composition of interests. I will not go into the tremendous organizational striations that go into the discovery, development, and final delivery of a drug to market. To create another litany, this would have to include, at the very least, a combination of big government and small government sops, the power of big pharma, intellectual property regimes, venture capital, large financial organizations, windfall-seeking hedge funds, the parcellization and outsourcing of research activities across transnational territory, the construction and reconstruction of legal subjects and biological definitions of the body, newly thickened strata of university administrators and deans, the cultivation of so-called star professors, not to rule out the active production, across these multiple terrains, of what we could call agnogenesis (the production of ignorance by dint of defending proprietorial knowledge), selective reporting of data, bogus claims, you name it. In the venture capital model, a product does not need to make it to market in order to be bought or sold to make money off of it. The mere rejection of truth criteria is therefore hardly adequate to understand the composition of commodity, of design. Capital is, at every stage, capital, ever and only incomplete, an endless valorization of its parts without a teleology of the whole: The M-C-M' cycle can be realized in every unit of a presumed production function.

Architecture, has, of course, fully echoed this trend—the book that I edited recently, *A Second Modernism*, speaks to some of the complexities of the relationship between disciplinary imperatives and funded research in great detail.[8] But Wigley's thesis still somewhat holds, although in an inverse way: In an era of Total Design, the scientists and adminstrators within the state more and more style themselves as designers, while designers find themselves scurrying around for a professional model. This is what Jesse Reiser misses about "bad science": its symbiotic relationship with and propagandist convenience for whatever is funded as "good science." The designers have no greater advantage if bad science were on the ascendant—two (if not more) can play at that game. The question, as I see it, should be put differently: In an era in which bad science was the norm, would architecture survive?

A critical question to ask would therefore be: Given this tremendous organizational and geographical striation of what is today called knowledge-driven capitalism, what is the status of this new architectural evanescence at the periphery of the university? Another way of asking the question would be: What is the place of the university as a node of knowledge production in these circuits of data-driven capital? From what I can discern, I would argue that never has this connection between knowledge and the knowledge economy been quite so tenuous. All the university perhaps offers today is perhaps something like a territorial locale, a kind of prestigious address so that capital that is in fact located elsewhere can claim to play at domesticity. The university is now, only, and ever, a piece of attractive real estate, which is to say, real estate through and through—and we could say that the humanities are like an inconvenient piece of old, rent-controlled housing—that is seen to be more in need of either demolition or, alternatively, gentrification, which is to say its conversion into promotional copywriting for the new state of affairs. What will our traditional conceptions of theory make of any of this? Very little, I suspect, other than lament the loss of former subsidies by invoking truth criterions that they were themselves (theoretically) devoted to demolishing.

1   Marshall Brown, "Kick the Architectural Competition Habit," *The Architect's Newspaper* (March 6, 2014), archpaper.com/news/articles.asp?id=7138.

2   Jean-François Lyotard, *The Postmodern Condition: A Report on Knowledge*, trans. Geoff Bennington and Brian Massumi (Minneapolis: University of Minnesota, 1984, 2002), 32.

3   Michel Foucault, *"Society Must Be Defended": Lectures at the Collège de France, 1975–1976*, trans. David Macey (New York: Picador, 2003), 25.

4   Donna J. Haraway, "Maps and Portraits of Life Itself," in Peter Galison and Caroline Jones, eds., *Picturing Science, Picturing Art* (New York: Routledge, 1997).

5   See Wolfgang Streeck, *Buying Time: The Delayed Crisis of Democratic Capitalism*, trans. Patrick Camillar (New York: Verso, 2014).

6   Daniel Defoe, *An Essay Upon Projects* (London: Thomas Cockerill, 1697).

7   See Arindam Dutta, "Design: On the Global (R)Uses of a Word," in *Design and Culture*, vol. 1, no. 2 (2009).

8   See Arindam Dutta, with Michael Kubo, Stephanie Tuerk, Jennifer Yeesue Chuong, Irina Chernyakova, eds., *A Second Modernism: MIT, Architecture, and the "Techno-Social" Moment* (Cambridge, MA: The MIT Press, 2013).

THE DISPOSITIONS OF THEORY
Keller Easterling

I wanted to say something simple about the dispositions we impose on theory. Beyond its content, beyond what we are making theory say, what are we making theory do? We shove it into segregating and quarantining dispositions. We force it into litigating binaries. We seal it into isomorphic arrangements. The disposition of theory—its temperaments or propensities—can even permit or deny information. It can shape theory into a provisional, temporary assumption on the way to an altered habit of mind or alternatively as an ossifying bully of thought. Dispositions not only permit or deny information—they color it, pinch it, deform it, or parboil it. What do we miss, what information do we delete with a segregating, binary, or isomorphic disposition?

CONSIDER THE SEGREGATING OR QUARANTINING DISPOSITION.

We remember the laughable segregation of theory and practice that used to dominate discussions and generate tireless circular conversation. Or we may still encounter the reactionary post-critical that would have the thought police lock away theory so that it would no longer muddle, with its dangerous woolliness, the purity of making. Equally segregating is the countering quarantining of the high-minded and the rhetorical to protect against the practical or the real. We segregated thought by generations or by a formalized discourse (e.g., semantics, deconstruction). We quarantine subspecialties in the discipline (e.g., theory, practice, research, history), even when we know that theory loves evidence and evidence loves theory—even when we know that they just want to be together.

CONSIDER THE ISOMORPHIC DISPOSITION.

Here, theory is shaped into religion. No longer the supposition that hopes to open onto more information, it becomes a technique for excluding information and arranging what's left in a self-referential array. Or theory becomes an elaborate locution to be chanted long enough for others to chant it and give themselves the authority to exclude those who can't.

In discussing the sciences, Latour has likened this isomorphic disposition of theory to that of a plant, which, having had so much success with photosynthesis, concludes that the entire world is run on chlorophyll. Scientific theory can be used to continually confirm assumptions rather than test and expand assumptions—to ingrain rather than change habits of mind.

The isomorphic disposition creates a control error that eliminates information and overlooks contradiction to maintain a solid state. This is the disposition of Jesus when he says, "You are with me or against me," making a childish category mistake that assumes the part for the whole. The disposition shares habits with the avant-garde, dramatically and nonsensically insisting that information must kill information and that knowledge must be successive rather than coexistent. In the isomorphic disposition: Stray from the family of disciples or stray from the central doctrine of, for instance, Capital, and you are either a dangerous enemy or a weak, vacillating, equivocal, interdisciplinary indeterminate. And you must be tolerated or eliminated. Still, we cling to isomorphic positions even when the cast-iron theories of, for instance, Capital, prevent us from seeing all the parallel markets that trade with other social logics, irrational desires, or dangerous masks. Even when, to be so determinate, *is not vigilant enough.* And telescoping down into any discipline we can hear the faint cries of even tinier isomorphic tempests, since it is well-known that the smaller the point, the more insufferable the unbeliever becomes to the believer.

CONSIDER THE BINARY DISPOSITION.

With this disposition, there can be no progress of thought without debate. It's a strange assumption on its own, like the assumption that we will only care about a story if there is a murder or conflict. Ideas can only emerge from dialectic. There is no other form of questioning or puzzling. Theory is litigation. Theory is scrimmage. And returning to the disposition of quarantine or segregation, there is great sport in agitating for segregated groups (theory, practice, history) to fight each other, challenge each other to duels, as if there were no other means by which thought could advance.

Debate is surely one source of the contradiction—the error, the extrinsic information—that can jolt theory forward. But when is our debate only the staged wrestling between known players that preserves a set of comfortable discourses intact? When is it an exercise in gaming strategies—like Schopenhauer's twenty-nine ways to win an argument? When debate itself becomes the object and the content, we can then get together regularly and throw ourselves against an open door—a satisfying exertion to stand in for work performed on the world's wicked problems.

Or do binary oppositions make us continually see enemies and innocents in our activism? Or do they continue to encourage histories organized around dramatic conflicts like wars? War, the favorite staple of history, creates epic tableaux that often upstage nerdier, less dramatic, but potentially more consequential evidence.

DIAGNOSTIC

So these segregating, isomorphic, and binary dispositions and other default dispositions may be diagnostics for assessing the propensities or the restrictions of our theory—restrictions that may delete the very information that we need. They can be worn on a string like a necklace and kept handy. Perhaps most important, they make it easier to see when theory is all disposition and no content. Maybe that would be something simple enough to say.

But beyond the meta-theoretical critique (and presumably we want a diagnostic for a political theater more consequential than that of architecture culture), if theory is about thinking hard, thinking differently, and seeing differently, what extra evidence and information might a dispositional register offer—what additional ways of knowing and speculating or theorizing?

There is nothing to succeed, correct, supplant, or oppose—just more expansive pastures beyond the one into which the overly adaptive architect has crowded.

I have been wondering about what this dispositional register reveals and what larger pastures it opens on to with regard to form-making and activism. Wondering how spatial variables might play a larger role as points of leverage in the extrastatecraft of global governance. You all know that I have been looking at a kind of infrastructural space, the matrix of repeatable formulas and spatial products that make most of the space—the Shenzhens and Dubais—of the world. It is like an operating system that makes certain things possible and certain things impossible. An operating system for shaping the de facto forms of polity—the protocols, sequences, routines, schedules—all activities or the rules of the game in the urban milieu. Like our theory, in addition to all the things it is saying, its real currency is what it is doing.

KNOWING HOW

When Mark Twain was a riverboat captain, he always said he sensed that the passengers were reading framed landscape views that passed by as if reading a pleasant graphic novel while he was reading a much more grave and dangerous story reflected in the face of the water. All the dimples and ripples that indicated shifting shoals. He was reading the disposition of the water like we are trying to read the disposition of theory, and it required almost instantaneous oscillations between evidence and theory.

To borrow from Gilbert Ryle's formulations, it was a situation in which you could not "know that" you could only "know how." Knowing how was dispositional, unfolding, latent. Knowing how was, ironically or not, indeterminate to be practical. Or theoretical to be practical. Or indeterminate to be vigilant.

The global infrastructure space that I study is the secret weapon of some of the most powerful because it is often doing sneaky things that are decoupled from what it is saying. One needs object forms like those we are usually trained to make, but one also needs to theorize active forms that are dispositional and time-released, like bits of code to hack the operating system. One needs form in another gear or register that is shaping things as well as an interplay between things.

And if we only recognize one way of making and knowing (like the pleasant landscape novel), think what we miss. If we can only address the world with objects and rhetoric, the world's most powerful players will run circles around us. The most powerful players are never satisfied with *knowing that*. It is too weak. They also want to *know how* to handle and deploy the world's dangers, uncertainties, irrationalities, duplicities.

At the moment, even though space is the durable outcome, the software for global infrastructure space is scripted by financial quants, McKinsey consultants, and World Bank yes-men in the language of econometrics, informatics, and managementese. Yet some of the most interesting thinkers in the social, political, and economic sciences are questioning the presumptions of their discipline or the supposed authority of their science. They want to know *how* as well as *that*. They are even searching for more complex contexts and discovering that space is clearly a useful testbed. At this juncture, one doesn't want to mistake a weak, diluted interdisciplinarity for its opposite—the chance to place spatial practices, undiluted, at a consequential crossroads between disciplines. It is a chance to work artfully on the irrationality that rules the world in ways that go beyond the rhetorical and foreground what we, as architects, know how to do. This possibility of leading with spatial variables—not only a dominant technical language like econometrics—is what, for me, lends some urgency to architectural theory.

Might we know how to ride in reverse over the space made with economic variables and power plays substituting spatial variables with different points of leverage—not only things but interplays, interdependencies, little engines of space. There may be dispositions of space as well as dispositions or temperaments of theory that allow us to lead or ally ourselves in this way.

If theory is something to think with while working on something that can't be figured out—something that doesn't look familiar—maybe one finds oneself, unannounced, suddenly doing what one set out to do. But mostly, theory simply causes us to continually say, "I don't know"—to rapidly oscillate between thinking and failing or thinking and making. Theory is then the opposite of rhetorical paralysis. It is something impractical on its way to a new practical, something illogical, risky, harebrained, or hard. We are theoretical to be practical, theoretical to be vigilant, or theoretical to be rigorous. We are theoretical to *know how*.

BROADCAST ARCHITECTURES
John Harwood

Page the Atlantic Ocean (will you please?)
  For one Cass Gilbert, architect-at-large
  Somewhere at sea beyond the twelve-mile marge.—
He's wanted by the ancient Pericles,
  (Since both Ictinus and Callicrates
  The elder members of the firm, have gone,—
  The architects who built the Parthenon
Whence Elgin hove away the famous frieze.)

Page every corner of the Briny Inn,
  Call out his name through all its corridors,
In every wave-length make a wireless din
  That shall be heard upon its farthest shores.
He's wanted on "long distance" (Time and space)
By one who's speaking for the human race.

—John H. Finley, "Call for Cass Gilbert," 1934[1]

In response to the rather generously broad prompt here to consider an urgency of architectural theory, and moreover an urgency that is somehow recent or current, I cannot resist the historian's vice of turning to a past urgency, one that has been repeatedly and even willfully forgotten: the demand for a response, on the part of architects and engineers, to the demands of a newly wired world, whose technical basis no longer quite seems to fit the conventions of architectural production. We remain, I contend, in an uncomfortable situation vis-à-vis the loops of wires threaded through our only apparently wireless world.

So a poem (the epigraph to this brief essay) and an anecdote, each delivered on the occasion of Cass Gilbert's death in 1934, by Gilbert's intimate friend John Finley and Gilbert's wife, Julia, are perhaps a good way to dramatize the problem. In the first, the "wireless" is both a technical means to defy or defer the passing of the architect from the stage of a world history, to reach him on his ship floating on the vast "Briny Inn," and to recall him to his duty of making spatial order on behalf of the "human race." In the second, which happened a few years earlier, there is the amusing but unsettling surrender of the usually comfortable arch-bloviator Gilbert to the terror of "mic fright."

Julia Gilbert, wife of Cass, recorded an amusing but illuminating anecdote about her husband's first encounter with the new mass medium. Long famous for his skill at delivering (rather pompous) improvised speeches at large gatherings such as professional associations, art societies, and the like, when Cass Gilbert was asked to deliver an address "live" over the radio, he was instructed by the producers to prepare his remarks in advance. When he refused, his family urged him to do so too. Grudgingly, he wrote the first half of the speech, trusting himself that once he had gotten started, the rest would flow naturally. Julia Gilbert retells the disaster that followed:

> We saw him leave the house, attended by a radio escort, and shortly after heard his voice over the radio—delightful, full, and rich. We listened with a sigh of relief, but the inevitable happened, of course. When the written part was over, the spoken words did not follow with their customary ease; a halting, inadequate, and unsatisfactory delivery was the result of unpreparedness, added to which he ceased speaking two minutes before his time was up, leaving the announcer in the terrifying position of having nothing to say or continuing to talk on the topic of which he was totally ignorant—and there was no orchestra or crooner to take up the slack left by Mr. Gilbert's sudden silence.
> I have always pitied that announcer, with the silent microphone before him and two minutes to go.
>
> When Mr. Gilbert returned to the family, he asked how the speech went. We told him tearfully that the first half was fine, but the last half was dreadful. This was his awakening to the fact that over the radio it is hearing, not seeing, that counts.[2]

There is an obvious reading here, which is that Gilbert was unwilling to learn the rigorous discipline of transposing one medium, public speech, to another, radio broadcast. Yet I think it worth noting that Julia Gilbert does not only note her husband's embarrassment but that of the "announcer," who, in the face of the architect's failure, is at a loss to fill in the dead air that followed. We architectural historians and theorists are, in the face of the inadequacy of our historiography to fundamental questions regarding technics, rather like that poor announcer, looking around the studio desperately for a crooner to fill in for us.

So how did Cass—how did we—get here? A book project I am pursuing currently, titled *Architectures of Mass Media: Telephony, Radio, Television*, is an attempt to answer that question through a thoroughgoing investigation of the architecture produced to realize the technical apparatus of telecommunications in the late nineteenth and early twentieth century not only as media but as *mass* media, with the sublime, hyperinfrastructural scale that such endeavors require. Such a history is not intended to be one of architecture "on," say, the radio—i.e., of architecture as the "content" of another medium, nor of the supercession of architecture by immaterial, miniaturized, and invisible technologies; rather, it looks to that architecture that was a necessary component of a larger mass-media apparatus. So, what follows is just a few notes from that history on the architecture of radio, by way of attempting to speak to our current perplexity in the face of an ever more dense wiring of the world that seems to silence us even as the noise of "chattering" and "texting" and "twittering" is deafening. See panel discussion → p. 115

Telecommunications was, in the first instance, wireless. But it always had walls. As the first "short history" of telephony written after the invention of the Bell system relates, the "ear trumpet" and "speaking trumpet" were early instances of communicating sound at great distance, allowing sound waves to travel farther through the medium of air because "the walls of the tube reduced the loss of energy from spherical action."[3] Whether it was the human voice projected through one of Athanasius Kircher's architectonic tubes meant to project the sound of a vocal performance outside of the walls of a house or public building, or one of Wolfgang von Kempelen's pneumatic "speaking machines," the increase in volume (or prevention of decay) of a given sound was accomplished through tectonic means.

Athanasius Kircher, speaking tubes connected to sculptural busts, from *Musurgia Universalis*, 1650

Even though many inventors can lay claim to the discovery of a means of telecommunication through a solid (as opposed to gaseous) medium well beforehand, the scientist, inventor, and entrepreneur Sir Charles Wheatstone deserves credit for picking up an often ignored observation from the preface to Robert Hooke's 1667 *Micrographia*. As Hooke boasted there, "I can assure the reader that I have, by the help of a *distended wire*, propagated the sound to a very considerable distance in an instant, or with as seemingly quick a motion as that of light—at least incomparably swifter than that which at the same time was propagated through the air—and this not only in a straight line, or direct, but in one bended in many angles."[4] Wheatstone resuscitated these experiments in a sequence that would lead him to share in developing the first commercial electrical telegraph, in parallel with his ongoing research into the nature of sound as propagated via vibrations in the air.

After reproducing Hooke's experiments and devising his own, Wheatstone demonstrated that a "Conducting-wire for transmission of Sounds" could be attached to the sounding board of a musical instrument such as a pianoforte or a harp at a perpendicular angle, which would then transmit the sounds to a similar instrument via its sounding board at the other end.

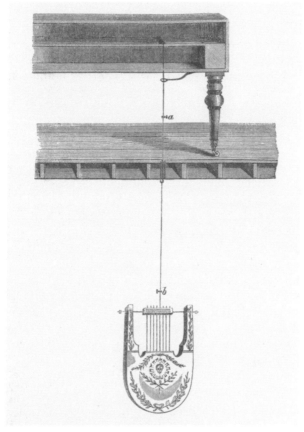

Sir Charles Wheatstone (engraver unknown), "Conducting-wire for the transmission of Sounds," 1831

Moreover,

> the sounds of an instrument may be at the same time transmitted to more than one place: for instance, communications may be made from a square piano-forte to a resounding instrument above, and to another below; and the communication may be even continued through a series of reciprocating instruments. If the instruments be not in adjacent rooms, but be further removed from each other, a person in the intermediate room, through which the conductor passes, will hear no sound but what is communicated by the ordinary means. Hence it would be possible to extend a horizontal conductor through a series of rooms belonging to different houses, and (provided the instrument connected with one of its extremities be constantly played upon) to hear at pleasure the performance in any of these rooms, by merely attaching a reciprocating instrument to the conductor; on removing this instrument, the sonorous undulations would pass inaudibly to the next apartment.[5]

Similarly, Wheatstone observed, one could produce a generic sounding board to "resound" all of the instruments in an "entire orchestra" in order to transmit them via the conducting-wire to another place. (Wheatstone noted that the sounding board could only register a faint signal; optimistically, though, he reported that "on placing the ear close to [the reciprocating instrument at the other end], a diminutive band is heard, in which all the instruments preserve their distinctive qualities... The effect is as a landscape seen in miniature beauty through a concave lens.")[6]

With this set of observations, the wired world was born, a mass media challenge to the primacy of print media, and Wheatstone was one of its most aggressive theorists. He noted that because sound travels roughly seventeen times faster through "iron wire, glass, cane, or deal-wood rods" than it does through the air (or, as many had it well into the twentieth century, the ether), it would be "as easy to transmit sounds through such conductors from Aberdeen to London, as it is now to establish a communication from one chamber to another." All that was needed was a means of "communicating sounds produced in the air with sufficient intensity to solid bodies." Microphones and amplifiers were some ways off yet, even if Wheatstone had developed the former device in a rudimentary way, but the conceptual organization of Wheatstone's experiments allowed for a full vision of communication from machine to machine over vast distances at high speeds.[7]* It is perhaps natural, but I do not believe it is reasonable or even sanely irrational, to focus on the medium of the wire as the primary protagonist of media history. This is precisely because the wire begets, in its various heydays, a complex of techno-ethical crises, appearing and disappearing seemingly at will.

The wired world, as even Wheatstone's interconnected musical instruments made clear,

* A few years after his early experiments on solid media transmission of sound, Wheatstone published a substantive article on "Reed Organ-Pipes, Speaking Machines, Etc.," which made plain his ambition to produce a "written language" adequate to "the articulations of speech." This would, in his view, overcome the obstacle of translating sound from gaseous to solid media for the purpose of telecommunications. Instead, as is well known, Samuel F.B. Morse solved the language problem the other way around in telegraphy, and many others in a wholly different way through "wireless telegraphy" or radio.[8]

See also Spyros Papapetros's discussion of wires and architecture → p. 176

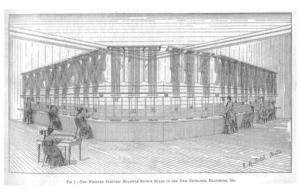

Fig 1.—The Writer's Electric Multiple Switch Board in the New Exchange, Baltimore, Md.

"Multiple Switchboard at Baltimore," engraving, 1884

was one in which the relationship of architecture to telephony—or, if you like, walls to wires—was inverted. Instead of serving as a direct means of bounding, reflecting and projecting sound, architecture had to be interconnected and penetrated by "solid media" of a different technical character. A glance at a multiple switchboard from the 1880s is, I hope, temporarily enough to carry the point. The intricate web of wires penetrates the architecture of the telephone exchange building according to its own logic and requires the design of an interface at the scale of furniture in order to make the business of switching manageable for its female operators.

By the time Marconi and an international coterie of inventors, engineers, and amateur enthusiasts had developed so-called wireless telegraphy near the turn of the twentieth century, these networks of wires had been threaded through buildings on urban, regional, and national scales by increasingly massive corporate concerns—such as American Telephone & Telegraph (the largest corporation ever to exist in human history) and Western Union, in the United States—and a wired infrastructure had bridged the oceans. But the "magic" of transmitting electromagnetic radiation through the air, as opposed to along wires, led to a temporary belief that these wires and the walls that served as their inconvenient adjuncts would no longer be necessary.[9] Radio is only ever *apparently* "wireless"—in fact, the complexity of the machinery needed for even an artificially simple live broadcast (i.e., leaving out recording and playback loops) demanded an amount of wiring an order of magnitude greater than even the largest of telephone switching installations. As a cantankerous "but on the whole reasonably friendly critic of broadcasting" in the earliest days of the BBC put it, "I do not like the description 'wireless': why describe the thing as a negation?"[10]

The first comprehensive published statement on the theory of radio station design appeared rather late, in the form of an article by the architect Dexter Purinton in the pages of *American Architect* in 1935. Purinton began "Radio... A New Architectural Problem" by noting that precisely because the physics of radio broadcasting was but poorly understood "even by the experts themselves...the architect faces not so much the problem of housing complicated machinery as that of providing a kind of insulated shelter in which a dangerously powerful force can be safely bent to the service of an engineering technique which is expanding with rapidity."[11]* Purinton's prod at the engineers, physicists, and inventors of radio puts one in mind of the criticism frequently made of Marconi himself, that he did not understand radio broadcasting technology; he just produced it, mostly by cobbling together other inventors' discoveries; Purinton was clearly at pains to stake out a role for architects in the exciting young field of radio station design through an appeal to a perceived risk that only architects could ameliorate.

* Similar, later articles covered many of the same bases as Purinton, albeit with greater detail; in particular, a special issue of *L'Architecture française* on "Maisons de la Radio" included an introductory essay by Léon Conturie, the chief engineer of French radio broadcasting. Conturie emphasizes the inversion of the relationship between walls and wires in his analysis of recording and broadcast studios: "These studios, which do not have, for the most part, anything in common with traditional theaters, must meet special and extreme acoustical conditions. Enclose these in a network of technical installations, a veritable nervous system that brings these programs ready to be broadcasted to a central point."[12]

The sources and character of this danger were multiple. In strictly physical terms, because radio frequency current passes through air and matter, it is most easily conducted, not in the body of a material, but along its surface and if not properly grounded, will collect upon a surface until it jumps viciously across space to the nearest point of contact. Electrical current shocks. But radio frequency burns, often so deeply that death results even though only a slight shock is present.[13]

Thus the architect needed to provide a redundant system of grounding throughout the radio station building or buildings—"the slightest spark" could destroy not only equipment but kill its human operators as well. Every piece of metal in the building, no matter how small, had to be connected with a secure bond to other metal pieces in a continuous connection to the ground: "The interior of a transmitting station must be completely enclosed with some sort of metallic shield," and since radio frequency ionizes dust and causes sparks (the same noted by observers of Marconi's earliest station), the control room of the station needed to be kept in a state of "absolute cleanliness."[14] Purinton recommended a central forced-air cooling system—the interiors of these metal buildings, with generators and resistors humming, would be extremely hot—with paper filtration, and all plumbing pipes kept at the exterior of the building as much as possible to isolate them from dangerous potentials.

These constraints on the architect's design produced other consequences as well. Since the safest and most efficient organization of the building involved the segregation, to the greatest extent possible, between the bulk of the equipment and the space inhabited by human beings, it was also necessary, in Purinton's view, to understand the architecture of radio as governed by a different geometry—rather than think of the building in terms of "square foot areas," he argued, "units for radio transmission are best arranged to minimize lengths of all bus and cable connections."[15] The inhabitable areas of the building would thus be organized so as to facilitate shortening the length of the wiring, by thinking of the building first as a long service chase that would house the dense web of wires—this meant that even when organized as efficiently as was then possible, a medium-sized 50kW station would require an absolute minimum of 60,000 cubic feet of space. The already minimal habitable interior of the building would also be as open as possible, since "interior obstructions" would produce dangerous electrical potentials "in spite of the most careful grounding." Therefore, the radio station as an architectural artifact became an intricately layered series of shells: The outer structure of the building corresponded roughly to conventional tectonic conventions, but this surrounded a layer of chases, which then surrounded a layer of insulation, which then surrounded two inhabitable interiors—one for the wires, the other for the engineers. All of this complex structure, and the sophisticated geometries of the wiring threaded out on and through various boards and boxes, was necessary to realize the relatively simple geometry of an undulating wave rippling outward in every direction from the top of the broadcasting tower.

Purinton offered up his own design for WOR's radio transmitting station in Carteret, New Jersey—done in his capacity as an architect working in the large New York firm Voorhees, Gmelin and Walker—as an exemplary instance of meeting

Voorhees, Gmelin, and Walker (Dexter Purinton, project architect), WOR Radio Transmitting Station, Carteret, NJ, 1935

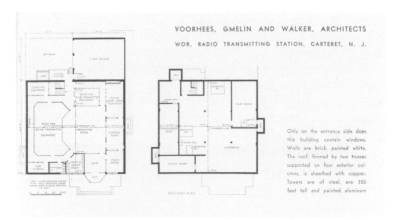

VOORHEES, GMELIN AND WALKER, ARCHITECTS

WOR, RADIO TRANSMITTING STATION, CARTERET, N. J.

Only on the entrance side does this building contain windows. Walls are brick, painted white. The roof, formed by two trusses supported on four exterior columns, is sheathed with copper. Towers are of steel, are 350 feet tall and painted aluminum.

WOR Radio Transmitting Station, plans

the heightened demands of a 50kW system.[16]* This relatively small-scale radio station illustrates much of the intricacy of radio architecture; however, there is much more than transmission to consider. Given that radio was produced through a massive complex of storage and playback media running

* As was the firm's practice in publishing their designs, the lead architect on a project was allowed to publish an article in the professional press on the building; however, the stripped-down Art Deco façade of the building, with its parallel bands of crisply organized bricks divided by recessed string courses, seems to indicate that Purinton was strongly marked by working alongside the firm's principal and lead designer Ralph Walker.[17]

from print to phonography to film to architecture to transmission towers, it is easy to forget the invisible origins of the radio signal: the administrative offices necessary to govern radio production, and the performance and recording studios in which the "content" of the new medium was played and captured, synchronized and transmitted. Perhaps the single most significant building from the period to accommodate both of these essential aspects of the radio apparatus was the headquarters of the BBC Broadcasting House. Designed in 1928 by George Val Myer and the first civil engineer of the BBC, Marmaduke T. Tudsbery, along with interiors by Raymond McGrath, Serge Chermayeff, Edward Maufe, and Wells Coates (among many

**George Val Myer and Marmaduke T. Tudsbery,
BBC Broadcasting House, London, 1928–31**

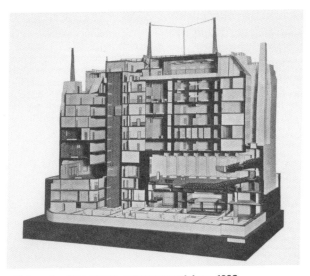

BBC Broadcasting House, cutaway model, ca. 1928

others), and completed (in its first iteration) in 1932, this Art Deco rabbit warren of offices and studios in Marylebone is far too complex an architectural work to address here.[18] But the strangeness of this building—a building in which a film called *Death at Broadcasting House* (1934) was shot using sets built inside Broadcasting House simulating the building itself—might be enough to return the reader to the core question. If "media determine our situation," then what situates those media?

It is as if the magic of the medium, the legerdemain that allows invisible waves to transport electricity and sound from one place to another via the "ether," has obscured the history of the architectural component of the radio apparatus—studio, station, home, vehicle—from view.* There can be little question that an architecture, one produced, as it were, by a lost theory, plays its role. One urgency, I am guessing, might be to recover that theory, in service of a description of the wired architectures that so sensationally deprive us of any sensation of the wires that bind us.

* Of course, this historical project is not one of an uncritical recuperative nature; instead, it is polemical, seeking to plunge other historical narratives into the darkness of forgetting by shifting historical method from monography to discourse analysis. As Friedrich Kittler writes in "Forgetting": "Discourse analysis practices a 'joyful positivism' [Foucault]. It accords not even a relative autonomy to philosophical discourse. It does not deal with the one *Urschrift* which every metaphysics of presence has supposedly forgotten, but rather with the many forgotten techniques which were invented to counteract forgetting."[19]

1   A longer essay on a similar topic was previously published in *Media-N*, vol. 10, no. 1 (Spring 2014), available at median. newmediacaucus.org/art-infrastructures-hardware/wires-walls-and-wireless-notes-toward-an-investigation-of-radio-architecture. My thanks to the editors for allowing republication of some portions of that text here.
    Published in Cass Gilbert, *Reminiscences and Addresses*, with "Reminiscences" by Julia Finch Gilbert (New York: privately printed, 1935). The poem is not dated, but from the context in which it was published it is possible to deduce that it was offered as a eulogy on the occasion of Gilbert's death in 1934.

2   J.F. Gilbert, "Reminiscences," 8–9.

3   John E. Kingsbury, *The Telephone and Telephone Exchanges: Their Invention and Their Development* (New York: Longmans, Green and Co., 1915), 7.

4   Robert Hooke, preface to *Micrographia: Or Some Physiological Descriptions of Minute Bodies Made by Magnifying Glasses with Observations and Inquiries Thereupon* (London: John Martyn, Printer to the Royal Society, 1667), n.p.

5   Charles Wheatstone, "On the Transmission of Musical Sounds Through Solid Linear Conductors, and on Their Subsequent Reciprocation," *Journal of the Royal Institution of Great Britain* 2 (November 1831), republished in Sir Charles Wheatstone, *The Scientific Papers of Sir Charles Wheatstone... Published by the Physical Society of London* (London: Taylor and Francis, 1879), 47–63, 57.

6   Wheatstone, *The Scientific Papers*, 58–59.

7   Charles Wheatstone, "Reed Organ-Pipes, Speaking Machines, Etc.," in the *London and Westminster Review* (1837; republished in Wheatstone, *The Scientific Papers*, 348–367).

8   On the intersections between Morse's contributions to telegraphy, cryptography, and the fine arts, see Jean-Philippe Antoine, "La démocratie à l'oeuvre: *The House of Representatives* et *The Gallery in the Louvre* de Samuel F.B. Morse (1791–1872)," unpublished lecture available at www.youscribe.com/ catalogue/rapports-et-theses/ savoirs/sciences-humaines-et-sociales/la-democratie-a-l-oeuvre-the-house-of-representatives-et-the-gallery-1547486, accessed March 3, 2014.

9   Numerous utopian paeans to the power of "wireless" in this period proliferated in magazines, newspapers, and books; there were even efforts to make this technology portable many decades before Bell Labs and others developed the "cellular" telephone network. See Grant Wythoff, "Pocket Wireless and the Shape of Media to Come," *Grey Room* 51 (Spring 2013), 40–63.

10   Lord Riddell, *Radio Times* (December 21, 1923), quoted in Asa Briggs, *The Birth of Broadcasting*, vol. I of *The History of Broadcasting in the United Kingdom* (London, New York, and Toronto: Oxford University Press, 1961), 15.

11   Dexter Purinton, "Radio... A New Architectural Problem," *American Architect*, vol. 146, no. 2,634 (June 1935): 68–76. An earlier article, "Engineering Problems of Radio Broadcasting Studio Design," had appeared in *American Architect* six years earlier (135 [February 5, 1929], 195–203), but it was much less comprehensive and mainly discussed the logistical organization of spaces in order to accommodate the needs of musicians, actors, producers, special effects producers, and so on.

12   Léon Conturie, "Maisons de la Radio," *L'Architecture française*, vol. 9, no. 77–88 (1948): 3–16 (quotation from page 3, my translation).

13   Purinton, "Radio," 70.

14   Purinton, "Radio," 70.

15   Purinton, "Radio," 70.

16   As indicated in a captioned photograph from *Broadcasting: Broadcast Advertising*, vol. 16, no. 7 (April 1, 1939): 24.

17   See Kathryn E. Holliday, *Ralph Walker: Architect of the Century* (New York: Rizzoli, 2012). On the firm's somewhat ambiguous attitude toward technology—it served as "house architect" to AT&T and many other high technology firms from the 1920s to the 1950s—see in particular Stephen F. Voorhees and Ralph T. Walker, "The Machine and Architecture," in Charles A. Beard, ed., *Toward Civilization* (New York: Longmans, Green & Co., 1930), 213–231.

18   On Broadcasting House, see Mark Hines, *The Story of Broadcasting House: Home of the BBC* (London: Merrell, 2008), and Colin Reid, *Action Stations: A History of Broadcasting House* (London: Robson Books, 1987).

19   Friedrich Kittler, "Forgetting" [1979], trans. Caroline Wellbery and David Wellbery, *Discourse* 3 (Spring 1981), 88–121, esp. 93. A wonderful recent book by Mark Goble, *Beautiful Circuits: Modernism and the Mediated Life* (New York: Columbia University Press, 2010), brilliantly explores this problem of the archive in chapter 4, "The New Permanent Record."

Conversation

CATHERINE INGRAHAM: I'd be interested in one point of clarification from Keller and Arindam. In your treatments of the problem of "urgency," you both to some degree referred agency to some other domain outside of architecture. It takes different forms—financiers or deans or administrators or bureaucracies or other offstage influences. I was struck by Keller's brilliant responsiveness to the theoretical possibilities in those outside domains, which can be both malevolent and ossifying but at the same time creative and eye opening, and certainly instrumental.

If this is the case, it seems odd that we keep reestablishing and insisting on a place for theoretical action to be happening within the university setting and within architecture schools in particular. Maybe this even relates to John's work on wireless broadcast, in that it refocuses our awareness outside the myopia of disciplinary discourse. So I'm wondering if this is true—should we be looking at these kind of displaced agencies for our theoretical urgencies?

ARINDAM DUTTA: I'll just premise my response by giving sort of a two-sentence definition of "agency" as I see it. When we talk about an agent of the East India Company or an insurance agent, we never presume that they're acting in their own interests. If we think of ourselves as free, there is a constitution that mandates that we are free—so in other words, agency is always a carriage of some other agency that places us in its place, right?

113

Second Panel

For me, the point isn't necessarily to understand that one is an agent only in the sense that one is carrying a certain institutional impetus—that's neither controversial nor problematic. As teachers, we teach curricula which are meant to carry some broader discourse in the names of the professors, which is thoroughly within that sense of agency. The real problem is to understand that these agencies are historically bound through and through, and not to eternalize a particular moment of consensus that we may have been used to thinking. The idea is to understand that there is no de facto ground on which one can truly stand, and it is only from there that one can begin to talk about ground.

In that sense, there is also a broader shift in the status of the university, which is pretty definitive. If you consider that theory is grounded in the vocation of the humanities broadly speaking, we have to remember that prior to the Second World War, the humanities were more or less ensconced within the salons of the liberal elite. Who could afford to do humanities but the rich? I mean, Walter Benjamin was rich. We have to accept that. What we see in the aftermath of the Second World War is an institutional impetus towards the democratization of the humanities, premised precisely on certain ideological value chains that we've already talked about. All I'm saying today is that these value chains probably no longer hold, and therefore the humanities, or creativity, is being pushed into a certain kind of para-economic activity, which makes itself apparent in its everydayness. For me, that is where theory must begin—at that ground where there is no ground.

KELLER EASTERLING: I was just trying to point out a split between what theory is saying and what it's doing—the dispositions that we impose on it that can permit or deny information, the ways in which it can erase the very thing that you're trying to create, and the ways in which it can give you all the information that you need. To model something like that in our architecture culture or in academia is potentially useful. Without being able to see that dispositional register, how do you deal with evidence in the world? I can't understand the political theater of Putin (or Putin and Snowden) just from the knowledge of their official statements. That's not going to help sort through the turns and shifting intentions behind what they're doing, which is so different from what they're saying. Theory can be evasive in the same way in the political theater of academia.

JOHN HARWOOD: One of the things that attracts me to this radio project is that while there's a ton of history written on the radio, it's all about what people were doing—who was singing what, who was giving what speech. If there's this divide between different dispositions of theory that produce different artifacts, in this instance we're contenting ourselves to this point with simply historicizing what a certain theoretical and political project would like us to worry about—which is Pevsner on the radio, and Benjamin's musings on the metropolis and "Enlightenment for Children"—and not the artifice that produces these effects, which is intensely complex.

INGRAHAM: There's a perpetual need to recalibrate theory, if you can say that, by marking the changing agency of parties or entities or postures or dispositions involved. There's an abiding structure. We want to say that theories are modeled on evidence, and that evidence also makes use of theory—(happy bedfellows)—but at the same time, each has its own domain, and there's a sort of will-to-power on both sides. Architecture continues to talk about a spatiality, that somehow lies behind political events; as if it embodied the potential for moving beyond what we mean by "space" as a geometric idea.

DUTTA: We've been discussing this at MIT a little bit—are architects really invested in space? I pose this to my design colleagues. Whatever happened to the plan? Are plans still viable? I mean, that's one representation of space that does not always seem endowed with theoretical promise today. I'm not entirely sure that architects today are actually interested in space.

WIGLEY: I just want to observe that A through H was unbelievably eloquent. An inspiration.

HARWOOD: We even got through I.

INGRAHAM: Yeah, that's right, thanks Mark. [Laughter]

PRIVACY AND PUBLICITY IN THE AGE OF SOCIAL MEDIA
Beatriz Colomina

Architectural theory, 2000+? What has really changed? What has become urgent?

In terms of media, the most striking thing is that in 2000 there was no social media. In 2000, Friends Reunited was launched in Great Britain to help people locate old school friends. This was the first successful online social network. By the end of the year, it had 3,000 users, and a year later 2.5 million. In 2002, Friendster got 3 million users in three months. The year 2003 was the year of MySpace. In 2004, Facebook started at Harvard as a collegiate version of Friendster; within a month, half of the Harvard College population was on it. Soon it expanded to other colleges, and in 2005 Facebook opened to high school students. The year 2005 was also the year in which YouTube was launched with an invitation to "Broadcast Yourself." The year 2006 was Twitter, as well as the year in which Facebook opened to anybody above thirteen years old. WhatsApp arrived in 2009 and is the most globally popular messaging app with 800 million users. Instagram, launched in October 2010, had 300 million active users as of December 2014. There are now about 1.5 billion monthly active users of Facebook. This short history could continue on and on. There has been an exponential acceleration of the number of available channels for broadcast of the self, matched by an accelerating number of people using them. It is estimated that by the end of 2015, 4 billion people—60 percent of the world population—will be connected to the Internet, most of them through mobile devices.

This represents a complete transformation of the way we live, with huge implications for architecture. Indeed, it is an architectural transformation. This is what is urgent for me, and for architectural theory, today. We need to understand the world we live in—architects and architectural theorists may be the last to realize how *architectural* this change is. What are the architectural consequences of this state of things? What is the architecture of social media?

But where to start investigating this massive event? Already in 1999, an article in the *New York Times* reported that a quarter of a million people were exposing their lives online, and that one million webcams had been sold that year alone. These were thought to be shocking numbers. Today billions are regularly exposing themselves online. The line between what is private and what is public, what is inside and what is outside, has been radically redrawn. Let's start then by asking the simplest architectural question: Where are we doing all of this? What is the space of social media?

In an Australian survey of 2013 it was found that 34 percent of social network users admitted to logging on at work, 13 percent in school, 18 percent in their cars, 44 percent in bed, 7 percent in the bathroom, and 6 percent on the toilet. What's most shocking about this report is how much of social life takes place not in public or even the living room, but in the car, the bathroom, on the toilet—and above all in the bed, floating alone without bedroom, house, or city. The bed has become the epicenter of the universe.

In what is probably now a conservative estimate, the *Wall Street Journal* reported in 2012 that 80 percent of young New York City professionals work regularly from bed. The fantasy of the home office has given way to the reality of the bed office. The very meaning of the word "office" has been transformed. Millions of dispersed beds are taking over from concentrated office buildings. The boudoir is defeating the tower. Networked electronic technologies have removed any limit to what can be done in bed. It is not just that the bed office has been made possible by new media—rather, new media is designed to extend a hundred-year-old dream of domestic connectivity to millions of people. The history of the office building has been shadowed by a secret history of the supercharged bed.

How did we get here?

In his famous short text "Louis-Philippe, or the Interior," Walter Benjamin wrote of the splitting of work and home in the nineteenth century:

> Under Louis-Philippe, the private citizen enters the stage of history… For the private person, living space becomes, for the first time, antithetical to the place of work. The former

is constituted by the interior; the office is its complement. The private person who squares his accounts with reality in his office demands that his interior be maintained in his illusions… From this spring the phantasmagorias of the interior. For the private individual the private environment represents the universe. In it he gathers remote places and the past. His living room is a box in the world theater.[1]

Industrialization brought with it the eight-hour shift and the radical separation between the home and the office or factory, between rest and work, night and day. Post-industrialization collapses work back into the home and takes it further into the bedroom and into the bed itself. Phantasmagoria is no longer lining the room in wallpaper, fabric, images, and objects. It is now in electronic devices. The whole universe is concentrated on a small screen with the bed floating on an infinite sea of information. To lie down is not to rest but to move. The bed is now a site of action. But the voluntary invalid has no need of their legs. The bed has become the ultimate prosthetic and a whole new industry is devoted to providing contraptions to facilitate work while lying down—reading, writing, texting, recording, broadcasting, listening, talking, and, of course, eating, drinking, sleeping, or making love, activities that seem to have been turned, of late, into work itself. Waiters in restaurants in the United States ask if you are "still working on that" before removing your plate or your glass. Endless advice is dispensed about how to "work" on your personal relationships, "schedule" sex with your partner. Sleeping is definitely hard work too, for millions, with the psycho-pharmaceutical industry providing new drugs every year and an army of sleep experts providing advice on how to achieve this apparently ever more elusive goal—all in the name of higher productivity, of course. Everything done in the bed has become work.

This philosophy was already embodied in the figure of Hugh Hefner, who famously almost never left his bed, let alone his house. He literally moved his office to his bed in 1960 when he moved into the Playboy Mansion at 1340 North State Parkway,

Chicago, turning it into the epicenter of a global empire and his silk pajamas and dressing gown into his business attire. "I don't go out of the house at all!!!... I am a contemporary recluse," he told Tom Wolfe, guessing that the last time he was out had been three and a half months before and that in the last two years he had been out of the house only nine times.[2] Fascinated, Wolfe described him as "the tender-tympany green heart of an artichoke."[3]

Playboy turns the bed into a workplace. From the mid-1950s on, the bed becomes increasingly sophisticated, outfitted with all sorts of entertainment and communication devices as a kind of control room. The magazine devoted many articles to the design of the perfect bed. Hefner acted as the model with his famous round bed in the Playboy Mansion in Chicago. The bed was first introduced as a feature in the "Playboy Townhouse" article of 1962, which presents a detailed but largely unrealized project in plans, sections, and renderings that had been originally commissioned to be Hefner's own house. Not by chance, the only piece of the design to be realized was the bed,

Burt Glinn, photograph of Hugh Hefner in bed, 1966

which was installed in the mansion. The bed itself is a house. Its rotating and vibrating structure is packed with a small fridge, hi-fi, telephone, filling cabinets, bar, microphone, Dictaphone, video cameras, headphones, TV, breakfast table, work surfaces, and control for all the lighting fixtures, for the man who never wants to leave. The bed was Hefner's office, his place of business, where he conducted interviews, made his phone calls, selected images, adjusted layouts, edited texts, ate, drank, and consulted with playmates.

Hefner was not alone. The bed may have been the ultimate American office at midcentury. In an interview in the *Paris Review* in 1957, Truman Capote is asked, "What are some of your writing habits? Do you use a desk? Do you write on a machine?" To which he answers:

> I am a completely horizontal author. I can't think unless I'm lying down, either in bed or stretched on a couch and with a cigarette and a coffee handy. I've got to be puffing and sipping. As the afternoon wears on, I shift from coffee to mint tea to sherry to martinis. No, I don't use a typewriter. Not in the beginning. I write my first version in longhand. Then I do a complete revision, also in longhand… Then I type a third draft on yellow paper… No, I don't get out of bed to do this. I balance the machine on my knees. Sure, it works fine; I can manage a hundred words a minute.[4]

From morning to afternoon to evening, the drinks, the paper, and the equipment changes, but his position on the bed does not.

Even architects set up office in bed at midcentury. Richard Neutra started working the moment he woke up with elaborate equipment enabling him to design, write, or even interview in bed. As his son Dion Neutra revealed:

> Dad's best time for creative thinking was early in the morning, long before any activity had started in the office below. He often stayed in bed working with ideas and designs, even extending into appointments which had been made

123

earlier. His one concession to convention was to put on a tie over his night shirt when receiving visitors while still propped up in bed![5]

Neutra's bed in the VDL house in Silverlake, Los Angeles, included two public phones; three communication stations for talking with other rooms in the house, the office below, and even another office 500 meters away; three different call bells; drafting boards and easels that folded down over the bed; electric lights and a radio-gramophone controlled from a dashboard overhead. A bedside table rolling on casters held the tape recorder, electric clock, and storage compartments for drawing and writing equipment so that he could, as Neutra put it in a letter to his sister, "use every minute from morning to late night."[6]

Postwar America inaugurated the high-performance bed as an epicenter of productivity, a new form of industrialization that was exported globally and has now become available to an international army of dispersed but interconnected producers. A new kind of factory without walls is constructed by compact electronics and extra pillows for the 24/7 generation.

The kind of equipment that Hefner envisioned (some of which, like the answering machine, didn't yet exist) is now expanded for the Internet and social media generation, who not only work in bed but socialize in bed, exercise in bed, read the news in bed, and entertain sexual relationships with people miles away from their beds. The *Playboy* fantasy of the nice girl next door is more likely realized today with someone on another continent than in the same building or neighborhood—a person you may have never seen before and may never see again, and it is anybody's guess if she is real (as in, exists in some place and time) or an electronic construction. Does it matter? As in the recent film *Her*, a moving depiction of life in the soft, uterine state that is a corollary to our new mobile technologies, the "her" in question is an operating system that turns out to be a more satisfying partner than a person. The protagonist lies in bed with Her, chatting, arguing, making love.

Advertisement by Bluebeam for working in bed

Joaquin Phoenix romancing his operating system from bed in Spike Jonze's *Her*, 2013

125

If, according to Jonathan Crary, capitalism is the end of sleep, colonizing every minute of our lives for production and consumption, the actions of the voluntary recluse are not so voluntary in the end.[7] It may be worth noting that communism had its own ideas of bringing the bed to the workplace. In 1929, at the height of Stalin's first five-year plan—with the working day extended and mass exhaustion of factory workers in the face of staggering production quotas—the Soviet government organized a competition for a new city of rest for 100,000 workers. Konstantin Melnikov presented the "Sonata of Sleep," a new building type for collective sleep, with mechanized beds rocking the workers to unconsciousness and slanted floors to eliminate the need for pillows. Centralized control booths with sleep attendants would regulate temperature, humidity, smell, and even sounds to maximize sleep. The inspiration was symptomatically American—Melnikov had read about a military academy in Pensacola, Florida, that taught language to sleeping cadets. Sleep itself had become part of the industrial process.

In today's attention-deficit-disorder society, we have discovered that we work better in short bursts punctuated by rest. Today many companies provide sleeping pods in the office to maximize productivity. Bed and office are never far apart in the 24/7 world. Special self-enclosed beds have been designed for office spaces—turning themselves into compact sealed capsules, mini space ships, that can be used in isolation or gathered together in clusters or lined up in rows for synchronized sleep—understood best as a part of work rather than its opposite.

Between the bed inserted in the office and the office inserted in the bed a whole new horizontal architecture has taken over. It is magnified by the "flat" networks of social media that have themselves been fully integrated into the professional, business, and industrial environment in a collapse of traditional distinctions between private and public, work and play, rest and action. The bed itself—with its ever more sophisticated mattress, linings, and technical attachments—is the basis of an intrauterine environment that combines the sense of deep interiority with the sense of hyper-connectivity to the outside. Not by chance, Hefner's round bed was a kind of flying saucer hovering in space in a room without windows, as if in orbit, with the TV hanging above as the reference to planet Earth. It is a circle, the classical image of the universe. The bed today has also become a portable universe, equipped with every possible technology of communication. A midcentury fantasy has turned into a mass reality.

What is the architecture of this new space and time?

In the 1960s and '70s, experimental architects devoted themselves to the equipment of the new mobile nomads in a whole galaxy of lightweight, portable interiors with soft reclining spaces as the core of a complex of prosthetic extensions (among many others, projects like Michael Webb's Cushicle and Suitaloon). All of these can be understood as high-performance beds complete with media, artificial atmospheres, color, light,

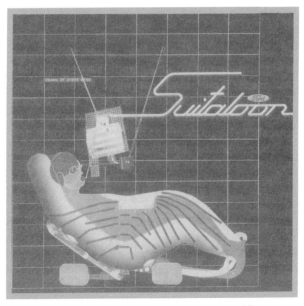

Michael Webb, Cushicle + Suit as Chaise Longue, 1968

David Greene, Inflatable Suit-Home, final stage of sequence of suit being inflated from Package to Home, 1968; suit made by Pat Haines based on the Suitaloon project by Michael Webb

and smell, a kind of pop-psychedelic Melnikov with the worker now sleeping inside the control booth. Reyner Banham wrote about naked Jane Fonda flying through space in her fur-lined horizontal bubble in the same breath that he enthusiastically embraced the architecture of *Playboy*. It was just a matter of time before John Lennon and Yoko Ono held a weeklong Bed-In for Peace in the Amsterdam Hilton Hotel during their honeymoon in March 1969. The idea of a Bed-In came from "Sit-In" protests and was intended as a nonviolent protest against war and to promote world peace. "Make love, not war" was the slogan of the day, but to the disappointment of journalists, John and Yoko were fully dressed in their pajamas, sitting in bed, as John put it, like angels. The bed had taken over from the street as the site of protest. They invited the world's press into their room every day between 9 a.m. and 9 p.m., treating the bed as an office in which they worked while journalists streamed in and images streamed out.

Promotional still for *Barbarella*, 1968

John Lennon and Yoko Ono, Bed-In for Peace, Amsterdam, 1969

What is the nature of this new interior in which we have decided collectively to check ourselves in? What is the architecture of this prison in which night and day, work and play are no longer differentiated and we are permanently under surveillance, even as we sleep in the control booth? New media turns us all into inmates, constantly under surveillance, even as we celebrate endless connectivity. We have each become "a contemporary recluse," as Hefner put it half a century ago.

In Laura Poitras's film *Citizenfour*, we see close-ups of Edward Snowden sitting on his bed in a Hong Kong hotel for days on end, surrounded by his laptops, communicating with journalists in the room and around the world about the secret world of massive global surveillance. The biggest invasion of privacy in the history of the planet is revealed from bed and dominates all media. The most public figure in the world at that moment is a recluse. Architecture has been inverted.

Edward Snowden in Laura Poitras's *Citizenfour*, 2014

1   Walter Benjamin, "Louis-Philippe, or the Interior," in *Reflections: Essays, Aphorisms, Autobiographical Writings*, ed. Peter Demetz, trans. Edmund Jephcott (New York: Schoken Books, 1978), 154.

2   Tom Wolfe, "King of the Status Dropouts," *The Pump House Gang* (New York: Farrar, Straus & Giroux, 1965).

3   Wolfe, "King of the Status Dropouts," 63.

4   "Truman Capote, The Art of Fiction No. 17," interviewed by Patti Hill, *The Paris Review* 16 (Spring–Summer 1957).

5   Dion Neutra, "The Neutra Genius: Innovation & Vision," *Modernism*, vol. 1, no. 3 (December 1998).

6   Richard Neutra to Verena Saslavsky (December 4, 1953), Dione Neutra Papers, quoted in Thomas S. Hines, *Richard Neutra and the Search for Modern Architecture: A Biography and History* (Los Angeles: University of California Press, 1982), 251.

7   Jonathan Crary, *24/7: Late Capitalism and the Ends of Sleep* (New York: Verso, 2013).

THE RISE OF THE SO-CALLED PRE-MODERN
Mark Jarzombek

We need to think critically about our historiographical formations, and in particular about an unstated and untheorized complicity between the discourses around contemporary practice and the broader disciplinary/theoretical frameworks of our understanding of modernism. The way to start is not to address the question head on but rather to look behind it, at its wake, so to speak, for we have witnessed a important secondary revolution in our field—a revolution that has been so silent that we are yet to discuss it even once. We have not noticed that as modernism became an established field, it produced a ghostly shadow of itself that is now a full-bodied discipline. It goes by the moniker "The Pre-Modern." The term was first used about fifteen years ago. Witnessing the birth of a new discipline is such a rare occurrence that it is usually celebrated; in this case, we have not even noticed it.

Part of the problem, of course, is that we (and by *we* I mean the architecture history/theory world) have abandoned much of our interest in a whole host of disciplines. In the 1970s, there was a sociologist at the Department of Architecture of the E.T.H., an anthropologist at MIT, a classicist at Cornell, and so on. All of these positions have disappeared, and indeed an ethos has disappeared along with them, perhaps for reasons that were relatively legitimate. Eduardo Souto de Moura stated it best when he pointed out that in the early 1970s, "context, structuralism, semiotics, anthropology, sociology, and economics predominated our training, and the mention of architecture was almost an insult."[1]

Even Renaissance architectural history fell victim to the vast housecleaning that began in the 1980s. Once thought to be the mainstay in architectural academia, it is now a dead discipline. The number of Ph.D.s in the history of Renaissance architecture that have been produced in the U.S. in the last ten years is close to zero. But who in my generation did not read James Ackerman's amazing analyses of Palladio's drawings? You didn't dream of talking to Colin Rowe without first having visited the Palazzo Pitti. And if you did not know quite a bit about Piranesi, don't even bother reading Tafuri. But today there is only one officially sanctioned academic position for Renaissance architecture left in the country, at MIT—and even there it is holding on by a hair.

But it gets worse. "Pre-Modern" has captured and embraced *all* that we "moderns" have ignored, and here I would include the field of global architectural history. Global history has finally come into its own in the last ten years, and architecture schools across the country are struggling to come to terms with this new disciplinary formation. But since it is being created at the same time as the discipline of Pre-Modern, the two are poised to be put into the same box. The potentially positive turn of the global will be undercut by the terrible negative of bracketing it off as somehow pre-modern. This is a very disturbing situation.

To prove my point, look at Harvard University's library catalog. The earliest references to Pre-Modernism start in the late '80s, and it has escalated from there. We see such titles as *Ceremonial Culture in Pre-Modern Europe* or *Pre-Modern Art of Vienna*. The venerable Max Planck Institute has just organized a conference called *Art and Knowledge in Pre-Modern Europe*. If Europeanists want to use the term to talk about the sixteenth century, then fine—but let them keep it focused on Europe. Sadly, that is not the case. There are now books like *Religions of the Silk Road: Premodern Patterns of Globalization* and *Multiples in Pre-Modern Art*. Even Gaudí is bandied about in reading lists as an example of "Pre-Modern art." A new periodization has even developed—the Late Pre-Modern!

I will say point blank: This concept is nonsense.

There cannot be such a thing as a Pre-Modern, for it would mean that modernism has become the Archimedean point of understanding history *backward* into all of time and space. Why should the rise of European technology, nation-states, and regimes of control—the concepts most associated with modernism—be the concepts against which human and architectural history is measured? It is the epitome of a civilizational arrogance, and it cuts to the core of our disciplinary project of research in the architecture history/theory world, casting a pall over its ascendancy.

The results are real. Many architectural history survey courses—90 percent of which deal with the so-called Pre-Modern—are taught by archaeologists, art historians, and anthropologists. These are all nice people, but where are the architects? Where is the architectural imagination, and the architectural history/theory world? Our recent Ph.D.s could no more tell you why Borobudur is one of the most important buildings in the world than they could See panel discussion → p. 159 the Pantheon. We have retreated from all of this; we allow these other disciplines to invade our world. My generation and our teachers fought the art historians and made architectural history/theory into a legitimate disciplinary enterprise—but we have now gone so far in that direction that soon we will be going back to them on our hands and knees, creating a situation that will be even worse than before.

My thought is this: Today's architectural history/theory world is less messy than it was in the 1970s, but this is because we have abandoned large chunks of our epistemological formation to people who do not have our architectural interests at heart. Admittedly, architectural education has become more efficient with regard to the problem of "the contemporary," but in so doing it has lost traction, ironically enough, with the broader problematic of modernity and its theorizations.

This is not the old and tired debate about history versus theory. Nor is this a question of how to integrate the proverbial humanities into architectural education. On some level it is simply a question of erudition. We live in a globalized world, and architecture students should know the range of issues associated with their discipline as they encounter that world. Their necessary erudition should include a critical take on that world's formation.

Take the example of Borobudur. It is a proto-computational building, designed completely around mathematical principles. Could we not spend some time thinking about it in a CAD studio? Its construction involved the tremendous reengineering of the surrounding hills. Could we not spend some time discussing it in the framework of buildings and landscape? In the last century, it underwent not one but two major rebuildings, the last one requiring serious transformation of its substructure. Could we not dwell even briefly on the thematics of the social construction of time? It is a UNESCO Heritage Site. Could we not discuss the nature of our officially sanctioned compulsion to restore buildings? It is a national landmark. Could we not spend time on the complex relationship between architecture and national identity in the modern world? The topicality of Borobudur continues endlessly, raising provocative, technical, disciplinary, and even philosophical questions about the status of architecture.

The main thing to recognize is that at the time of its construction, Borobudur was a *modern* building. Whenever I say something like that, I get asked, "Well, what about postmodernism? Are there then many postmodernisms?" Though I understand the nature of the question, it puts the wrong train on the track. I am not interested in modernism as an art-historical category. My definition of *modernism* is purposefully simple: Modernism is a condition of rupture. I realize full well that modernism could be other things as well, but this is my working definition, which I like in its simplicity since there is always a backward and a forward to any rupture—there will always be an erasure and a projection.

The ruptures that help us understand Borobudur are numerous. First of all, this was a building exported from India and placed (from the Indian perspective) in a remote rain forest. The idea of designing a building as a mandala at the scale of a mountain was particularly innovative. It was borrowed, however, from Hinduism. In that sense the building is significantly different from the traditional stupa, which may be big but is not "a mountain." To design a building/mountain so that it is not just accessible, but accessible in a certain complex way that allows the devotee to both become Buddha *and* visualize his life, is part of the unique genius of the design. No building today in our secular world can even try to approach this operation—to inscribe the identity of Buddhism in your being through the architectural trace. The building is a launching into the realm

Borobudur, Buddhist temple at Magelang, Indonesia, ninth century

Borobudur, Buddhist temple at Magelang, Indonesia, ninth century

of metaphysics. To say it crassly, all this boggles the mind, and was designed to do just that.

I could continue, but my point is only that this building—as a representation, as a philosophy, as an operative space of devotion, as a mathematical puzzle, as a feat of engineering—was entirely astonishing in its day. If you were a young architecture student in the year 800, where would you want to go to see the latest? To Europe? No way. Most buildings there were squat and posed few design challenges. Byzantium and Armenia had lost their charm, and there was little money for great building given all the political turmoil in the area. But in Southeast Asia—that was where it was happening. Architecture students would have flocked to Borobudur just as they go today to a building by Le Corbusier or Rem Koolhaas. We should reclaim that energy rather than simply situating Borobudur in the context of "history" and "preservation." In reclaiming that history and the excitement that architecture brings to the question of cultural definition, we are tapping into the most philosophical condition of architecture.

Hegel was the first to identify this condition. He argued that architecture and philosophy emerged at the same historical moment. He also argued that architecture over time lost its philosophical edge to the other arts, and indeed I think that our emphasis on modernity *über alles* almost proves him correct, or at least we associate "the modern" with our contemporary world. The truth is that only some buildings rise to the level of "modern." Only some buildings "rethink" the present in new terms. In that sense, I would argue that if Rem Koolhaas had lived in the ninth century, chances are good that we'd know him as the architect of Borobudur.

I admit that this is all a type of mind game, and you might think that I have abandoned my identity as a historian. Let me worry about that. What I want to convey is the basic fact that history is filled with moments in which architecture discovers new potentials to speak to its times, and beyond. This is why the category "Traditional Architecture" is as absurd as "Pre-Modern." A lot of so-called traditional architecture is indeed "traditional" in that it blandly replicates what has been done before, and perhaps for good reason. But to think that everything that has come before the modern is traditional is absurd. One sees the problem at the University of Virginia, where the course ARH 581: The Architecture of East Asia is described as "a survey and introduction of traditional architecture and allied arts in China, Japan, and Korea."[2] Just as it makes no sense to say that modern exists exclusively after 1890 (or whatever date you choose), it makes no sense to argue that Asian art before the era of modernism is "traditional."

There have been many modern moments, most associated with changes in power and economy. Borobudur, to continue the example, was built as a magnet for Indian traders and colonizers who settled in the area and turned it from a rain forest to a rice-producing region. It was a building at the frontier of reality. Like Timgad for the Romans—which was in a sense also overdesigned so as to attract settlers—this building was meant to attract devotees as a means of building the economy. It was a bravura building. What better way to import and inspire workers than to bring religion to their doorstep? It would be just as true now as then. In other words, there is more to Borobudur than just Buddhism.

Scholars describe the whole process of India's cultural expansion into Southeast Asia as Indianization. It began in the fifth century and lasted until the tenth, by which time the local regions had more or less internalized both Buddhist and Hindu practices as their own and made wealthy empires out of them. The time between the ninth century and the thirteenth century was the great high point of Southeast Asian civilization. Borobudur was perfectly timed at the turn from experiment to success, its influence spreading from Indonesia to Cambodia and up to the Kingdom of Dali (centered in what is now Yunnan province of China). The modernist experiment of re-landscaping the environment (i.e., adding a "sacred mountain"), of reengineering the plains for rice, and administering the resultant economy (as empire) was the prototype of the Khmer. They copied the success of what you might call the "Borobudur Effect," and magnified it to produce Angkor.

But like all modernities, this was all built on massive amounts of risk. The rice economy is fragile since it by necessity requires an export and import economy, open to the vicissitudes of regional and macro-regional conflict. The landscapes were also fragile, whether because of volcanoes or deforestation. Just as economies in the modern world can be here today and gone tomorrow—as in the "Rust Belt" of the United States—so, too, in Southeast Asia. Once Borobudur lost its edge (because of flooding, cheaper markets elsewhere, and even the rise of the Mongolians, who shifted the global economy to the far north), the whole thing collapsed in the thirteenth century. People still made rice, but the great Borobudur was not needed. It fell into disrepair and was soon little more than a heap of stones until the arrival of the European colonialists, who, touching it with the wand of their own modernity, thought that it should be restored. But as much as we might be interested in the preservation story, should we not be interested in the larger historical arc of the building? It is not an arc of "history" or "tradition," but the arc of modernity. Like all modernities, it belongs to us, as moderns.

In our current academic world, one that saps our understanding of the history of the so-called "Non-West," these questions are simply absent for architects. The building might be discussed by an art historian in a survey class. He or she will most likely emphasize the Buddhist representations on the walls of the temple and its sculptural profile, for that is where most of the literature concentrates, but what about the questions that interest us? There is no reading list on buildings like these, or a paltry one at best, since we—on the architecture side—don't write about these things. Nor do we try to excite the architectural student or the history/theory world to speculate about these things. Compound this by the thousands of missed opportunities with students, and then compound that by the hundreds of architectural schools, and you begin to see why I think that this is a major disciplinary problem.

The consequences are real and palpable. If we abandon these historical territories as just "history," or as just a question of archaeology and preservation, then don't imagine for a moment that those disciplines will respect our interests. The first line of defense is to refuse the creation of history positions in the "Pre-Modern." We must at all costs avoid adding legitimacy to the division between those who teach modern and those who teach Pre-Modern.

But we can do more. We must go on the offense. We must take back what is ours. Our history/theory world does not begin in the 1920s, or the 1890s. It even precedes the era of colonial entanglements. I am not saying that we should all be experts in Southeast Asian architecture of the ninth century, but if we are truly interested in "the modern," then we should realize that in the ninth century, Borobudur *was* the modern. The Borobudur Effect was just as palpable then as the Bilbao Effect today. So it is in this context—in the context of innovative design and architectural teaching—that we need to reimagine some of these places. We need to take these buildings out of what we sadly call "history" and put them back in what I hope we can all proudly call "architecture."

1   *Eduardo Souto de Moura, 1995-2005: El Croquis* 124 (2005), 16.

2   Online course description at www.virginia.edu/registrar/records/97gradrec/chapter6/gchap6-3.5.html, accessed July 15, 2014.

THE URGENCIES OF THEORETICAL STUFF
Mari Lending

I

Theory is in fact urgent, virtually a matter of life and death. This struck me recently when reading a piece in the *New York Times* titled "Legal Debate on Using Boastful Rap Lyrics as a Smoking Gun" (March 26, 2014). To me, it was breaking news that it is possible to be convicted of murder and imprisoned for life (or worse, if you happen to be in the wrong state) with poetry as the only evidence presented in court. Briefly summed up: In 2007 two young men were shot dead in Virginia. There were no witnesses and no murder weapon, and the case went cold. In 2011, a detective saw a YouTube video in which a rapper with the stage name Twain Gotti performed a song apparently describing the murders in sufficient detail to be arrested, charged, and prosecuted. The case is currently one of more than three dozen prosecutions in which rap lyrics (handwritten, published, recorded, or performed) play a prominent role as evidence in U.S. courtrooms.

Now, what could this possibly have to do with theory? The idea that rap lyrics can be considered a confession to crime belongs to a centuries-old, troubled liaison of literature and law, including the obscenity trial over Flaubert's *Madame Bovary* in the 1850s (a novel accused of being too close to reality), and a century later, the dubious conviction of an elderly, illiterate French farmer for the murder of a British couple, as the "plot" of the killings fit perfectly with the nineteenth-century novel that was, according to Roland Barthes in one of his finest mythologies, unconsciously haunting the imagination of the French judges. "If you aspire to be a gangsta rapper, by definition your lyrics need to be violent," a criminologist commented. And indeed the *New York Times* did present several smashing examples of poetry glorifying violence, played out by the colorful personas of various rappers. The one-to-one translation from the imagination of an artist to the act of manslaughter is, of course, like blaming Dostoyevsky for Raskolnikov's dark deeds—for most of us, simply an impossible and media-insensitive translation. This impossibility has been established for at least a century

145

thanks to a series of theoretical reflections on signatures, intentions, and truth. Barthes's *effet de réel* springs to mind. The mimetic power of realistic art obviously made the exchange of poetry and reality an easy one for the detectives investigating the Virginia murders, as well as for the judge and the jury. Certainly, this could be considered a victory for art, way beyond the artistic ambitions of the imprisoned rapper. However, any juror with only a vague familiarity with aesthetic theory from Freud and formalism to post-structuralism and beyond, would have had to conclude "not guilty." Art simply has other claims of truth than action, and a very different epistemological basis. However guilty the convicted rapper might be and despite his imaginable pleasure in bragging about assumed brutal accomplishments, the verdict represented a blatant blurring of the real and the imagined, of action and its representation. However far aesthetics might reside from the law, the fact that a jury (i.e., civic society) ruled guilty with lyrics as evidence reminds us that theoretical insights from the field of aesthetics may be trapped in a way too exclusive realm, on a disturbing distance from political, social, and ethical realities.

Yet, the Virginia case also evokes the reality desire of theory. Theoretical deliberation always deals with, is integral to, springs from, and changes reality. That goes for this murder case as well as for, say, a plaster cast of a fragment from the Parthenon. In the framing and definition of evidence dwells a most tangled constellation of theory and materiality. It is an entanglement that cannot easily be disentangled, it seems, whether the subject matter is performed on YouTube, displayed in a gallery, or stored out of sight.

II

As our host for this symposium has been instrumental in fashioning the territories of architectural theory since the 1980s, the invitation to speak about "The Urgencies of Architectural Theory" may be understood as a bequest, a claim, or straightforwardly as a question. Read as a question, my immediate answer would simply be no. No particular urgencies—architectural theory is fine. Just like the world in general, architecture hardly exists without theory; at least we would not be able to make sense of anything of importance without theory. That makes theoretical affinities both personal and existential. Theory has to do with how we think and feel, with what we see, and with how we understand the phenomena surrounding us, be they aesthetic, social, political, or architectural. Theory has to do with passion, with imagination, etymologically, of course, with speculation, and thus it pretty much covers everything of significance. Theory is the way we look at the world, what the Germans call *Weltanschauung*, in the most basic and classical sense.

Thus, one might find the way architects sometimes talk about theory a bit puzzling, as if theory is something else and different from architecture, a world of its own, so to say, detached from practice, history, stuff. Brutally and bluntly, let me name the phenomenon I am thinking about, "anthology," or rather, let me borrow Sylvia Lavin's encircling of a certain "Will to Anthology"; with edited volumes of architectural theory striving at lending stability to "an otherwise promiscuous body of material," designating "the literary merger of museums and psychotherapeutic counselors at trauma sites."[1] The anthology industry that for decades has sprinkled extracts of theory of the most disparate origins with the epithet "architectural" might successfully have consolidated "theory" in architecture schools and as an integral part of architectural discourse. Yet, this integration of theories of many kinds into architecture can also be seen as a disintegration of architecture from its wider place in the world and theory as disentangled from history. One might wonder if the ordering of theory into neatly botanized canons (schools, -isms, decades, and trends) of particular relevance for architecture might eclipse the historicity of theory and its historical, empirical preconditions. That was exactly what George Kubler seems to have thought when he, in the early 1960s—in polemic contrast to what he found as the "bristling ugliness" of the concept material culture favored by anthropologists to

147

distinguish ideas from artifacts—launched a history of things
to "reunite ideas and objects under the rubric of visual form."
The things he had in mind included "both artifacts and works of
art, both replicas and unique examples, both tools and expres-
sions," and as he so beautifully put it: "From all these things a
shape in time emerges."[2]

At the moment, I often think about Kubler's lovely shape
in time and his history of things, while trying to make sense of
a particular, historicist phenomenon: the proliferation of full-
scale casts of architectural monuments that in the latter part
of the nineteenth century proudly furnished museums from
Moscow to Chicago. A major mass medium, plaster monuments
were fundamental in the reframing, invention, and canonization
of ancient monuments. Turned into portable exhibits, plaster
was in fact the medium in which grand audiences experienced
architecture. Just to mention one example: In 1881 an American critic was reporting to his home audience on the Pergamon
excavation and the first public display at the Altes Museum in
Berlin of the fragments that were later constructed and exhibited
as the Pergamon Altar. Mesmerized by the still disintegrated
Hellenistic wonders, he announced that they make "us ardently
long for the day when we shall see casts from them added to the
collections of Art Museums in America."[3] His wish was soon
fulfilled. Traces of the busy transatlantic trade in monuments
in the last decades of the nineteenth century can still be found
in a museum cluster in Springfield, Massachusetts, even though
the collection first installed in the 1890s is today eclipsed by
more popular attractions, such as the Dr. Seuss museum. In a
deserted gallery hangs a full-scale panel from the Gigantomachy
frieze showing the Goddess Athena fighting a giant, accompanied by a rare and incredibly interesting wall label verifying
the provenance of the cast: "Plaster cast by the Formerei der
Kgl. Museen, Berlin, Germany." Just as the Parthenon had been
catapulted out of London and into an international orbit of exhibition, the new origins of a circulating Pergamon soon became
Berlin. Obviously, only as casts could the two monuments be
displayed in the same room.

The dissemination of architectural monuments from different times and places was a grand cultural enterprise championed by the most prominent European archaeologists, architects, art and architectural historians, as well as by directors and curators at the finest museums of antiquities, such as the Louvre and the British Museum. The benefits of casts resonated with a variety of nineteenth-century scientific taxonomies, among them chronology, evolution, style, and comparison, unachievable in even the best-equipped museums of originals. Only a well-selected museum of casts allowed for the display of architecture as profoundly historical, in one space, at full scale and in three dimensions, "in one synoptical and simultaneous view," as Charles Newton of the British Museum and the later excavator of the Mausoleum in Halicarnassus put it in 1851: Detached from their place of origin and massively displaced in time, materiality, and discourse, bits and pieces of reproduced monuments allowed for an ordering and reordering of architecture through the "great principle of chronological arrangement."[4]

However, more or less overnight, these veritable showcases of theoretical historicist ambition were conceived as an awkward liability, and many museums started the process of transferring the casts to storage, destruction, and oblivion, deeming them worthless junk. Modernist aesthetics of authenticity, new conceptions of purity, and an increasing obsession with originality had contributed to this change in taste, for which any copy was morally and aesthetically flawed. The plaster cast with its disembodied materiality, even more so.*

"As the trend away from theory's abstraction has moved the tectonic plates of research more and more towards materiality, so has its manifestation in 'things' attracted greater interest," Alina Payne states in her superb book on objects and ornaments.[6] Payne

* Getting rid of full-scale casts became an urgent matter in schools as well as in museums. As Barry Bergdoll has written: "It was precisely in opposition to this culture of models of emulation, of classical casts and relics as exemplars and as trophies of culture, that the modern movement in architecture established its credo of invention without models, of an architecture that could unburden itself from tradition."[5]

Theory in storage: More than 100 years of Parthenon casts and molds produced by the British Museum, in storage on the outskirts of London

points to a current interest in the physically perceived past, which I believe is making itself palpably present in a new vocabulary saturating architectural discourse. It is marked by a certain prefix that reveals a new affinity for returns and can be traced in the proliferation of words and objects such as replicas, reconstructions, reproductions, restorations, remakes, re-creations, repetitions, reenactments, reinventions, remediations—and flanked by an army of supportive verbs: *recycle, reuse, recompose, reimagine, restage, reactivate, reconnect, reexamine, redefine*, and many more. None of these words are new. Yet, the concurrence and current configurations of the re-glossary is noteworthy. If architectural culture might be recovering from a slight hangover caused by decades of theoretical excess, it is, I believe, a very specific theoretical backdrop that enables the current reassessment of objects, buildings, and spaces. The fundamental destabilization of the original/copy dichotomy inherited from philosophical deconstruction has slowly meandered from the realm of texts to a wide territory of objects. In lieu of nostalgia and ideas of permanence, origins, and authenticity, we are witnessing a stark preoccupation with how objects behave, change, move, work, and fluctuate, with how they circulate in time and space.

Products of scientific aspiration, historical imagination, and aesthetic appreciation, the plaster monuments belong in such a trajectory of circulating, fluctuating objects. In their heydays, they mirrored empirical preconditions and theoretical speculation. The galleries displayed contemporary debates on the history and future of architecture, theoretical deliberations that were channeled into a historiographic backstage when the casts were exiled from the galleries. The remaining collections appear enigmatic, mute, and idiosyncratic, also spatially, as Mark Wigley observes in his prosthetic genealogy of the School of Architecture at MIT, where the architectural casts once "so obscured the walls that the collection became the walls, defining, subdividing, and rearranging the space."[7]

That is, I believe, because the theoretical climate and passions these collections were once rooted in and which they once articulated is lost from sight. In hindsight, the monuments and documents (a crispy paper topography spanning from constantly updated sales catalogs of casts and photographs to cablegrams and shipping insurance documents) left behind from nineteenth-century cast culture, appear in fact as a Kublerian shape in time of their own, as true conflations of ideas and objects expressed in visual form.

10,11. Rogers Building, architectural drawing rooms, 1876

12. Rogers Building, architectural lecture and drawing room, 1876

16

Casts becoming architectural: The cast collection at the School of Architecture at MIT, as illustrated in Mark Wigley's "Prosthetic Theory"

III

The Parthenon is the superstar, also in plaster heaven. For 200 years, plaster Parthenon has been a venue for the discrete theorization of the monument, investigating the relation of the parts to the whole. A recent presentation of the ongoing work on the actual Athenian temple by the director of the Acropolis Restoration Service and a professor of chemistry at the University of Crete at the Center for Hellenistic studies at Yale University made me think, again, about the urgencies of theory; at least the slightly horrifying prospect of architecture stripped of theoretical consideration.

The Parthenon, a novelty: The north side of the ongoing building of the Parthenon, 2014

The Parthenon is all about change. Few buildings of this celebrity have changed as radically through the course of history: The Parthenon is a true monument in flux. When Virginia Woolf, just to name one of innumerable witnesses, confides to her diary in 1932 that she found the temple much more solid and assembled than she remembered it from her first Acropolis visit in 1906, it testifies to a pretty acute recollection, See also Lucia Allais's account of the Balanos restorations ← p. 33

as she was an eyewitness to Nikolaos Balanos's restorations. Yet, the changes that the Parthenon is currently living through are of a somewhat different kind. The *re-* prefix will not let anyone who has seen the temple from time to time, even only in images, over the last decade miss the fact that the current restoration is about building a monument yet unseen. The director of the endeavor showed no will to discuss the theoretical boldness of such an Olympic ambition, while the chemist, with his alluring aura of science, forensics, and materiality, made it a straightforward matter liberating patina from dirt and speeding up the weathering of new fragments of shiny white Pentelittic marble with what appears to be a randomly chosen forty years. This positivist Parthenon suddenly appeared as an uncanny, headless monster run wild in the hands of an anonymous collective of restorers now in their fourth decade of building and cleaning, where even the authorship of this new Parthenon appears unclear and bureaucratic.

See panel discussion → p. 160

While the Parthenon in Athens may be in the process of becoming disturbingly stabilized, trapped in a theoretical cul-de-sac and detached from change and speculation, the fluctuating plaster Parthenon still represents delicious convolutions. An early, lapidary manifestation of this versatile, scientific, historical, and theoretical phenomenon was posted in the *Times of London*, June 7, 1822. Calling the attention of "the lovers of Antique, Architects, and Others," a small advertisement announced the "valuable contents of the GALLERY OF CASTS, from the antique, the property of John Samuel Hayward, esq. deceased" for auction at Mr. Christie's Great Room at Pall Mall the following day. Among the particularly valuable objects offered for sale were casts from the "Elgin Marbles, taken by favour, previous to the removal of the originals to the Museum." For a present-day reader, the attribution of these casts might appear slightly anachronistic. One could assume that the dismembered parts from the Parthenon became "the Elgin marbles" the moment the British Parliament in 1816 purchased the collection from Lord Elgin, and that the temple

The Elgin Room at the British Museum before all casts were exiled from the galleries, ca. 1923

fragments were turned into exhibits when almost immediately put on their first public display in the Temporary Elgin Room at the British Museum, then under construction, in Bloomsbury. For contemporary readers, however, the dating of the casts prior to this much-debated acquisition must have made perfect sense. Lord Elgin had molds made from the temple already in 1802 while assembling objects from the Acropolis, and these casts were circulated and collected even before the marbles were shipped from Athens to London. Cast in situ, the pieces auctioned at Christie's were early and already rare appearances of what were to become a rich assortment of an increasingly perfected series of casts. Orders for casts were placed at the British Museum already in 1816, and new molds were made in accordance with new findings and theories about the possible entirety of the temple.[8] The Parthenon soon became ubiquitous (take a shortcut from 51st to 52nd Streets between Madison and Fifth Avenues, and you will pass one of these series of casts; another set, also produced in London, can be admired in the Acropolis Museum in Athens). Until all casts were expelled

155

from the British Museum in the 1930s, the Elgin Marbles were always displayed with casts, sometimes accompanied with two different sets, to display archaeological and art historical developments—that is the history and the theories on the Parthenon, in constant flux. Together with its fellow plaster exhibits from an obsolete nineteenth-century cast culture, the Parthenon emblematically shows that there is a history of theory lurking in stuff, even in something as banal as plaster. These are theories that cannot easily be anthologized.

1   Sylvia Lavin, "Theory into History or, the Will to Anthology," *Journal of the Society of Architectural Historians*, vol. 58, no. 3 (September 1999): 494.

2   George Kubler, *The Shape of Time. Remarks on the History of Things* (New Haven: Yale University Press, 2008), 8.

3   Charles C. Perkins, "The Pergamon Marbles. II: The Gigantomachia and Other Sculptures Found at the Pergamon," *The American Art Review*, vol. 2, no. 5 (March 1881): 192.

4   Charles Newton, "Remarks on the Collections of Ancient Art in the Museums of Italy, the Glyptothek at Munich, and the British Museum," *The Museum of Classical Antiquities: A Quarterly Journal of Architecture and the Sister Branches of Classic Art*, vol. I, no. III (July 1851): 226–27.

5   Barry Bergdoll, "The Paradoxical Origins of MoMA's Model Collection," in Mari Lending and Mari Hvattum, eds., *Modelling Time: The Permanent Collection, 1925–2014* (Oslo: Torpedo Press, 2014), 160.

6   Alina Payne, *From Ornament to Object: Genealogies of Architectural Modernism* (New Haven and London: Yale University Press, 2012), 11.

7   Mark Wigley, "Prosthetic Theory: The Disciplining of Architecture," *Assemblage* 15 (August 1991): 15.

8   For an amazing and detailed study of the production and distribution of the Elgin Marbles casts, see Ian Jenkins, "Acquisition and supply of casts of the Parthenon sculptures by the British Museum, 1835–1939," *The Annual of the British School at Athens* 85 (1990), and also his *Archeologists & Aesthetes in the British Museum 1800–1939* (London: British Museum Press, 1992).

Conversation

KELLER EASTERLING: It would be ridiculous to try to be synthetic about these three very different talks, but they do make me think about those things that have escaped architectural bombast, like the bed. Because it's been kind of under-theorized in architecture; it's been something of a butterfly left unpinned to the board, and has been able to absorb all kinds of technologies and experiments. The lack of theorization has left it free to do those things, you might say.

BEATRIZ COLOMINA: It's an interesting point—the thinking is coming not from theorists but from those young architects who are more attuned to what is happening in the world, perhaps because that's the world they inhabit, which is more naturally their own than theory's. Maybe the butterfly pinning is left to the old guard, since the kinds of concerns that a new generation has are completely different from those of an older generation.

I didn't talk about this today, but it's not just that where we work and where we live have fundamentally changed—spaces are changing more generally. Is it so great that we're doing all that work in bed? Is it so great that we're working 24/7? We used to have office hours and that was it, right? Just as I sat down here in this conference, you wouldn't believe how many emails popped up from students and colleagues. I'm supposed to answer them, but the day goes by quickly, and then the weekend comes and the night comes. What is work and what is rest? What is night? These are fundamental questions for architecture.

MARI LENDING: I'm interested in this idea of
the bed as the collapse of order between what
was work and rest. I'm wondering if it could
stand for a collapse of order more generally.
From my perspective, the separation of history
and theory was a distinctly American thing that
looks a bit weird from Europe and also from
outside architecture, from the field of aesthetics—because where do you draw the line? The
metaphor of the bed asks us to break that distinction down some.

COLOMINA: Did that happen? I don't remember a
radical distinction between theory and history.
I got my hands really dirty in Le Corbusier's
archives, and spent hours and hours with my
evidence, which I was in love with. Then when I
produced all of that evidence, people would say
things like, "Oh, she's imposing contemporary
concerns of post-structuralist theory." And I'd
say, "What are they talking about, exactly?" I
think that's a caricature of the work that was
going on in the field.

But doing serious historical work doesn't mean
that we were blind or deaf to the world
around us. We did that work precisely because
we were not. We were all immersed in certain
preoccupations that came out in the work, but
it didn't determine them. I must confess
to you that I never read Derrida very closely.
It didn't captivate me the way that Walter
Benjamin did. I can recite Walter Benjamin
backwards, but I cannot Derrida. Foucault was
much more important to me. But you also absorb
things by a kind of osmosis, by carrying the

books or by being close to people that carry the books. [Laughter]

EASTERLING: I'm still curious about what's driving some of your urgencies. Mark, you've turned out amazing Ph.D. students who have been enriched by your school to make this field, I would say, messier or greater or richer. So I'm curious about this segregated wasteland that you see happening.

JARZOMBEK: Well, one issue is that there are just not enough of us. There's a huge void, and there's a limited number of people that Ph.D. programs and even architecture schools can produce who are interested in these type of things…there are literally not enough bodies, currently.

I just came from a conference with a lot of anthropologists and sociologists, and they're going, "Wow! We haven't done architecture in a long time." And I'm saying, "Don't go there. That's what we're supposed to be doing. We're supposed to be sending our guys out into your discipline." We're going to be a minority voice in all of this—in ten years, they're all going to have Ph.D.s, and they're going to sound fancy, and they're going to get tenure… Mark, you've got to stay on! There's going to be another dean and you're going to have an anthropologist walking around here. [Laughter]

AUDIENCE: This question is for Mari. I'm interested in this aura of monuments, and you mentioned that the changes in restoration techniques are a result of the discoveries made in

archaeology as the restoration is occurring.
So does that mean that the restoration itself
is, in fact, constantly being revised? And
do you think it would be better to let the Parthenon decay?

LENDING: That's a big question, I cannot even
answer that. But I was just thinking about
something similar the other day, because while
it seems like this is surely from the '80s
or the late '70s, the restoration project is
going on now. Right now. There are people in
this room that know much more than I do about
that, but I think that it has run a bit wild.
It's way beyond the initial plans, so now it's
actually turning into architecture proper, and
not just restoration—because they're building.
It's not "re-" anything. It's a completely new,
unforeseen temple on the top of the Acropolis. There are now actually architects of that
structure called the Parthenon, but we don't
know their names.

JARZOMBEK: My question is this: Where's the
outrage? The history/theory world should be
on the front lines of this. So I'd go even
further—I think that what's happening is a
complete fraud, and evokes all sorts of really
interesting theoretical questions on a whole
range of issues. Where is the outrage in the
architectural schools? And this is just one of
dozens of topics where one could say, "This is
really bad." When do we just stand up and point
to that, instead of allowing sort of certain
types of preservation industries to control 90
percent of the discourse about these questions?

WIG[G]LE-Y ORNAMENTAL, OR, (THE PROSPECT OF) THEORY AS ORNA-MENTATION

Spyros Papapetros

(PRE-)THEORY

Karl Philipp Moritz's 1793 publication, *Preliminary Concepts for a Theory of Ornament*, offers not only an intuitive theory of ornament but also an alternative model of what "a theory" of any object might ultimately be.[1] Eschewing any systematic representation of its subject, the slim volume (consisting of previously published articles and letters) initially appears as a discordant assemblage of short sections on a variety of topics.[2] Moritz's eye leaps from the frames of paintings to the clothing of statues, and his argument follows, making speculative reflections on "unity and multiplicity" in decoration and offering historical accounts of the ornamented altars and temples of the ancients. Moritz jumps media, going from detailed descriptions of Raphael's stanzas and the iconographic programs of the rooms of Ancient Roman and German Renaissance palaces (replete with ancient mythological references) to equally elaborate observations on the costume of the human character types that may occupy some of these spaces (such as an elegant Roman matron, a princess from Parma, and a stiff Renaissance Burgermeister). This "(pre)-theoretical" book on ornamentation gives us an *image* of theory that is equally startling as its variegated subject.

This aspect or even *prospect* of theory is characterized by perpetual transformation and frequent shifts of focus and objective—a theory animated by distraction, surprise, and even conceit. There are no enumerated principles, fixed rules, or carefully arranged analytic expositions one may normally associate with the theoretical structure of contemporary scientific, philosophical, or architectural treatises of that era and beyond. Each brief section has its own logic and method developed to an intricate level of consistency only to change again in the next one. Moritz, in other words, offers us fragments not only of a theory of ornamentation but of ornamentation as a form of theory, a case in which the very anti-theoretical character of ornament traces its own theoretical pattern. Here, theory and practice, description and intuition interweave with one another to create a textual fabric whose very brilliance illuminates and concurrently obscures ornamentation. Using the most luminous category of objects, ornament, Moritz appears to be making a mockery of the Enlightenment and its principles of judgment and aesthetic taste.[3]

Ornamentation, according to Moritz, is a practice of "perforation" (*Durchbrechung*, which literally means "breaking through")—the tracing of a gap, slit, or hole on a continuous surface, as in the art of fretwork (*Durchbrochene Arbeit*) common in building and furniture decoration. Similar to the way that the ornamental carvings of a Gothic cathedral, "the buckle of a shoe," or "the steel button in clothing" have the capacity to "cut through" the uniformity of objects that they decorate, these small incisions can deflect attention from the normative contour of an artifact and subvert its functional hierarchy.[4] Ornament then would designate not only a "crime," *Verbrechen*—as Adolf Loos more than a century later would declare—but also a more general process of "breaching," *Durchbrechen* in Moritz's terms. This is a decorative gap that breaks not simply the law but also the larger epistemological system that supports any social and aesthetic norm. Ornament as crime, ruse, or sin opens up the possibility of a deviant behavior that stringently resists, subverts, and breaks down the consistency of any architectural structure as a solid theoretical or material construct. Therefore, any genuine theory of ornament is essentially a "pre-theory," an intuition or anticipation toward a theoretical conceptualization, as the term *Vorbegriff* used in Moritz's title projects.

It is precisely this intuitive "break" established by the practice of ornamentation that provides the space for performing a chronological leap from the end of the eighteenth to the closing of the twentieth century, which witnessed the resurgence of ornament as a disruptive theoretical object in the architectural and other literatures of deconstruction. There, ornament would once more create an ambivalent space, at once marginalized to a distant part of the page, picture, or discourse and yet still transformative, charging these zones as an itinerant center of investigation.

Continuing to think ornamentally, I propose to examine the work of a singular author, the honoree of this conference on the legacy of architectural theory at the beginning of the third millennium, by sampling certain fragments of his theoretical work related to ornamentation. Without authoring a book-length theoretical treatise or collection of essays on ornament like the one by Moritz, Mark Wigley has extensively theorized ornament, either directly, as in his early work on deconstruction, or implicitly, as in his most recent articles on networks, and continues to think and theorize ornamentally. Ornament may remain a *parergon*, or "side work," in the author's *main* work, but in the Derridean sense, it is precisely its supplementary role that allows it to suffuse the body of his theoretical production.

Moving beyond the work of individual authors, ornament becomes a heuristic subject or connecting medium that binds a multiplicity of theoretical and practical discourses. It is precisely ornament's unparalleled capacity for creating analogies and correspondences among buildings, texts, and epistemological systems that might partly explain its resurgence from 1990s' deconstructivism to the architectural theory, historiography, and building practice of the 2000s.

I   PROSTHESIS

We start then with the photograph of a prosthetic limb, an inorganic arm made of metal, leather, and pliable rubber that appears to be holding a book. Extracted from a 1915 German treatment manual for wounded victims of the Great War, the photograph of the reading mechanical arm serves as an allegorical frontispiece for Mark Wigley's well-known 1991 article in *Assemblage* on "the disciplining of architecture"—a meditation on prosthetic theory, or perhaps more aptly, on theory as a prosthesis to building.[5]

Within the photographic frame of this modern allegorical frontispiece, it is as if the prosthetic arm itself performs the act of reading; the human reader is a ghost—a body elided

165

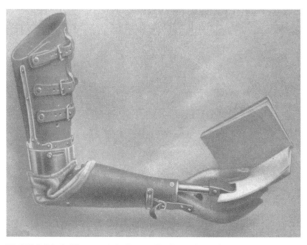

"Artificial Intelligence? Orthopedische Behandlung Kriegsv-erwundeter," 1915, as illustrated in Mark Wigley's "Prosthetic Theory"

from the picture by the very prosthesis that is supposed to enhance it. Supplementation confers the eradication of the subject it supports, and perhaps so does theory to the practice it embraces. Similar to a prosthetic attachment, ornament is an active entity that becomes autonomous from the body, artifact, or building on which it is initially appended. Instead of being carried by a subject, it is now the subject or supporting structure that is *carried away* by the very levity of its detachable extensions.

The excursus on prosthetic theory in Wigley's introduction and epilogue serve as brackets enveloping the core of the article—a study on the origins of architectural education in America in the late nineteenth century, particularly the first design schools at MIT and Columbia. Wigley offers an incisive reading of the spaces, such as lecture halls, design studios, and drawing rooms, some of which are used for the copying and analysis of ornament: Long, vertical, one-to-one plaster copies or drawings of spiral tendrils and other motifs to be applied as building ornaments animate the barren walls on which they are pinned with a projective form of vegetation.[6] Here, ornamentation turns the inorganic prosthesis of architectural education into an organic form of cultivation (a similar *line* of education via ornament would be retraced a few decades later by the anti-academics Sullivan and Wright).

An "architecture lecture and drawing room" in the Rogers Building at MIT, 1876, as illustrated in Mark Wigley's "Prosthetic Theory"

In the article's conclusion, we encounter an illustration with the engraving of a mechanical iron hand from a sixteenth-century treatise on "supplements to the defects of the human body."[7] Supplements can be offensive and protective, lethal as well as restorative, and so is the archi-tecture they support in its traditional allegiances with military technology. Surveying metal dec- **See panel discussion → p. 234**orated artifacts from ancient times in the second volume of his *Style*, Gottfried Semper noted that "implements of war and hunting" are "the most beautiful adornments—true orna-ments for men."[8] Ornament in this case is a supplement that supports its carrier in battle both by the solidity of its struc-ture and power of its beautifully decorated surface. Semper's statement equates ornamentation with military and political power, even if the same proclamation appears to connote the very emasculation of power in the (male) subject that carries no ornament. Conversely, one may argue that the architect's true

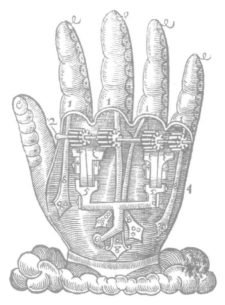

"The form of a hand made artificially of iron," from Ambroise Pare's *A Supplement on the Defects in Man's Body*, 1579, as illustrated in Mark Wigley's "Prosthetic Theory"

weapon and/or supplement is *ornament*—a form of prosthesis that enhances his buildings with social, political, and rhetorical power—and whose supplementation calibrates the communicative and even combative power of his projects.

Either as a form (or *space*) of education or as a supplement of military technology, ornament proliferates by weaving inside and outside of the body or the building it enhances. Ornament produces more ornament. Like a tendril plant on a wall, it has an almost animistic power of self-(re)generation, and so does the literature that trails behind it. However architectural theorists around the late nineteenth century would strive to establish laws controlling the production of ornament, the only principle that ornament ultimately follows is that of uncontrollable proliferation. Theory and historiography have no other choice than to follow its rhythmically undulating loops across the ages.

II   GAP

Let us then move a year earlier in terms of the author's production and more than a century later in terms of the chronology of his subject. The March 1990 issue of *Ottagono* contains a special section on the subject of ornament. Next to articles by Marco Pogacnic on Semper's *Style* and Anthony Vidler on "The Architecture of Adornment" (which surveys the shifting manifestations of architectural ornamentation from postmodernism to deconstructivism and from Michael Graves to Daniel Libeskind), Wigley publishes "The Decorated Gap."[9]

Cover of Ottagono 94, "*Ornament,*" March 1990

Notice that in the bilingual journal, the article's Italian title is *La Contradizzione decorata* ("The Decorated Contradiction"), which, without exactly contradicting the English title, suggests that the unstable object of decoration oscillates between "gap" and "contradiction"—a formal and an epistemological discontinuity, which traces the *origin* of ornamentation.

The article, in fact, starts with references to Robert Venturi's *Complexity and Contradiction* and ends with observations on a series of building projects by Denise Scott Brown and Venturi described by Wigley as an architecture of the "gap"—a gap added to the building in lieu of decoration, or more precisely, a gap between ornament and structure that covers up and finally obliterates the decorated surface. As Wigley argues, "The architecture is literally in the gap. It is not decoration that is being added to [Scott Brown and Venturi's] buildings but the gap between them."[10] The two architects do not cover the gap between ornament and structure but augment it by making their profusely decorated façades (often allegorically broken or fragmented) detachable and independent from the core simply to show unabashedly that they "live" as decoration. The locus of ornament here is not a designed artifact or a building frame but a relentless gap, as if the object of decoration had been replaced by a void, indicative of or even *allegorical* of its present condition. If in Moritz's (pre)theory of ornament, the minuscule gaps of fretwork rhythmically punctuated the Gothic façade, here the gap is the vast ornament *behind* the façade performing a covert act of perforation.

Ornamentation is as much an act of ostentatious display as it is of occlusion and concealment, and this expands to the literature that describes ornament. For example, a similar contradiction between occlusion and display, according to Wigley, permeates Scott Brown and Venturi's most popular project, their studio (and later book project) *Learning from Las Vegas*. Particularly in its first and larger-format edition, the book appears as a "decorated shed," akin to the ornamented buildings it displays—a book literally "cladded" by a detachable cover, semi-transparent and semi-opaque to the authors' celebration of an architecture of billboards and other image signs. The regular conglomeration of photographs of the same building signs on the book's illustrated pages creates a multidirectional decorative fabric that further diffuses the "stardust" originally emanating from Las Vegas's urban labyrinth.

In *Learning from Las Vegas*, building, billboard, and book illustration appear identified on one surface, as if all distance were eliminated, and with this very loss of distance lies a "gap," the "decorated gap" of contradiction. The book, which itself was turned into a mechanical prosthesis when it was attached as a photographic image to the frontispiece of "The Disciplining of Architecture," is now another supplement or ornament that displays the very failure of ornament to unite the erudite surface and its bodily substructure.

III   SPACE

Wigley's most extensive theorization of ornament appears in *The Architecture of Deconstruction*, first published in 1993 but partly based on the author's 1986 dissertation. In terms of visual material, the book is decisively unornamented, as it eschews illustrations, yet it contains a section on "the structure of ornament" as well as numerous references to ornamentation in other sections.[11]

The book index lists *ornament* next to *decoration* (in brackets) as if the two terms were interchangeable.[12] Nevertheless, the parenthetic term *decoration*, especially in its uses in twentieth-century French literature on art and architecture, connotes a more expansive term describing a total design system that transcends individual surface elements and extends into three-dimensional space. Akin to an eighteenth-century *roccaille* leaf motif, twentieth-century decoration spills over and extends in space to encompass all aspects of architecture.

One could indeed read the entire book as a type of ornament—both a theory and practice of a verbal form of decoration. While seemingly marginal or supplementary, ornament punctuates and ultimately suffuses the text as if it were its primary object, or even its constantly unattainable objective.

One of the main themes of the book is the triad of "ground/structure/ornament," not as a linear horizontal progression but as a "vertical form of hierarchy."[13] As Wigley describes, both Western architecture and philosophy rely predominantly on the "ground"—a rational and/or metaphysical foundation supported by Kant and Heidegger and undermined by Derrida. For Wigley, the same basic hierarchy supports two further oppositions between ground and structure and structure and ornament. The higher we move, the freer the scheme becomes. As Wigley writes, "with each additional layer the bond is weaker. The structure is supposedly bonded to the ground more securely than the ornament is bonded to structure."[14] However, by its very distance from the ground and relative independence from structure, ornament gains in plasticity and freedom. Ornament often revolts against the very structure that carries it. Structure then tries to "control" ornament and when it can no longer do so, it tries to eliminate it. This ostensible elimination forecasts the fate of ornament in twentieth-century modern architecture, which purports to be unornamented.

Attempting to challenge the polarity between core structure and surface ornament as crystallized by both Kant and Hegel, Wigley presents ornament as that which already *is* or can *become* structural, "like a scaffold added to the structure."[15] This ontological reversal is already presaged in the theoretical writings of nineteenth-century architectural theorists like Karl Boetticher and later Gottfried Semper, both of whom investigated the distinctions and analogical correspondences between building *core* and ornamental surface.[16]

It may at first seem contradictory that the section on "the structure of ornament" is included in the book's third chapter, titled "The Slippery Art of Space,"[17] but for Wigley, the very question of ornament, either in philosophical or architectural practices, *is* spatial, since ornament, just like the "supplement," is about "the distinction between inside and outside. It is ornament that defines space. There may be no space without ornament, and no thought about ornament that is not a thought about space."[18]

The spatial dimension of ornamentation echoes its nineteenth-century reinvention by Semper and his coining of a new type of adornment that he named "directional ornament (*Richtungsschmuck*)." Examples of such ornament include the fluttering edges of helmets or the pointed contours of acroteria attached to ancient ships and temples.[19] In all of these cases, ornament is both a material *and* a theoretical object that expands beyond the physical limits of the body or building that carries such ornament. Directional ornament points to a destination that far exceeds the spatial limits of the decorated artifact. The very object supposed to attract attention to itself redirects and diffuses attraction among a spatial network of relationships. This is a *selfless* and socially active type of ornament—an ornament redeeming its self-absorbing nature to a network of other objects, bodies, and spatial directions. Here, in fact, lies not only the spatial but also the social, aesthetic, and political potential of ornament in its capacity to both concentrate and redistribute power, to freeze or reanimate social energy at an individual or collective level.[20]

The spatial expansion of ornament in the late nineteenth century marks its reinvention from the domain of theory and the practices of applied arts to that of history and archaeological investigation. I refer here to the endless historical and theoretical treatises on ornamentation published around the turn of the century that supplement ornament's global circulation.[21] The same explosion of literature on ornament also supports the invention of the inaugural histories of architecture, such as those by James Fergusson and Banister Fletcher, in which architectural styles are classified (and ostensibly ossified) according to morphological and/or typological developments in the forms of ornamentation. The history of architecture then emerges as a supplement, moreover a textual prosthesis, to a theory of ornamentation.

IV WALL

A similar move from theory to historicization is performed by Wigley in *White Walls, Designer Dresses*, in which he transitions from the philosophy of Kant, Heidegger, and Derrida to the rhetoric of Semper, Loos, and Le Corbusier, showing a spectrum of views for or against ornamentation.[22]

The story of ornament in the early twentieth century coincides with an essential aspect of the history of modern architecture apropos of its disavowal of historical ornamentation and reinvention of cladding as a second mask covering smooth building façades. The new ornament is the *lack* of (conventional) ornament as a prestigious sign of distinction. What Le Corbusier called "the decorative art of today" appears entirely different from that of yesterday yet is essentially the same in its totalizing impact. From dress to implement to building enclosure, this decisively unornamented type of modern decoration projects a new form of cosmic decorative extension.

Ornament historicizes itself precisely by its absence and clandestine transformation into a smooth but richly textured surface, manifested, for example, in the white ripoline-coated surfaces celebrated by Le Corbusier. No longer a series of isolated motifs, ornament survives as a larger decorative system based on the harmonic correspondences between inorganic and organic materials. Here, smooth bodies and shining furniture textures rehearse the patterned symmetries of traditional ornamentation by means of a reciprocal form of substitution. From now on, ornamentation consists not of the imitation of human, vegetal, animal, or mineral motifs but of an abstract network of analogies or even homologies between building and (infra)structural systems. The essential *skeuomorphism* of twentieth-century ornamentation lies less in its resemblance to specific implements than to its rehearsal of and identification with processes that produce larger systems of objects.

The apparent eclipse of ornament also signifies its ultimate expansion into space via its transubstantiation into a network of information and communication systems—telephone cables,

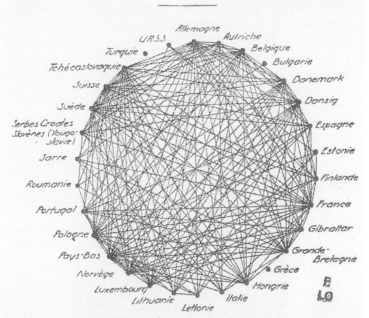

"International telephone network, from the file cabinet collection of material for illustrations in *L'Esprit Nouveau*," as illustrated in Mark Wigley's *White Walls, Designer Dresses*

electrical wires, radio and television waves, and pipelines as they interlace with one another to "weave" what Wigley via Semper characterizes in *White Walls, Designer Dresses* as the new textile forms of modernity.[23] An image of the globe covered in the threadlike lines of international telephone networks reproduced in *L'Esprit Nouveau* shows the totalizing dimension of these systems—intricate circuitries that frame the technological architecture of modernity.[24]

See also John Harwood's "Broadcast Architecture" ← p. 96–112

The reciprocal move from invisible service network to conspicuous ornament can be illustrated by a series of late-nineteenth-century designs, almost contemporary to Loos's articles on plumbing and against ornament and bodily decoration mentioned by Wigley, such as Henry Van de Velde's mirror and

Henry van de Velde, hair-cutting furniture for the Haby hair salon, Berlin, 1900–01

faucet-board unit design for the 1900 Haby hair salon and barbershop in Berlin. Here, the exposed hot- and cold-water metal pipes attached to the faucets interweave with similar pipes that do not carry water but serve as object stands or have no use value, i.e., they are *mere* ornaments.[25] Ornament grows like vegetation into implement and vice versa; such is the vicissitude of the "decorative drive," what Semper called *Verzierungstrieb*, which has a tendency to *corrupt* the structural systems that support it.[26]

V   NETWORK

Wigley's more recent work on "network fever" retraces the information and infrastructure systems that transfer the interior to the exterior by remaining conspicuously exposed.[27] Such networks are simultaneously usable implements and useless decoration but with a highly symbolic value. Ornament has not disappeared; it has been reunited with the world by returning to the ground and becoming one with the infrastructural systems that produce it. Its spatial orientations appear to fold back into the skin of the earth traversed by linear networks reminiscent of patterns of tribal or archaic geometric tattooing. From supplement to ornament to structure to ground to network, the circle of decoration appears closed via a totalizing circuitry of design production. If decoration was originally produced by an "explosion of the world" (the Greek *diakosmisis*), its modern clandestine survival is marked, as Wigley has already remarked, by a total (design) implosion.[28]

   Going back to the epistemological categories and vertical hierarchy of ground/structure/ornament articulated in the *Architecture of Deconstruction*, here, it is as if ornament has merged not only with structure but with the ground, including both underground and over-the-ground systems. Technological ornament has essentially become the *background*, a preliminary scaffolding that supports the original structure still insistent on remaining ornamentally visible after its completion.

Gordon Matta-Clark, "Pipes," 1971, photograph of installation at Holly Solomon Gallery, New York, 1994

Several decades after van de Velde, Gordon Matta-Clark would offer his own version of exposed infrastructural systems in his installation titled *Pipes*. First shown in Boston in 1971, the original work consisted of an existing gas pipeline projecting through the wall and running parallel to a series of photographs showing he trajectory of gas pipelines "from the street into and through the building."[29]

This form of decoration transforms former structure into ornament via its photographic exposure. Flatness and the reduction of structure into an image do not eliminate spatiality; on the contrary, they augment the multidimensionality of the former structure by unearthing its ornamental potential. Let us recall here that Matta-Clark is the same anarchitect who proclaimed that "one of [his] favorite definitions of the difference between architecture and sculpture is whether there is plumbing or not."[30]* In this installation, this singular difference between architecture and sculpture is ostensibly obliterated since here plumbing has been transformed into a decorative element, a feature that is less functional implement than ornament added to the building to camouflage it into sculpture and vice versa.

* **Matta-Clark continues: "So although it is an incomplete definition, it puts the functionalist aspect of past-due Machine Age Moralists where it belongs—down some well-executed drain."**

VI   RUDIMENT

From total eclipse to immanent resurgence, the modern evolution of ornament appears to follow a parabolic historiographic scheme rehearsing a grand theoretical pattern. In their book *L'Évolution régressive en Biologie et en Sociologie* (1897, English edition *Evolution by Atrophy*, 1899), Belgian theorists Demoor, Massart, and Vandervelde describe how previously well-developed animal organs gradually lose strength and are reduced to rudiments that sometimes pose as ornamental extensions.[31] The same theorists compared transformations in declining social

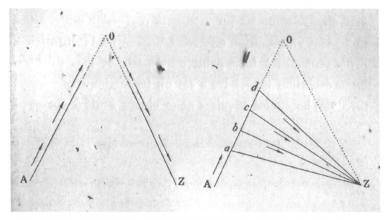

Jean Demoor, Jean Massart, and Emile Vandervelde, *Evolution by Atrophy in Biology and Sociology*, 1899, diagram

and political organisms, showing how the British monarchy managed to thrive through costumes, pageantry, and festival decorations at the same time that their gubernatorial powers were drastically diminished. Here, the loss of power is ostensibly compensated by the efflorescence of ornamentation.

The process of ornamental rudimentation as a form of change is illustrated by a diagram. Once an organism evolves from point A to an imaginary peak, or point O, and then starts to atrophy, it will never go back to point A but to a new point Z, which is symmetrical to A and displays several links with previous stages of its evolution, *but it is not the same.*[32] The ornamental rudiment is not simply a symbolic link to former transformations but the active representative of organic changes that may still occur. Ornamental survivals are not the stubborn and/or ossified representatives of an irretrievable past but the catalytic agents of a future condition that strives to acquire shape.

Developed during the turn of the century, such evolutionary theories are close to an era that was about to witness the abrupt demise and transference of power during major political, cultural, and architectural revolutions. More than a century ago, the explosion of literature on ornament was followed by radical architectural practice, including one that prescribed the ostensible demise of ornamentation. The recent resurgence of interest in theories, historiographies, and practices of ornament makes us wonder what all of these new ornamental excrescences might collectively augur.

VII (AFTER-)THEORY

The cultural and epistemological reversals rhetorically annunciated by ornament may also rehearse the undulating trajectory of architectural theory in recent decades, a unique part of which remains a theory of ornamentation. Even if theories of deconstruction and postmodernism appear as mere rudiments today, their vestiges survive as "structural ornaments," prostheses that have d/evolved into atrophied organs so as to symbolically represent the unfulfilled potential of their former stages.

Like ornament itself, the theory of ornamentation survives by informing the very *method* of the historical text—a method evident in the proliferating use of marginal and/or subversive details that start flourishing as soon as the historian starts "looking at the overlooked." This more encompassing historiographic attitude includes not only minor objects like ornament but also "minor" or forgotten characters, ideologies, and tendencies, whose hitherto concealed presence resurfaces on the very wall that previously inscribed their removal. Such theory does not pretend to be an original invention or a comprehensive system in the manner of a grand architectural master plan drawn on a historiographic tabula rasa but a more subtle act of supplementation to former organic developments—another line, another twist, another *wiggle* that may sway architecture's arboreal hierarchy beyond its ossified boundaries and regulations.

Recent architectural discourse is permeated by an almost neurotic resistance not only to theory but also to the very act of reflecting and "looking back." It is a "projective" attitude that claims that architecture may only look forward, but it is also this attitude that results from and leads to a form of historical (as well as hysterical) blindness. Theories of ornamentation display not only the value but also the inevitability of a symbiotic relationship with the historical past, including the furtive existence of rudiments, remnants, ornaments, and failures.

Reflecting on the state of architectural theory in 2000+, it is perhaps time to look back and study the intricate ornamental patterns it traced and the minor pathways it followed. Not to rehearse the same trajectory but, as the theorists of "regressive evolution" would support, to build (*by unearthing*) a new one. Theory's current rudimentation or ornamentalization caused by its dispersal and decorative fragmentation (what was previously described as *diakosmisis*) into an infinite number of theoretical and historiographic perspectives (echoed in the variety of presentations of this conference) will perhaps result in its regressive evolution into a more liberating form of *pre-theory* recalling Moritz's kaleidoscopic compilation of fragments. Such new *pre-theory* can only come *after-* or *post-*theory. In other words, it will be a *preposterous* theory—the prospect of a theory historically conscious of the temporal incongruity traversing its many origins and endings.

1   Karl Philipp Moritz, *Vorbegriffe zu einer Theorie Der Ornamente* (Berlin: Karl Matzdorf Buchhandlung, 1793). The term *Vorbegriff*, used in German philosophy of that era (including the introductory section of Hegel's *Science of Logic* [1816, 1833], connotes a "preliminary or inchoate concept). See "Vorbegriff," in the *German Dictionary of Philosophical Terms*, ed. Elmar Weibl and Philip Herdina (Munich, New York: Saur, Routledge, 1997), vol. 1, 328.

2   For an astute analysis of Moritz's "theory" see Alina Payne, *From Ornament to Object: Genealogies of Architectural Modernism* (New Haven: Yale University Press, 2012), 31–32.

3   The last section of Moritz's *Vorbegriffe* is dedicated to "the judgment of taste (*Geschmacksurtheil*)" apropos of matters of ornamentation; see Moritz, *Vorbegriffe*, 140–42. In his Third Critique on "The Power of Judgment (*Urteilskraft*)" concerning matters of aesthetic taste (first published in 1790), Kant criticizes decorative details, such as "the frames in pictures" and "the draperies in statues" as "additions" and not "intrinsic constituents in the complete representation of an object." These are precisely the objects celebrated by Moritz in the first sections of his book. See Immanuel Kant, *The Critique of Judgment*, ed. and trans. James Meredith (London: Oxford University Press, 1952), 68 (translation modified).

4   See the section on fretwork "Durchbrochene Arbeit," in Moritz, *Vorbegriffe*, 138–39.

5   Mark Wigley, "Prosthetic Theory: The Disciplining of Architecture," in *Assemblage* 15 (August 1991): 6–29. See illustration captioned "Artificial intelligence? Orthopedische Behandlung Kriegsverwundeter, 1915" on page 8, fig. 1.

6   See the 1876 photograph of an "architecture lecture and drawing room" in the Rogers Building at MIT in Wigley, "Prosthetic Theory," 17, fig. 14.

7   See illustration "The form of a hand made artificially of iron" from Ambroise Paré, *A Supplement on the Defects in Man's Body* (1579) in Wigley, "Prosthetic Theory," 23, fig. 19.

8   "The first and probably the most important forged objects were tools of war and the hunt. From the earliest times they were objects of careful functional study and at the same time models of the highest decorative art. They were always seen as both necessary tools and the most beautiful adornments—true ornaments for men." Gottfried Semper, *Style in the Technical and Tectonic Arts, or Practical Aesthetics*, trans. Harry Francis Mallgrave and Michael Robinson (Los Angeles: The Getty Research Institute, 2004), 864.

9   Mark Wigley, "La Contraddizione decorata/The Decorated Gap," in *Ottagono* 94 (March 1990): 36–55. In the same issue, see also Marco Pogacnic, "Gottfried Semper: Il Governo dello Stilo/Gottfried Semper: The Government of Style," 7–15; Anthony Vidler, "Dal Tatuaggio al Monile: Archittetura come Ornamento/From Tattoo to Trinket: Architecture as Adornment," 16–35; and Jacques Lucan, "La Decorazione come Costruzione: Un Paradosso?/Decoration as Building: A contradiction?" 56–67.

10   Wigley, "The Decorated Gap," 45.

11   Mark Wigley, "The Structure of Ornament," in *The Architecture of Deconstruction: Derrida's Haunt* (Cambridge, MA: The MIT Press, 1993), 83–88.

12   See entry "Ornament (decoration)" in the index of Wigley, *The Architecture of Deconstruction*, 277.

13   Wigley, *The Architecture of Deconstruction*, 93.

14   Wigley, The *Architecture of Deconstruction*, 11.

15   "The scaffolding that originally supports a structure is the part of structure that becomes ornamental. The structure of structure is, in the end, ornament." Ibid, 16. For a different evaluation of Wigley's writings on ornament see the section "Wigley und Hays: Ästhetisches Objekt versus theoretischer Text," in Jörg H. Gleiter, *Rückkehr des Verdrängten: Zur kritischen Theorie des Ornaments in der architektonischen Moderne* (Weimar: Universitätsverlag der Bauhaus-Universität, 2002), 317–19.

16   Karl Bötticher, *Die Tektonik der Hellenen* (Potsdam: Ferdinand Riegel, 1844–52). On the distinction between structure and ornament or "core-form (*Kernform*)" and "art-form (*Kunstform*)" in Bötticher's tectonics, see the chapter "'Tectonics' and the 'Theory of Rainment,'" in Werner Oeschlin, *Otto Wagner, Adolf Loos, and the Road to Modern Architecture* (New York: Cambridge University Press, 2002), 44–63.

17   Mark Wigley, "The Slippery Art of Space," in *The Architecture of Deconstruction*, 59–95.

18   Wigley, *The Architecture of Deconstruction*, 85.

19   Gottfried Semper, "From Concerning the Formal Principles of Ornament and its Significance as Artistic Symbol" (1856), trans. David Britt, in *The Theory of Decorative Art: An Anthology of European and American Writings, 1750–1940*, ed. Isabelle Frank (New Haven: Yale University Press, 2000), 91–104.

20   For the sociological permutations of adornment see Georg Simmel's classic essay "On Adornment," in *The Sociology of Georg Simmel*, trans. and ed. Kurt Wolff (New York: Free Press, 1950), 338–44.

21   On the historiographic repercussions of the global circulation of ornament in the second half of the nineteenth century, see my "World Ornament: The Legacy of Semper's 1856 Lecture on Adornment," in *RES: Anthropology and Aesthetics* 57/58 (Spring/Autumn 2010): 309–29.

22   Mark Wigley, *White Walls, Designer Dresses: The Fashioning of Modern Architecture* (Cambridge, MA: The MIT Press, 1995).

23   "The telephone, like all systems of communication, defines a new spatiality and can be inhabited. It is the modern equivalent of Semper's weaving." Wigley, *White Walls*, 28.

24   "International telephone network. From the file cabinet collection of material for illustrations in *L'Esprit Nouveau*. Fondation Le Corbusier," in Wigley, *White Walls*, 28–29, fig. 1.11.

25   See van de Velde's haircutting furniture (*Frisiertisch*) made of mahogany, brass, and glass for the hair salon Haby, Berlin (1900–01), Klassik Stiftung Weimar, Museen, reproduced in the recent exhibition catalog on the architect, *Leidenschaft, Funktion und Schönheit: Henry van de Velde und sein Beitrag zur Europäischen Moderne*, ed. Thomas Föhl and Sabine Walter (Weimar: Klassik Stiftung Weimar, 2013), 193.

26   Gottfried Semper, "From Concerning the Formal Principles of Ornament."

27   Mark Wigley, "Network Fever," in *Grey Room* 4 (Summer 2001): 82–122.

28   I refer to the global "explosion" and simultaneous psychological "implosion" in postwar total design systems described by Wigley in his article "Whatever happened to total design?" *Harvard Design Magazine* 5 (Summer 1998): 1–8.

29   Gordon Matta-Clark, *Pipes*, first installed in Boston in 1971. See photograph of installation at Holly Solomon Gallery, New York City (1994), collection of Los Angeles County Museum of Art, Los Angeles, reproduced in *Gordon Matta-Clark*, ed. Corine Diserens (New York: Phaidon, 2003), 48 and 51, fig. 57.

30   Gordon Matta-Clark, quoted in Donald Wall, "Gordon Matta-Clark's Building Dissections," *Arts Magazine* 50 (May 1976), 74–79, reprinted in *Gordon Matta-Clark*, ed. Corinne Diserens (London: Phaidon, 2003), 181–86.

31   Jean Demoor, Jean Massart, and Emile Vandervelde, *L'Évolution régressive en Biologie et en Sociologie* (Paris: Alcan, 1897), translated into English in *Evolution by Atrophy in Biology and Sociology* (New York: Appleton, 1899).

32   Diagram in Demoor, Massart, and Vandervelde, *Evolution by Atrophy*, 248.

"TAKING TIME"
Felicity D. Scott

My contribution takes the form of brief speculations on the subtitle of this event—the "urgencies of architectural theory"—a notion I want to refract through two interrelated contexts: first, landmark events within the period of recent history alluded to in the primary title, "2000+"; second, certain turns taken by theoretical research during this period. (I am thinking primarily of theoretical texts, although I wouldn't want to confine theory to the written domain.) But first I want to stress a point of continuity with theoretical projects or practices related to architecture during what I guess we would call "2000-": Architectural theory in the 1980s and '90s, or at least the more cogent streams of it, shared the project of opening up spaces or spheres (including conceptual ones) within and through which architecture was able to think otherwise about itself, to question its assumptions and mandates, even to scrutinize and put pressure on what seemed to be the dominant urgencies within architectural practice in the more conventional sense of the term. These openings facilitated variegated forms of theory-design encounters, and theory-history relays that, if demonstrating a mutual imbrication—of theory, design, and history—retained (at times) productively nondeterministic or non-instrumental ambitions with respect to each other. Unlike architectural theory in the traditional sense of the term, theoretical work from this recent period (in its more critical form) was not conceived as a prescriptive tool or disciplinary framework that would map easily onto or help determine practice—like a treatise telling architects what to do—nor did it simply legitimize or help to define certain streams of extant work. Theory did, however, offer, and continues to offer, an array of conceptual tools, and it touches down upon, and often unsettles, disciplinary and professional norms to productive ends. Theory maintains, to stress, a non-identical relationship to design practice, even while having an impact upon it; it initiates a relationship or spacing that can also take on a certain untimely, or differently timed, character: Theory can be critically out of sync, or seemingly out of sync with the forces affecting contemporary practice; it can even look like history. At stake in this revisiting of theory, I think, is continuing

187

to identify the sorts of concepts and strategies that theoretical work helps to open up within architecture, identifying the nature of critical and political spaces theoretical interventions might help launch, the voices whose entry they might facilitate: In sum, the question at stake is what theory might allow us to "think" about architecture and the manner in which it touches down in the world, how it might productively haunt, even creatively deflect the discipline's current playing field.

I

"Perhaps the battle no longer looks quite the same. Well, are we really still in the same relationship of force, and does it allow us to exploit the knowledges we have dug out of the sand, to exploit them as they stand, without their becoming subjugated once more? What strength do they have in themselves? And after all, once we have excavated our genealogical fragments, once we begin to exploit them and to put in circulation these elements of knowledge that we have been trying to dig out of the sand, isn't there a danger that they will be recoded, recolonized by these unitary discourses which, having first disqualified them and having then ignored them when they reappeared, may now be ready to reannex them and include them in their own discourses and their own power-knowledge effects?"[1]

This epigraph comes from Michel Foucault's opening lecture to "Society Must Be Defended," presented at the Collège de France in January 1975. First published in French in 1997, it was translated into English in 2003 as the inaugural volume of Foucault's series of lectures at the college. Along with other anthologies of his writings, this series has had a significant impact on Foucault's legacy, including within architectural theory. It was not that Foucault's thinking from the '70s—from his conception of power as relations of force, a paradigm modeled on war (hence his attention to the rhetoric of battles, struggles, strategy, and tactics), to his theorization of biopower, biopolitics, territory, and the arts of government—had not already found their way into architectural discourse earlier. Rather, the reception of Foucault's work within architectural discourse was dominated (for many reasons) by the important earlier books—*The Order of Things*, *The Archaeology of Knowledge*, and *Discipline and Punish*—and by the seemingly more architectural, or material tropes related to disciplinary paradigms as evidenced in the panopticon. Foucault famously theorized the intimate coupling of power and knowledge during this period—marked at times by their very hyphenation—tracing, among other things, the impact of the human and social sciences upon broader domains within modernity. Yet it was the overtly strategic nature of discourses—their functioning within relations of power—that came increasingly to the fore in the 1970s and beyond, along with rendering those strategic operations historically legible. Discourse was now conceived as strategic games played out on a battlefield, knowledge (at least in part) a participant in and effect of those battles. "Discourse battle and not discourse reflection," Foucault stressed of its strategic character in 1976: "Discourse—the mere fact of speaking, of employing words, or using the words of others (even if it means returning them), words that the others understand and accept (and, possibly, return from their side)—this fact is in itself a force. Discourse is, with respect to the relation of forces, not merely a surface of inscription, but something that brings about effects."[2]

As Maurizio Lazzarato has argued, at stake in Foucault's reading of power relations as fluid and strategic games (rather than power as the property of individuals or the product of institutional frameworks) was insisting upon the potential that ethical and political agency could emerge within the instabilities and mobilities of positions within such a field of players. It was a conception of power that entailed the possibility or imminent condition of a strategic reversibility of power, an undermining of the status quo. Hence the importance of Foucault's tripartite distinction between modalities of power— "states of domination" (the focus of conventional notions of how power operates), strategic relations of power, and techniques of government that in some sense mediate between them. Concomitant to this conception of power as unstable, and as effectively reversible, was recognition of the productive or creative function of resistance. No longer "conceptualized only in terms of negation," as Foucault put it, resistance could be reconceived as an active form of participation that catalyzed processes of transformation: Moreover, such creative acts could open onto new forms of life.[3]

This understanding or paradigm of power emerged within Foucault's theorization of biopower, his reading of how techniques of power and of government were exercised within territories and over populations and ultimately bodies, and it is in this sense that many of us have been thinking with Foucault's expanded conception of power and subjectivity. Foucault's arguments also attended to the political analysis of discourse—"it is a matter of exhibiting discourse as a strategic field," he posited—an argument with theoretical, institutional, and historical implications for architecture, and perhaps an important subtext at play within current debates.[4] When we more overtly refract Foucault's reading of power back onto disciplinary and institutional formations within architecture we can suggest that although architectural canons, Pritzker prizes, historical narratives, professional norms, and other congealed discourses and institutes operate to stabilize certain relations of power, to in effect translate them into states of domination, we can also imagine other contributions to the field taking the form of creative interruptions or strategic reversals. In this regard we find ourselves back at the task of theory. To come back to the epigraph: Foucault did not assume, naively, that strategic reversals of power would give rise to states of liberation, but rather that this very dynamic harbored the potential of annexation, a type of incorporation into the system that had to be assumed within the temporal logic of one's practice. If typically working against the ethos of radical struggles, this dynamic of learning from dissent also implicitly harbored opportunities for subtly redirecting the wider apparatus.

See also Arindam Dutta's comments on disciplinary formations ← p. 73–74

II

In 2006, in the midst of the Iraq War, I sat in on a seminar titled "Politics as War," taught by Etienne Balibar at UC–Irvine. Balibar used the occasion to undertake a close reading of a series of classic texts on war and politics—Tolstoy's *War and Peace*, Clausewitz's *On War*, Carl Schmitt's *Concept of the Political*, and some of Karl Marx's later writings, explicating the notion of, and contradictions inherent to, a global war (a generalized situation of war that entailed the loss of distinction between civil wars and foreign wars, as with the Bush administration's launching of the highly ambiguous War on Terror). Balibar initially planned also to address Agamben's *The State of Exception*, Giovanna Borradori's *Philosophy in a Time of Terror: Dialogues with Jürgen Habermas and Jacques Derrida*, and Foucault's *"Society Must Be Defended"* (the recent publication and translation of which was, in part, the occasion for the course). The class never reached (at least explicitly or in detail) these more recently published texts. I mention Balibar's course here for the following reason: In introducing his motivation for returning to classical texts at this volatile moment, he offered a formulation of the role of the humanities that left a powerful impression. He posited that it was precisely when there seemed to be no time to spare, when on account of contemporary events it seemed most urgent to act, immediately, in order to intervene, that one might take time to reflect or think, in this case in order to reassess key concepts related to war. This was not instead of action, but as a sort of supplement to it. He suggested that one might proceed "as if" this mode of reflection was equally urgent, and indeed his explication elicited remarkable insights regarding the opacity or slipperiness of the contemporary definition (or redefinition) of war and its relations to political maneuvers. At stake, we might say, was learning to recognize the strategic blurring of political and military goals in regard to then-current events: the attacks of 9/11, the U.S.-led wars in Iraq and Afghanistan, Hurricane Katrina in New Orleans, etc., as well as forging theoretical weapons through which to enter the discursive register of this battlefield. If terms like *war, security, justice, conflict, sovereignty, peace, emergency, public,* etc., were in the process of gaining new valence, even new definitions (their meaning being subtly, or sometimes not so subtly transformed to particular political ends), then those terms were, implicitly, also unstable and hence might also be recast to take on other resonances. Here again emerged a role for theoretical work, one of strategically reversing or redirecting emerging valences at play.

Balibar also raised a question familiar to all of us who work with historical material: that of how to address seeming coincidences between philosophical issues addressed in classic texts—in his case largely derived from the domain of political philosophy, but not exclusively—and issues raised by both historical and contemporary events. How, that is, do we think the reciprocal determination and interaction between philosophy (or theory) and life/history/experience, to which we might add, or within which we might inscribe, architecture? There are many ways of reading such affinities within architecture, and the terms of those readings differ or shift with the particularities of discourses and events at play. Sometimes there are direct or overt connections—an architect reading or producing theory; a theorist taking architecture as a starting point, or site, through which to reflect on forms of life—but on other occasions the mediating factors are less evident, the connections more spectral, requiring a broader matrix to unpack. In most cases such affinities or intersections can, I want to suggest, be read as offering historical symptoms or clues that point to cogent stakes; they often serve as moments of legibility or intelligibility, crystallizations of historical and political forces at work. In this sense, theory is marked by historical events, just as architecture, as a discipline, a practice, and a discourse, is in turn highly—and rightfully—porous to contemporary transformations in technological, economic, social, and geopolitical terrains: Indeed, architecture often quite literally attempts to operate at the vanguard of such transformations (even sometimes posing as an avant-garde). To elucidate this porosity, and to cite some questions informing my current research, we could point to architecture's complex relationships: to the rise of cybernetics and systems theory in the post–World War II era and hence proximity to the military-industrial academic complex; to the strategic announcement and mobilization of threats of insecurity (of places, territories, populations, environments, etc.) in the interest of justifying forms of defense, regulation, management, and control, including under the rubric of humanitarian emergencies; to the emergence of Big Data and data management systems, and in turn the problematic of NSA surveillance, etc.; or to various moments of protest, struggle, and occupation targeting emergent techniques of power.[5]

Returning to the issue of how to "think" the coincidence or intersection of theory or philosophy and, let's say, life or history, I want to underscore that it is on account of the ambiguous resonances and often-unstable relays across these domains that such moments of convergence require us (maybe *require* is too strong a word; perhaps *prompt* is better) to take a position with respect to their political valence as well, and to consider their possible critical reorientation or strategic deployment. This ambiguity and instability, that is, marks the valence of these coincidences as urgent, as "urgencies of architectural theory." Thus we might ask whether, why, and how to engage a resonant contemporary event or—to come back to Foucault—to dig something out of the sand. I am not suggesting that theoretical and historical work is always reactive or that it simply responds to "urgencies" such as war, political cynicism, and the millions of lives it can put at risk, or threats to privacy, or environmental catastrophe, although they can all be good motivations. Nor am I suggesting that because architecture, in the more conventional sense of practice, often itself reacts to major historical events and changes that theory should blithely follow, like a lap dog. But insofar as theory has long served as a site of ethical questioning and political conscience within architectural debates, and insofar as it facilitates the circulation of concepts that can help open architecture up to its outside or to that which the discipline often attempts actively to foreclose in the name of asserting its autonomy, it seems warranted to speculate on the prospects for such an unsettling role.

III

So, I have found myself faced with a seeming paradox: Urgencies both mark the contemporaneity of, and serve as potential traps for, theory. Engaging urgencies comes with risks. As should be evident, many of the urgencies to which I have alluded have a militaristic character, one that has infiltrated not only aspects of my subject matter but also my rhetoric, wavering between the register of the allegorical and that of the literal in this respect. In the face of a global apparatus of capital driving this militarism, an apparatus often marked by cynicism and violence and with which architecture intersects in complex ways, it does appear urgent to act or respond in some way but also to take time to reflect and theorize, and to seek spaces in order to do so. Theory both produces and occupies or activates those spaces, emerging to fill gaps or interrupt architectural assumptions. So it remains urgent to theorize, to find ways to "think" with the present but not necessarily in alignment with it. My own work most often takes history as a medium to help constitute such spaces to think (albeit laterally) about the present, even to attempt to reflect upon it. It is not the only way to do history, and certainly not the only way to do theory, but it allows for a type of figuration of *urgency without urgencies*. It situates one's work in the manner of constructing knowingly asymmetrical platforms from which to enter into contemporary battles, albeit not always through the terms in which extant struggles within the field are offered up to us as relevant or central. They are platforms that, I hope, exhibit certain discursive and conceptual tools and from which the strategic arrangements of forces on those battlefields are rendered more intelligible. I try to identify moments when the outcome of a battle, or the terms of a discourse, are still undecided (even if not evident at the time): With historical retrospect, we can obtain a grasp on the path such a story subsequently took, through identifying key points of instability as well as the effects of decisions made. We can also mark out the contours of other potential moves in the game, trajectories that never came to pass or that left few traces. If

theoretical-historical work implicitly lays out prospects for strategic games, it is not, to return to where I began, in the interest
of being prescriptive with respect to others' practice but rather
to help imagine alternative possibilities, scripts, narratives,
or even simply questions for leaping forward, terms that are,
strictly speaking, not identical to those of the past.

I want to finish by recalling that central terms at play within
contemporary architectural research—territories, populations,
bodies, environments, security, insurgency, defense, injustice,
militarism, neoliberalism, neocolonialism, communication and
control technologies, media and management strategies—were
around before 2000, in 2000-. We can find numerous traces in the
historical record, notably during the 1960s and 1970s, as I try
to develop in my research. Hence the importance of Foucault's
work from the 1970s to this particular project, work that was so
decisively marked by that moment's increasingly evident nexus
of neoliberalism, globalization, and militarism. In addition to
tracing archaeologies of the art of government and its relation
to an emerging biopolitical apparatus, Foucault implicitly spoke
to recent events: He recognized in postwar struggles for liberation from colonial rule, and battles against neocolonial incursions
such as those played out in Latin America and Indochina, a type
of asymmetrical but strategic struggle against dominant relations
of power, a struggle that could be read within a longer historical trajectory and in other contexts (such as Europe) and that
offered ongoing lessons. Hence, too, the importance of the recent
publication and translation of his lectures, a dissemination that
coincided with a moment during which that nexus of neoliberalism, globalization, and militarism became increasingly impossible
to ignore, a moment (coincidently? I am not sure) marking the
end of the rule of architectural postmodernism and its eclipse by
battles over the discipline's embrace of digital technologies and
their paradigms of management and regulation. After 2000, that
is, this conjunction of militarism, globalization, and neoliberalism
emerged into heightened visibility and hence into the domain (to
return one last time to this event's subtitle) of the "urgencies of
architectural theory." Whether one liked it or not, it became a

context through which to read architectural battles. At stake for theory, then, is how to contribute new or updated tools to help interrupt that dominant apparatus, to reverse its hierarchies, or to help redirect architecture's possible relation to it. At stake is taking time to do so.

1   Michel Foucault, *"Society Must Be Defended": Lectures at the Collège de France, 1975–76*, trans. David Macey (New York: Picador, 2003), 11.

2   Michel Foucault, "Le Discours ne doit pas être pris comme..." (1976), cited by Arnold I. Davidson, "Introduction," in *"Society Must Be Defended,"* xx.

3   Maurizio Lazzarato, "From Biopower to Biopolitics," *Tailoring Biotechnologies*, vol. 2, no. 2 (Summer–Fall 2006): 17.

4   Foucault, "Le Discours ne doit pas être pris comme..." cited by Davidson, "Introduction," xx.

5   See Felicity D. Scott, *Outlaw Territories: Environments of Insecurity/Architectures of Counter-Insurgency* (forthcoming from Zone Books).

TRANSVERSAL MATERIALISM: ON METHOD ARTIFACT, AND EXCEPTION
Pelin Tan

To rise in the middle of a feeling of discouragement. To make coffee. To warm some milk. To take vitamins. To wait for the storm. To listen to the news and let one believe that things, later, will be much better.[1]
—Etel Adnan

In the text that follows, I will try to do three things and ask one question. The question: How should we better understand the situational relationships between architectural or spatial artifacts and their landscapes and environments? I will explore this question by looking at three interrelated problems—method itself, the inherently anachronic nature of artifacts, and the design of spaces of exception. This is not a suggestion for a construction of a theory as such; rather, I am interested in focusing on how thinking and practice proceed in a transversal way. This transversal exchange—rather than the formulation of new theories—is one way in which architectural theory holds urgency for the present.

ON METHOD

The spatial productions of our everyday lives are often understood as the architectural outcomes of many layers of influencing factors and independent actors (to use a familiarly Latourian word). But releasing that dependent relationship of object and subjectivity opens up other methodologies. The social sciences and applied design generally still refer to a dualism of object and subject, based in Cartesian thought. While this dualist structure was altered and to some extent undermined by philosophical post-structuralism, those changes were never entirely adopted by applied design and architecture. How might a more transversal form become possible? What is its method? How might this transversal form take root between normative dualistic criticism and the discourse of "new materialism"—a term coined by Manuel DeLanda and Rosi Braidotti in the late 1990s, as linguistic post-structuralism was on the wane, but which has developed and spread substantially in the last eight years?

New Materialism is a critical methodological approach and contextual frame that examines the dualist structure of subject/object that marked much of twentieth-century thought. The main criticism stems from the tendency of linguistic post-structuralism to center the production of knowledge within human subjectivity. There are many layers of New Materialism that differ from field to field—feminism, geography, the anthropocene, or biology. But in general, the ways in which humans shape landscape, territory, and spatial production as outcomes reveal a process of interrelation between things, as well as the biopolitical power relations that undergird the representation of spatial production and process. In understanding the production of space as a constellation of processes, objects, and things no longer require justification simply from twentieth-century phenomenological methods or dryly positivist empirical materialism; rather, this New Materialism brings a "speculative realist" method to bear on understanding spatial environments. Thus, some routes of New Materialism embrace a kind of fetishism of objects while others support Latourian actor-network methods that can lead to another kind of hierarchy in subject/object dualist structure, highlighting the dominance of object.

The transversal method—which by its very nature resists dwelling only on questions of objects or subjectivities—helps us question what we think we know about architectural practice. It invents newly fluid territories. It allows us to rethink the common definition of architectural "form," opening up more heterogeneous understandings than the prevailing, largely neoliberal sense that architectural form is an assemblage of the economic processes of production and representation in which both remain ambiguous. New Materialism, by contrast, suggests that the material that constitutes the form becomes present in its combination of function and physicality, and the ensuing possibilities for architectural method and practice flow from that more multiple sense of form.

We can think, for example, about working *against* the materiality of the architectural form—searching for a more *discursive* form that coexists in certain relationships and creates transversality. Gordon Matta-Clark offers a historical example. His creation of form by way of demolition—commonly understood as a critique of modernist object-formalism—was not only a bodily attack against physical material of architecture, but also against the meanings that the material represents. Stephen Walker describes Matta-Clark's formalism as something of a discursive spiral: "Form returns there after pursuing something of a detour, and when it returns it does so in a mode that is different from that of modernism... Form no longer bears the absolute, eternal truth, but is now raised as a question."[2]

Matta-Clark's approach remains a vital criticism of modernist formalist tradition (and until the last decade, his work was generally considered within the epistemology of *artistic* formalism), but it also has much to say about our contemporary means of questioning form and representation in *architecture*. The criticism of formalism in architecture is still founded in the separation of materiality and the senses—or body and mind. The "de-functioning" of form—deconstructing the meaning of form and questioning its function—is a rare practice of criticality in architecture. When Deleuze claims that "dualism is what prevents thought," he means that dualisms (like materiality/senses, for example) neglect the processes of thought, focusing instead on its outcomes.[3] Deleuze's philosophical approach—not unlike Matta-Clark's anarchitectural method in this regard—asks us instead to consider the incomplete relations between mind and body.

Somewhere between the rigid separation between subject and object of Cartesian thought and the criticism of that binary found in post-structuralism, we might locate the beginnings of subjectivity. A more nuanced understanding of "form" and "material" might be advanced from the theoretical perspective of new materialism (or, as we might call it instead, transversal materialism), which has taken a critical stance against linguistics-based post-structuralism. In their book of interviews with major thinkers of this tendency, Rick Dolphijn and Iris van der Tuin explain:

> Working through Cartesian or modernist dualisms, new materialism has set itself to practice the Spinozist dictum that the mind is always already an idea of the body, while the body is the object of the mind. In terms of artworks, for instance, a new materialist perspective would be interested in finding out how the form of content (the material condition of the artwork) and the form of expression (the sensations as they come about) are being produced in one another, how series of statements are actualized, and how pleats of matter are realized in the real.[4]

How might architectural form be defined according to the approach of new materialism? Matter and form in architecture—generally speaking, but especially in formal modernism—have often been interpreted according to functional context. An architectural practice that concerns spatiality and matter beyond the functional pragmatism demanded by neoliberalism is nearly unthinkable.

Manuel DeLanda (read by many architects since the 1990s) has defined the material world through the concept of morphogenesis. Neither monist nor dualist structures should be denied, in DeLanda's account, but neither offers an adequate explanation of the material world, which develops in a "non-linear" way, outside of the categories placed on it by the human mind. His interest resides in "unformed and unstructured morphogenetic flows...this flowing reality animated from within by self-organizing processes constituting a veritable non-organic life."[5] Unsurprisingly, given his interest in both materiality and a Deleuzian sense of "becoming," he points out the question of matter in Deleuze's philosophy:

> The question of the objective existence of problems is a crucial issue in Deleuze's philosophy of matter and form,

a philosophy which attempts to replace essentialist views of that genesis of form (which imply a conception of matter as an inert receptacle for forms that come from the outside) with one in which matter is already pregnant with morphogenetic capabilities, therefore capable of generating form on its own.[6]

To undertake this work of replacing essentialist views of form in architecture, the fundamental base of how we understand the distinction of matter and form is one place to start. Whether a simple block, a model of a form, the spectacular realities of luxury housing in Dubai, a migrant dwelling capsule, or a temporary refugee camp, the singularity of each form is found in the interplay between its own spatial organization and its location within the sedimentary layers of other forms. What makes this "transversal" is the methodology by which we might think about the possible morphogenetic capabilities of these architectural matters.

Thinking transversally about architecture allows for trans-local, borderless knowledge production that rhizomatically extends beyond the familiar terrains of architecture and design to encompass questions like citizenship, militant pedagogy, institutionalism, borders, war, being a refugee, documents and documenting, urban segregation, the commons, and others. Transversal practice—"neither institutional therapy, nor institutional pedagogy," as Félix Guattari puts it, but rather an analytic method that cuts across multiple fields—is often affiliated with models of knowledge and pedagogy such as "assemblage methods" or "affective pedagogy."[7] Methodology is not only a system for describing realities; it is a political tool that takes part in the process of knowledge production. "Method assemblage," as described by John Law,

is the process of enacting or crafting bundles of ramifying relations that condense presence and (therefore also) generate absence by shaping, mediating, and separating these. Often it is about manifesting realities out-there and depictions of those realities in-here. It is also about enacting Othernesses.[8]

Law's work, which mainly concerns critical approaches of methods for the social sciences, also reveals methodological openings for architectural research and pedagogy. How might we understand the possibilities of creating such transversalities that enact these states of Otherness? "Affective pedagogy," meanwhile, refers to Deleuze's reference to Spinoza's concept of "affect/affections," a type of perception that moves beyond the body and assemblages of form: "Affect is a starting place from which we can develop methods that have an awareness of the politics of aesthetics: methods that respond with sensitivity to aesthetic influence on human emotions and understand how they change bodily capacities."[9] The discursive potentialities of form—and how the matter of a form can be outside of the control of the architect's mind—moves us beyond the post-structuralist critique of Cartesian dualism. These concepts allow us to think of new multiplicities for pedagogy and practice, and make possible a more transversal form of architecture.

Eyal Weizman has asked: "What should creative architectural research 'learn from the domination of Gaza' and apply in London?"[10] The moments of testimony, negotiation, resistance, and design practiced by the various actors within the spaces (and architectures) of conflict that he studies point to an extra-disciplinary ontology in which practice and theory are inseparable, and are thus beyond the possibility of simple physical reconstruction or an "architecture of peace." The methodological and theoretical concept of the "forensic"—developed in recent years by Weizman and his team, as well as others like Anselm Franke—has brought vital attention to the production of public "truth" in architecture.[11] Returning to the Latin root of *forensis*, Weizman observes the critical link between *forum* (as negotiation) and *forensics* (as a methodology of examining crime): "Forensics is thus the art of the forum—the practice and skill of presenting an argument before a professional, political, or legal gathering. Forensics is in this sense part of rhetoric, which concerns speech. However, it includes not only human speech but also that of things."[12] In this context, architectural production and the presentation of objects, things, testimonies, and forms exist in multiple relations to both the event and the space in which it occurred or is constructed. "Forensics is thus concerned both with the materialization of the event and also with the performance of the object within a forum."[13]

Weizman's theoretical approach has many connections with methodologies of approaching things as well as modifying the object/subject dualism of post-structuralism. Bruno Latour's "actor-network theory" and the more recent developments of "object-oriented ontology"—two fields of thought that have become prominent enough to become widely known by their acronyms—influence Weizman's forensic spatial practice, but as a *multiple* practice and production, it goes well beyond both methods. In his work on similar questions relating to the anthropocene in architecture, Etienne Turpin eloquently describes the pitfalls of both methods when applied on their own: "Where the former approach valorizes the connectivity of the network, and the latter position emphasizes the irreducibility of nodes as the primary constituents of the network."[14] Transversal method is intrinsic in the form.

ON ARTIFACT

This focus on the reconstituted relationship between objects and subjectivities demands another question: How might a contextualized "form" move from being a metaphorical, affirmative experience into a more discursive realm? The philosopher Quentin Meillassoux has introduced the concept of the "arche-fossil" as framework for looking at "not just materials indicating the traces of past life…but materials indicating the existence of an ancestral reality or event."[15] This temporal co-existence informs us about current conditions (whether of the socioeconomic means of production or the layered representation of a given object) but also its past and future. How might we experience this intertwined arrangement of layers—whether of social, geological, or architectural strata? The artistic practices of Emre Hüner (Istanbul, 1977) and Anton Vidokle (Moscow, 1965) invite us to dig into these questions. Both deal in their video works with architectural models, the modernist approach to form, contemporary problems of representation, and the spatial artifacts of neoliberal production.

Hüner's work focuses especially on spatial imaginaries, architectural entities, possible settlements, and uncommon arrangements between subjectivities and objects. Of interest here are his visits to Fordlandia—a now-ruined industrial set-tlement in the Amazon rain forest that was built by Henry Ford in 1928 to produce rubber for Ford company—and Doris Duke's orientalist villa in Hawaii known as "Shangri La." Through these experiences of landscape, Hüner questions both the forms of capitalist modernity in exotic physical environments and evokes the colonial evolution of such economic artifacts. In each case, Hüner's work moves between the realized projects and the fragments and models that underpin the larger forms but are often detached from them. These fragments and models are not directly linked to the architectural object but are rather traces of a realized material that could have been realized in other ways. In his 16mm film "Diamond Head Diving Man" (2012), for example, we see found fragments of the intricately detailed model first proposed for "Shangri La" in the 1920s. The model as rendered in the film carries its own time and space that embody it as an artifact separate from the meaning of the realized mod-ern villa. In his project "Fordlandia" (2010), the experience of Hüner's artistic excursion is made visible through fragments of ceramic, found objects, linin, magazines, and photographs exhibited in a vitrine, as a sedimentary layering of forms. These artifacts illustrate a kind of ruination, in Jalal Toufic's sense that ruins are a place "haunted by the living who inhabit them."[16]

The question then becomes: Can we experience other possi-ble "times" and "spaces"—lived or not lived—and how might their forms be represented? As artifacts? As ruins? Perhaps we can approach Hüner's metaphorical spatial forms as arche-fossils. This

Emre Hüner, stills from "Diamond Head Diving Man" (2012)

Emre Hüner, "Fordlandia," wooden vitrine, linen, ceramics, found objects, magazines, and photographs, as installed at the Rijksakademie Open (2012)

would lend itself to DeLanda's "geological approach" to human history, which offers us a known but perhaps still uncommon argument about how we should understand material culture:

> Human culture and society are not different from the self-organized processes that inhabit the atmosphere and hydrosphere (wind, circuits, hurricanes), or, for that matter, no different from lavas and magmas, which as

self-assembled conveyor belts drive plate tectonics and over millennia have created all the geological features that have influenced human history.[17]

Hüner's own aim in these artistic investigations was "to create an abstraction of utopian or imaginary architecture, planetary landscapes, and possible settlements on planets, the idea of flight and remains of civilizations, while keeping my focus on materiality and texture of ceramic and the other materials."[18] His sensitivity to the surfaces of materials and their transforming forms can be seen in both works. The process and the details of the materials become an expanding "still life" that he observes in his studio, conveying a relation to the history of the formation of artifacts often found in earth.

Might an architectural model be understood as an "artifact of an artifact"? In an architectural context, in both Hüner and Vidokle's works, architectural models and anachronic forms are conveyed as dialectical narratives.[19] Vidokle's "Two Suns" (2012), meanwhile, is a video narrative of a personal experience with the architectural form commonly held to be the twentieth century's first fully modern house—Gerrit Rietveld's Schröder House in Utrecht (1924).[20] In the video we witness people engaged in the construction of a dwelling, located in a

Anton Vidokle in collaboration with Hu Fang, "Two Suns," 22 minute HD video with sound (2012)

Anton Vidokle in collaboration with Hu Fang, "Two Suns," 22 minute HD video with sound (2012)

rural part of Taiwan along the new constructed highways that connect satellite cities—the recent post-Fordist hubs of global digital technology—across the country. The filmmaker's voice tells us about the house in Utrecht and the story of its architect, as well as Vidokle's own experience of the current Taiwanese landscape that we see in the video. The façade is built out of a grid of mirror-like windows, reflecting the landscape in the surface of the building. It is an anachronistic architectural experience, listening to this narrative of the Schröder House while seeing the production of an architecture so intimately tied to the contemporary, neoliberal moment of anthropocene (and vice versa). Watching the reflection of the landscape and highways of Taiwan in the mirror-covered dwelling raises the issue of whether the knowledge of form is informed either by architectural models—utopias or artifacts as the decay of forms.

Warfare, ecological disaster, and technological collapse have deep effects on our everyday life and will continue to influence our future spatial infrastructure. Ecological disasters also cut both ways, having now become useful reasons for governments to further demolish ecological landscapes and the lives of their inhabitants. This phase of anthropocene will be defined by the co-productions of governmental and other actors as they seek to control the ecological landscape. The ambivalence of experiencing artifacts and the decay of forms forces us to consider and dwell more on the discourse of timeless terrestrial experience.

ON EXCEPTION

Another artifact of an event, an architecture of decay, is a refugee camp. "Decay" is for me a key concept in understanding form, time, and putrefaction—giving "decay" a meaning that is not exclusively negative. Reza Negarestani asks, "Is decay a positive of a negative building process?" and answers by arguing that "the building process of decay is subtractive" and "is concurrently intensively negative and extensively positive."[21] The contraction of the negative and positive sides of the process of decay shows that the subtraction of forms are *potentials*—the infinite latitudes of forms. Negarestani's first axiom is as follows: "Decay is a building process; it has chemical slant and a differential dynamic distribution...the process of decay builds new states of extensity, affect, magnitude, and even integrity from and out of system or formation without nullifying or reforming it." The decay of forms confronts us to deal with anachronisms that prevent the contraction of the "inhumanity" that is rooted in human history. Urbanized refugee camps and settlements are forms of decay, a building process of subtraction that is both anachronism and a potential decay of architecture itself.

Refugee camps are often described as the spatialization of exception—the infrastructures of sustenance such as dwelling, food, health, and emergency issues are the basic forces of zoning for a *tabula rasa* camp plan. This form of dwelling and its zoning is a production of space whose process reflects the continuous negotiation of public space, based on things like border politics and their juridical justification, the negotiation of humanitarian aid, and political agencies. The design program of a camp aims to supply the needs of a community at the spatial scale of a neighborhood, a village, or a small city in which the community is seen as a homogenous entity (with particularities like kinship,

211

religion, and tribal networks having been disregarded). These camps, as the anthropologist Michel Agier puts it, "gradually become the sites of an enduring organization of space, social life and system of power that exist nowhere else. These are paradoxical devices, hybrids that, for lack of an appropriate term, I shall call city-camps (*camps-villes*)."[22] While the link between the concepts of camp and city paradoxically signifies the problems of normative design—a term that describes an early twentieth-century approach to urban planning based on social normative engineering as well as upending public participation in planning processes—Agier conceptualizes camps as an *urban* space with a heterogeneous everyday life, as well as a *biopolitical* space, with its networked practices of the actors and agencies.

The architect Manuel Herz has claimed that refugee camps are not "non-places," in the way that they have often been described in the social sciences. Rather, in keeping with Agier's idea of the city-camp, it is a settlement, a territory of political, economical, and judicial relationships that also transforms the relations of the world outside. But Herz goes further, claiming that refugee camps are the direct materialization of a dynamic political act against those urban forms that are idealized by the West.[23] Seen as a biopolitical space of an anti-colonial city, the camp for Herz becomes a potential spatial practice against Western-oriented modernism and global colonial dwelling forms.

The architect Alessandro Petti—whose practice DAAR, with Sandi Hilal, focuses instead on public space and ways of commoning in refugee camps—asks a counter-question:

> If a citizen's political identity is played out in the public space of the city, what is found in the camp is its inverse: here, a citizen is stripped of his or her political rights. In this sense, the camp represents a sort of anti-city, a constitutive void of a political order. But what effect does this anti-city produce on the public and political space of the city?[24]

Through the problematization of public space, Petti claims that the camp has a potentiality as an "anti-city." As a biopolitical space, camps cannot be conceptualized through a dichotomy of inside/outside—it is beyond such a dualistic structure.[25] Moving past more Western discussions of public space and nation-state citizenship, Petti and Hilal focus on a new term—a practice called *Al-Masha*. The meaning of the word is equivalent to the English "common," and the practice has an Ottoman legacy of cultivating land as a collective:

> The notion of Al-Masha could help reimagine the notion of the common today. Could this form of common use be expanded by redefining the meaning of cultivation, moving it from agriculture to other forms of human activity?... But how to liberate the common from the control of authoritarian regimes, neocolonialism and consumer societies? How to reactivate common uses beyond the interests of public state control?[26]

Al-Masha offers Petti and Hilal a potential new formation of citizen and space beyond the usual public/private dualism.

In my own work at the Architecture Faculty of Mardin Artuklu University, we have been examining the camp settlements of southeastern Turkey that have sprung up in the wake of the Syrian civil war and conflicts in south Kurdish zones. Our spatial research has focused on camps that consist of official camps run by Turkish Government (AFAD Department), Ezidi camps run by Kurdish municipality, temporary camps created within in existing buildings, and several types of architectural formations (bus stations, sports halls, empty factories) that embody the political/social negotiations that are central to camp life.[27] The research focuses on four factors that we find fundamental to the design and informal space production of camps:

1 A biopolitical analysis of camps that are constructed, controlled, and run by the Turkish Government and the UN

2   The shifting usage of the camps' public spaces and facilities in the everyday life practices of refugees

3   Gestures of design without architects in the camps

4   Infrastructure in temporary camps officially run by the state and camps created by self-initiations in already existing buildings such as bus stations, art gallery, sports halls, unfinished constructions, and empty factories.

One such example of a biopolitical space that hosts the negotiations of a complex set of actors can be found in the Midyat Refugee camp, north of Mardin near the Syrian border and designed in March 2013 to host 10,000 people (its population is

Schematic plan of Midyat Refugee camp (2013)

currently 6,500). Habat Mehmet Yıldırım, a former graduate student of Mardin who led the team that designed the camp on behalf of the Turkish government, noted three major determinants of the camp's form—topography, demands from the Assyrian community, and surveillance.[28] The topography was a rugged terrain that had to be flattened into a smooth surface ready for water, electricity, and dwellings. The Christian Syrians in the camp asked to be separated from the Muslim Syrians, requiring zoning into religiously segregated areas—the north part of the camp was designed for administration, the middle part for Muslims, and the south part for Christians. Separating these two communities led to further security needs, so the administration tents were placed in the north of the camp, in order to control easily the rest from above (both directionally and topographically). The two communities are further separated by the buffer of a security road; other roads in the camp, such as those that convey people, goods, or livestock, are fenced in. Notably, however, there is not any serious threat from inside and outside the camp—the surveillance and security play the role of empty signifiers, and the design is justified biopolitically rather than geopolitically.[29] See panel discussion → p. 231

The recent temporary tent encampments for the Ezidi communities that escaped from Shengal and Kobéne to Turkey are mostly in self-initiated tent camps around the towns of Mardin and Suruç or, somewhat paradoxically, erected inside of existing buildings. The major actors in this case (alongside the refugees themselves) are the Kurdish municipalities, solidarity groups, and several international NGOs that intervene through politics of humanitarian aid and solidarity discourses. Despite this official emphasis on solidarity, the refugees are generally self-organized around their tribes and families and have created ad-hoc design solutions according to commoning practices. For example, the newly designed local bus station of Mardin hosted around six hundred refugees from Shengal, in an arrangement managed by the Kurdish party and the municipality. The kitchen of the camp was run by the youth of a leading family of the community. Local voluntary teachers ran a school inside a big tent from Mardin. These sorts of everyday practices of life open up several self-organized modalities in which design remains as an ad-hoc solution instead of a form of biopolitical control.

The refugee is an archetype of the subjectivity that claims a right to the city and urban participation. Gypsies, refugees, nomads, the homeless...such biopolitical subjectivities are the artifacts of survival strategies in urban life, straddling the border of exclusion and inclusion or shaped by the ecological contingencies of the anthropocene. In the philosophy of Emmanuel Levinas, a refugee experiences the Otherness, *being* the Otherness. Or, as the poet Etel Adnan has put it, we are all refugees. A refugee is the subject of unconditional hospitality within an experience of radical space.

As Giorgio Agamben has put it—following in theoretical constellation of others like Carl Schmitt and Levinas—subjectivity is defined in the condition of exception.[30] But by defining refugeehood in this theoretical frame, the refugee's subjectivity is constrained and emancipation is disallowed. This emphasis on exception (on victimhood, aggrievement, and Otherness) diminishes the potential transversal subjectivity of the refugee. Agamben's frequently cited definition of this state of exception points to its ubiquity:

> If the essence of the camp consists in the materialization of the state of exception and in the subsequent creation of a space in which bare life and the juridical rule enter into a threshold of indistinction, then we must admit that we find ourselves virtually in the presence of a camp every time such a structure is created, independent of the kinds of crime that are committed there and whatever its denomination and specific topography.[31]

While understanding the camp as a biopolitical space based strictly on otherness can be ontologically justified, this approach clearly leaves out the potentialities of subjectivity as well as the on-the-ground territorial conditions. Therefore, the becoming of the refugee's subjectivity as it is commonly understood is trapped in victimhood as well as the idea that the camp is the subject of sovereignty.[32] Thus, we may claim, the contemporary experience of "exception" as a form is a multiple constellation that exists in tension between territorial facts, objects, and subjectivities. Transversal materialism offers a channel for understanding these tensions in both theory and practice, where both are understood to be ontologically inseparable. The three registers of transversal materiality discussed here—method, artifact, exception—could be defined and developed separately, or approached in a way that allows them to be folded together. The contemporary spatial demarcation of the tension between territorialities and subjectivities forces us to invent, and to move beyond our existing architectural methods and theory.

My thanks to James Graham, Mark Wigley, Anton Vidokle, and Emre Hüner for their discussions and assistance in developing this text.

1   Etel Adnan, *In the Heart of the Heart of Another Country* (San Francisco: City Lights Books, 2005), 13.

2   Stephan Walker, *Gordon Matta-Clark: Art, Architecture and the Attack of Modernism* (London: I.B. Tauris, 2009), 31, 40.

3   Gilles Deleuze, "Dualism, Monism and Multiplicities (Desire-Pleasure-Jouissance)," seminar, March 26, 1973, *Contretemps* 2 (May 2001), 92–108.

4   Rick Dolphijn and Iris van der Tuin, eds., *New Materialism: Interviews & Cartographies* (Ann Arbor: Open Humanities Press, University of Michigan Library, 2012), 91.

5   Manuel DeLanda, "Chaos/Control: Complexity," *Amerikastudien/American Studies*, vol. 45, no. 1 (2000), 33–41. Manuel DeLanda, "Deleuze, Diagrams and the Genesis of Form," *ANY: Architecture New York* 23, Diagram Work: Data Mechanics for a Topological Age (June 1998), 30–34. Manuel DeLanda, "The Geology of Morals, A Neo-Materialist Interpretation" www.t0.or.at/delanda/geology.htm.

6   Manuel DeLanda, "Deleuze, Diagrams and the Genesis of Form," 30–34.

7   Pierre-Félix Guattari, *The Guattari Reader*, ed. G. Genosko (Oxford: Blackwell Publisher, 1996), 121.

8   John Law, *After Method: Mess in the Social Science Research* (New York: Routledge 2004), 122.

9   Anna Hickey-Moody, "Aesthetics and Affective Pedagogy," *Deleuze and Research Methodologies*, eds. Rebecca Coleman and Jessica Ringrose (Edinburgh: Edinburgh Press, 2013), 92–93.

10   Eyal Weizman, *Oyuk Topraklar: Israil'in İşgal Mimarisi* (İstanbul: Açılım Yayınevi 2015), 259–60 (Turkish translation of *Hollow Land*).

11   See www.forensic-architecture.org.

12   Eyal Weizman, *Forensic Architecture: Notes from Fields and Forums* (Ostfildern: Hatje Cantz, 2012).

13   Eyal Weizman, Paulo Tavere, Susan Schuppli, Situ Studio (2010), "Forensic Architecture," *Architectural Design Journal* 28 (September 2010), 60.

14   Etienne Turpin, ed., *Architecture in the Anthropocene: Encounters Among Design, Deep Time, Science and Philosophy* (Ann Arbor: Open Humanities Press, 2013), 7.

15   Quentin Meillassoux, *After Finitude—An Essay on the Necessity of Contingency* (Bloomsbury Academic, 2008), 22.

16   Jalal Toufic, *Vampires—An Uneasy Essay on the Undead Film* (Station Hill, Post-Apollo Press 2003), 34.

17   Manuel DeLanda, *A Thousand Years of Nonlinear History* (Cambridge, MA: The MIT Press, 2005).

18   See my article on Emre Hüner in *Domus*, August 22, 2013, www.domusweb.it/it/arte/2013/08/22/emre_h_ner.html.

19   For Massimo Scolari, architectural models are tools for design processes, but nevertheless remain the best form of representing architecture: "When it has survived to testify to an architectural ambition, it is often the sole representation of a procedure that in the conceptual sense has ended and that will always remain unknown."

20   "Two Suns" (HD Video, 22", 2012), Anton Vidokle in collaboration with Hu Fang, is set in an abandoned house in the Taiwanese countryside, situated between a banana plantation and a highway.

21   Reza Negarestani, "Undercover Softness: An Introduction to the Architecture and Politics of Decay," *COLLAPSE VI: Geo/Philosophy* (January 2010), 382.

22   Michel Agier, "Between War and City: Towards an Urban Anthropology of Refugee Camps," *Ethnography* 3 (2002), 322.

23   Manuel Herz, "Refugee Camps—or—Ideal Cities in Dust and Dirt," *Urban Transformation* (Berlin: Ruby Press, 2008).

24   Alessandro Petti, Architecture of Exile. See also Sandi Hilal, "Abu Ata, Architect: A Play in Four Acts," (2008), www.campusincamps.ps/wp- content/uploads/2012/12/Sandi-Hilal_Fawwar-play-Final.pdf.

25   Alessandro Petti, Architecture of Exile.

26   Alessandro Petti, Sandi Hilal, and Eyal Weizman, *Architecture After Revolution* (Berlin: Sternberg Press, 2014), 183.

27   Midyat Refugee Camp research studio, March 2014. Studio leaders: Pelin Tan and Markus Miessen, MAU Architecture Faculty, Mardin. Forensik Mimarlık—Socio Spatial Research of Refugee Camps in Southeast Turkey, Principal Researcher: Assoc. Prof. Dr. Pelin Tan, Researcher: Architect Ömer Faruk Günenç, funded by Mardin University Scientific Research Project Department (BAP), 2015–16.

28   Interview with Habat Mehmet Yıldırım, architect/ designer of Midyat Refugee Camp, Urban Planning Department of Turkish Government, Mardin (March 3–5, 2014). Yıldırım was a master's student of MAU Architecture Faculty, Mardin). See also "Midyat Çadırkent (Mülteci Kampı) Planlama Süreci, Sonrası ve Alternatif Kamp Önerisi" (The Process of Midyat Tent Camp and Alternative Camp Design Proposal), term paper of seminar by Habat Mehmet Yıldırım, in "Things, Animizm, Territory" postgrad course by Assoc. Prof. Dr. Pelin Tan, MAU Mardin.

29   This point was made by Mark Wigley in the conference discussions, and helps make clear the relationships between the zoning plan, the design of the camp, and the unknown embedded knowledge in the camp and around the camp.

30   This discussion is a bit beyond the aim of my article and cannot be fully dealt with here. However, I suggest strongly a Ph.D. thesis in Turkish by Duygu Türk, which compares the ideas of ethics and politics between Levinas, Schmitt, and Badiou. See Duygu Türk, *Öteki, Düşman, Olay: Levinas, Schmitt ve Badiou'da Etik ve Siyaset* (Istanbul: Metis Publishing, 2013).

31   Giorgio Agamben, *Homo Sacer: Sovereign Power and Bare Life* (Stanford: Stanford University Press: 1998), 98.

32   Although Critchley interprets Levinas's primary ethical ontology as "active nihilism" for the emancipation and the ethic of the subjectivity through the Otherness; he might see Agamben's camp of space of exception as prevention of the potentialities of emancipation by default. Simon Critchley, *Infinitely Demanding* (New York: Verso, 2013). "If you think the way someone like Agamben argues, if you work with legal history and philology and a more or less Heideggerian understanding of history and ideas of fate, then the world is a concentration camp for sure. But I don't think it is." Pelin Tan, interview with Simon Critchley, "Breaking the Social Contract," *e-flux* 38 (October 2012), www.e-flux.com/journal/ breaking-the-social-contract.

SOME
NOTES ON
ARCHITECTURAL
THEORY
Bernard Tschumi

In architecture, as in several other areas of knowledge, theory and practice are so closely intertwined that any attempt to negate one term at the expense of the other means the extinction of both. Kill theory and practice dies. Kill practice and theory dies. This could be the summary of my position.

Think theory is dead? Don't worry: It will come back when everyone is bored with the hegemony of good feelings and widespread complacency. Practice is dead? Unlikely, unless a moratorium on building becomes a norm.

Designing and building works of architecture takes so long that these works will always be described, excoriated or praised, and, hopefully, debated. Without debates, architecture becomes a predictable dictionary of received ideas and clichés. For example, in architectural education, the fight against the received ideas of mainstream ideologies—modernism, postmodernism, regionalism, and the many other "-isms" of history—has generally been achieved through debates with an inescapably theoretical slant. I would go further: Theory is, by nature, critical or polemical. Theory emerges whenever the conventional discourse on architecture is questioned.

It is never easy to fight what others consider common sense, namely opinions shared by the mass media, clients, and most competition jurors. Theory is the opposite of "common sense." Theory is about being critically conscious, not only about what others do but also about what you yourself are doing. Theory is about asking questions, taking nothing for granted, knowing nothing with certainty. Hence, theory is not a method or a technique; its role is to be suspicious of all methods and all techniques, raising questions about them.

Should theory be opposed to practice? Does one precede the other? Do you theorize first and then practice what you theorized? Is it the other way around? Neither theory nor practice alone will teach you how to invent concepts or attain the most pertinent idea on an intelligent way to resolve contradictory constraints, from zoning regulations to programmatic demands, from waterproofing membranes to a so-called iconic presence.

Since the invention of schools of architecture in 1666, with the Academy Royale, and through a large part of the twentieth century, most theories of architecture have been prescriptive, asserting that "*this* is the right way to design; *that* is the wrong way."

Much of nineteenth- and twentieth-century theory was both prescriptive and ideological, since it advocated specific ways to articulate forms, functions, and materials at the exclusion of other ways. The precepts of the modern movement, along with the so-called postmodern ones (think "New Urbanism"), were prescriptive and ideological. I would suggest that most architecture has no theory but instead has ideology—namely, a dictionary of received ideas.

Architectural theory tends to be either prescriptive or descriptive. I'll defend a descriptive theory every time over a prescriptive one. A descriptive theory is meant to be objective and analytical; it analyzes positions or practices. It is not about being the thought police, requiring this or forbidding that. It seeks to expand knowledge rather than to narrow it.

Is there one theory of architecture or several? Should one talk about "theory" or "theories"? If theory is about asking the right questions, then let's use the singular. But since theory is about rejecting the dictionary of received ideas, it is also inevitably polemical. There is nothing wrong with different polemical positions, each resulting in a different theory, each asking different questions.

Antoine Compagnon, professor of literature at Columbia, to whom I owe credit regarding several of these issues, suggests by analogy that one should make a distinction between a "theory of architecture" and "architectural theory."[1] The "theory of architecture" would be the body of works and thoughts about the state of the field over a given period of history. "Architectural theory" would, on the contrary, be more oppositional and critical, including about the "theory of architecture."

Some Notes on Architectural Theory

Architectural theory raises questions, but about what? Let me venture a succinct but not necessarily finite list:

— What is architecture?

— What is the relationship between architecture and its use, including its social use?

— What is the relationship between architecture and its materiality?

— What is the relationship between architecture and ideas or concepts?

— What is the relationship between architecture and representation (or notation)?

— What is the relationship between architecture and its architect/author?

— What is the relationship between architecture and its viewer/user?

An example of a question: What makes this particular construction "architecture" rather than just a building? My answer (contradicting Nicholas Pevsner): A bicycle shed with a concept is architecture; a cathedral without one is a building.

In the mid-'60s, the late Austrian architect Hans Hollein proposed that "everything is architecture." This definition, close in spirit to the conceptual art of the time, could be countered by asking: If "everything is architecture," what distinguishes a brick arch from a glass of water? Long before, the philosopher Hegel had suggested that architecture is all that does not point to utility.

Hegel's supposition brings us to another pair of questions:

— Does architecture speak about the world, relate to the world? (Is it inclusive, intertextual, popular?)

   or

— Does architecture speak to architecture, relate to architecture? (Is it autonomous, exclusive, elitist?)

These are two clichés whose opposition is, in itself, a cliché. Let's note that the cliché is not specific to architecture but instead is prevalent in cultural histories that include art, literature, and cinema, among other fields. These few points about theory are just another way to think about several open issues in architecture and stay wary of complacency about others' presuppositions. Don't believe anyone. Think for yourself.

   Therefore, the answer to the question "what is architecture?" is by no means a given and depends on the relationship between architecture and use. Architecture is not simply a game of forms. Some of the simplest things in architecture are highly theoretical. For example, while people may say their architecture is about detailing or construction methodology, these fields are not only discrete but also theoretical. If you examine a simple wall detail, it is made up of different components— some inside, some outside, and some in between. One is called insulation, and whether you put it on the outside or the inside has different implications, at once aesthetically, historically, technically, and, of course, thermally. Something as simple as a wall section can lead to a whole discussion on the nature of inner and outer envelopes. Where you locate insulation is simultaneously theoretical, ideological, and practical. The same goes for waterproofing. Do you locate it behind a so-called rain screen (which, paradoxically, does not keep the rain out, but acts purely as a visual envelope on the outer surface)? Or, is it the outer surface that is "waterproofed"? Again, the question is simultaneously theoretical, ideological, and practical.

Some Notes on Architectural Theory

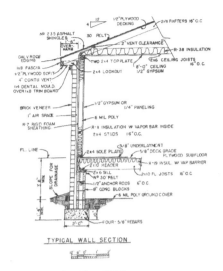

TYPICAL WALL SECTION

Typical brick and stud wall section

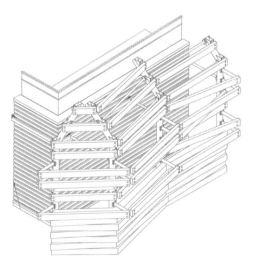

Bernard Tschumi Architects, Paris Zoological Park, 2009–14, drawing of envelope

In other words, nothing is innocent. When you place a wall of glass 30 feet away from your building as a way of responding cleverly to the zoning regulations of a particular city, you are taking both a theoretical stance and a very pragmatic one. But let's take our recent project for the Paris Zoo as an example. When you study the relationships of the inner and outer envelopes, here drawn as a skeleton, and place the circulation in between, or select the materials of those envelopes, you are actually investigating a theory about the nature of enclosure in architecture. This has nothing to do with language or linguistics,

Paris Zoological Park, detail of functional envelope and visual envelope

although you will certainly find texts by Foucault or Deleuze that might help support your argument. The argument really starts with the nature of architecture.

It is increasingly a condition of our time that the functional envelope and the visual envelope are separate, each with its own respective autonomy. This also happens in our design for the Paris Zoo. The project has two main arguments. The first one is that the architectures for the animals and the visitors are identical. For example, the entrance pavilions for the public share the same mesh as the aviaries for birds and small animals.

Restaurants and public amenities have the same wooden screens as the shelters for the rhinos and the giraffes. The two types of species, human and animal, are treated equally.

Paris Zoological Park, animal enclosures

The second point argues about an inner, functional envelope used for shelter and an outer envelope that provides the visual perception of the whole. While envelopes have been heavily theorized in other contexts, here they are made to investigate an evolving dissociation that is common to the twenty-first century. Every project operates within a specific discourse, and with the Zoo we explore the discourse of architecture and envelope—something that is neither simply theory nor practice, but inevitably involves both.

1   Antoine Compagnon, *Le Démon de la Théorie* (Paris: Seuil, 1998), 22.

Conversation

MARK WIGLEY: The conceit of this conference is that there's no coherence, that each person speaks as an individual. But then, of course, coherence might ambush the panel. Coherence would be, for example, the fact that this is 2014, and therefore certain shared concerns arise. Ornament might be one, or the presence of the aesthetic within theory, or whether theory is a thing that we deploy in the traditional sense. Pelin, you said you didn't want to use theory. You were very strong on that point. But then you described camp as being an empty signifier, sounding relatively theoretical.

PELIN TAN: I used some theoretical language because we're in the space of this conference, and theory is part of your provocation. But we all like to deal with theory. We all like to deal with concepts and we all try to make links with architectural history and philosophical sorts of theory and history. It's a desire that's always there. So when I say that I don't want to do any theory, that I don't want to write, it's in the sense of theory as a dry chain of references from somewhere. I don't want to speak as a sociologist, but when architects do theory—if I can be a bit of a devil's advocate—it tends to be a sprinkling of a bit of Deleuze and Guattari, a bit of this and that. This is the sense of theory against which I'm asking whether we need theory in architecture.

BERNARD TSCHUMI: I do not see why the names Deleuze, Guattari, or Foucault should be inevitably connected to theory. I would propose that architecture theory has existed for as long as humans have had a language. The reason why I use the word "language" is that the language of building is not quite the same as the language of drawing or of talking—therefore, you can articulate different thoughts through different means, but all the thoughts are there in the act of building. To equate theory with so-called post-structuralism is, I think, a very reductive notion.

I'd be far more interested in going back to Mark Cousins's earlier point that when you're standing in a lecture hall and you turn to look at the window, there's quite a difference between the window for a philosopher and the window for an architect. I found that idea very interesting because he used the word "window" as if the word "window" was an acceptable reference point. I could reply that a window is a received idea. It's a cliché. That's a problem that both architects and philosophers have when the philosophers say, "Let's open a window to the future"—using an architectural metaphor to try to think, and therefore not thinking very far.

TAN: Yeah, yeah. But it's not that simple. Firstly, I really just said Deleuze and Guattari because they were very much cited and used in the last decades. And the other thing is that they are actually quite practical philosophers at the same time—they are very much involved and Guattari is an activist.

TSCHUMI: Yeah. Sure.

Conversation

FELICITY SCOTT: And they get some of their ideas from architects, of course.

TSCHUMI: That's correct.

WIGLEY: But Pelin, since you are a sophisticated theorist, when you say—

TAN: "Sophisticated." [Laughter]

WIGLEY: —you are!—when you say, "I don't want to use theory," we all wake up to this anti-theory theory. So I thought it was interesting that you used the phrase "empty signifier" to refer to this security apparatus that was not really being used as a security apparatus. It is being used to represent security. If Spyros is right that I think everything is ornament, then it would certainly be interesting to me to see theory dropped into your talk around what could be considered the ornamental use of security.

Maybe I could frame that as a question, because, of course, you didn't use theory when talking about the digging up of the bones. Which implies that theory could arrive when ornament was the issue, but perhaps not as much when it was about life and death. Maybe that's a way of connecting to Felicity's talk, because if there are 45 million people living in camps, there may not be any more urgent question for architects than, "Is there such a thing as a well-designed camp?" or, "Were you given the commission, would you do it?"

A well-designed camp may include an attitude
toward ornament that's not entirely unlike
Bernard's, which so beautifully addressed the
giraffes with their own extraordinary ornament.
They may pretend that they need that particular set of spots for survival reasons, but it
seems to me much more flirtatious. Another kind
of camp for the animals, then. For you, Pelin,
perhaps architecture is another kind of camp
since you're a refugee from sociology, and you
have taken up camp within architecture—and you
even find yourself responsible for the electricity and lighting of your own camp.

TAN: Firstly, I think architecture certainly
borrowed extensively from structuralist and
post-structualist theories. But we are looking
into this idea of before and after 2000, and
I think that one current urgency is to ask
whether architecture is capable of dealing
theoretically with the discursive relation of
subject and object, or subjectivity and form
outside of academia. Any current architectural
form doesn't represent any single unique or
multiple meaning, and the knowledge of the form
has a more complex process that is related to
economy, politics, policy, social agents... A
"camp" is just a "form." Besides representing
an urgent social reality, it is a form of common dwelling of facts in which many complex
relations of agents are involved. The issue
here is how a "camp" enables us to discuss it
as an architectural form that is also a form of
knowledge and social production.

WIGLEY: So I'd just throw it back to Felicity—
and, of course, I love that idea about "2000-."

You also ask questions about camps and human rights, and therefore as a theorist you have a sense of urgency about thinking that through. Is there a place for ornament in that kind of historical work?

SCOTT: Oh, that's a very good question.

WIGLEY: It may not be.

SCOTT: Well, Rudofsky's work and thinking are saturated in the question of ornament and its relation to architecture, these are inseparable things for him. He will quite literally read surfaces as a symptom of forms of life, so there's no question that ornament plays out there, albeit in less familiar ways. But in my current work on human unsettlement, when ornament comes in it often articulates with other questions, such as more familiar claims to meaning. It's not the same discourse on ornament that Spyros was speaking to at all—it doesn't have the same intellectual coordinates, or at least didn't at the historical moment I refract it through.

But I certainly wouldn't want to give up on the aesthetic, or the various forms of signification in architecture. They definitely play out within my current work. I tend to ask to what ends are they mobilized, as opposed to what role they play structurally within the conception of architecture, which is a slightly different move.

WIGLEY: But just to stay with that point, you were very clear that your strategy for theory

233

would be what you called "knowingly asymmetrical platforms," invoking the language of resistance to amorphous globalized systems. When you first spoke I heard "asymmetrical," of course, as an aesthetic category, as in "not symmetrical." [Laughter]

SCOTT: Yeah, yeah.

WIGLEY: So again, I suppose it's the old argument about whether aesthetics and politics have any resonance.

SPYROS PAPAPETROS: There definitely is. Maybe we don't need to go back to the nineteenth century, but Semper was all about that. At the same time that he is writing a treatise on military projectiles, he's also writing a treatise on ornament. When he says that weapons are the true ornaments of men, I think there is something to that.

Ornament is an instrument of power: You attract or repel, defend or attack, the same way that you can do with missiles. You institute social relationships. And ornament is shaped by and in turn reflects social, political, and other forces. That's Semper's theory about ornament—precisely that it's shaped by forces that are not just gravity and universal harmony. They are real economic forces, political forces, which he knows very well at that time of his exile in London when he was writing on decorated artifacts following the 1851 Crystal Palace exhibition.

So ornament is a kind of elusive device. It has to disappear in order to survive, those are the very dynamics of its historical ontology. And, in fact, I want to redirect the question to you: Why ornament for you at that time—

WIGLEY: Not just at that time.

PAPAPETROS: —I meant between the late '80s and early '90s?

WIGLEY: Why always ornament? For example...this is a deflection. [Laughter] I love the drawing that Bernard showed, which I realized afterwards was the drawing of the basic detail of the giraffe enclosure. It's a sort of anti-tectonic manifesto, because on the inside you have a more or less orthogonal system that looks like the beginning of a system of shutters, but displaced outside of it is a bigger, heavier system of shuttering, which is almost kitschy but actually behaves irresponsibly, in a way. It's bigger and heavier than it should be, and it moves when you least expect it, and it turns out to be these big wooden pieces suspended. So it is a kind of in-your-face deployment of ornament as weapon.

PAPAPETROS: You see, this is why we are so happy that Mark Wigley is going to go back to writing. [Laughter]

WIGLEY: But you mean it like that.

TSCHUMI: Oh, absolutely, yeah.

WIGLEY: And you also drew the detail—I always hate this word—abstractly, as if it was actually a drawing in a tectonic manifesto.

TSCHUMI: Sure. It was.

CATHERINE INGRAHAM: I'm almost now persuaded that there is never an absence of something ornamental in whatever we would call architectural at any given moment. There's always something developing.

MATTER AGAINST MEMORY
Eyal Weizman

This conference is organized around the question of theory and practice in architecture, but rather than foreground architecture here, I'd like to speak instead about a wider field of "aesthetic practices." Thinking about a problem through aesthetics is always necessarily and simultaneously about both theory and practice. Aesthetic practice is where politics, theory, and practice meet.

The work I will present here stems from the growing archive of the Forensic Architecture project, which seeks to address the question of how architectural intelligence can intervene in the world and perform in different forums.

Forensic architects are building surveyors who deal, in the words of one practitioner, with "the application of architectural facts to legal problems."[1] Such facts, according to another practitioner, are the "cause and origin of architectural defects such as construction, window, wall, and roofing failures; floor problems; accessibility issues and architectural design errors."[2] In presenting architectural evidence, Forensic Architects make use of drawings, photographs, models, computer simulations, and sometimes 3-D laser scans. The context is most often the arbitration and litigation processes of insurance disputes, which have increasingly become a major part of the contemporary building industry. That forensic architects often mobilize evidence against designers does not add to their popularity. The practice occupies a specialized and rather marginalized place in architectural practice and is shunned by architectural education.

Building survey might seem too ordinary and unimaginative a practice, but forensic architects understand a crucial thing about buildings that is often missed by architects: Buildings are not static things. Rather, they undergo constant transformation in response to forces. Different building materials—steel, plaster, stone, glass, concrete, or wood—respond differently to changes in environment and climate. Shifts in weight distribution—indicative of changes in the way a building is used—affect floors and beams. It is in these changes and movements, undertaken on both micro and macro scales, that history is registered in built form. Just like political history, the "structural history" of a building includes environmental "root causes," architectural "pathologies," "crises," "building failures," and "transformative structural events."[3]

Building surveyors understand the multiple material processes collected under the term "decay" as slow and diffused "formative forces" that shape the building beyond the architect's work (indeed, despite it). If material deformations are the result of force fields, inversely, these forces would be recorded in mutation, deflection, and sheer. Buildings are thus sensors; as material assemblages in formation, they are—in the hand of surveyors—*information*. But reading history from built form is not a straightforward process. This is because buildings do not move in a linear fashion, in the same linear way by which quicksilver, for example, translates temperature into volume. This makes buildings *weak* or indeterminate *sensors*. The different material components of a building move in different speeds in relation to others, every material on which a trace is registered is not neutral or passive. Different materials can act as mediums that record some things but not others. Events are imprinted against a constantly mutating surface, and retained for longer or shorter periods. Inscription is never perfect, information is lost in matter and in its transmission, matter forgets as much as it remembers; it is full of gaps and absences. The sensorial capacity of matter is the first layer of the forensic aesthetics.

Forensics—the mode by which political claims are made public—must thus be thought of as an *aesthetic* practice.[4] The forensic aesthetics has several layers: The first is "material aesthetics" and describes the function of material objects as sensors. This layer of forensic aesthetics is a primer for and primary to human perception, apprehension, and judgment. It follows the Greek origins of the term, which refer to sensation. To sense is to be aestheticized, in an inverse logic to the way an anesthetic specialist numbs one's perception to pain. The second refers to the ways by which material reality—if architecture is to be interpreted as a sensor—needs to be captured by other sensors, such as analog or digital photography or other remote sensing technologies. The presentation of finds within public forums calls for other technologies, rhetorical and aesthetic mediations. It is in these forums that history becomes politically "present" and "true" in its appeal to affect. "Forensic aesthetics" is thus a field of anarchic mediality: All things are mediated and performed through other things.

Forensics, which includes both research and the presentation of research, has a dimension of in-the-field study—which we are familiar with as architects—but also of in-the-forum presentation, which we are less familiar with. These are the two entangled forms of our aesthetic practice. Field research is about the aesthetic quality of matter, leading me toward very close material interrogations, an intimacy with matter and the texture of architecture and other surfaces. It demands that architecture be defined as a media form, but forum-work mobilizes aesthetics in a completely different way, as the art of presentation and of making our research political.

See panel discussion
→ p. 293, 301

I will narrate just one of now more than twenty investigations that we have undertaken in the context of the Forensic Architecture project, which has more or less transformed the Center for Research Architecture that I ran at Goldsmiths into a forensic agency. But rather than being a forensic agency that employs scientists, we employ artists and architects. Initially we did not have much work, but gradually, by continuing to practice the art of forensics, we have received an increasing flow of commissions. This forensic agency is not simply about providing service—we have also instituted another form of critical, historical, and theoretical research into the very foundations of forensic practices. So in a sense we are both constructing and questioning the very terms that we were using. Some of our work is historical and theoretical, some of it is propositional, and some of it is articulated as a service to various prosecution teams around the world; the latter is mainly in the context of war crimes and human rights violations. These aspects of our work are sometimes in contradiction with each other.

I will focus here on research commissioned by the United Nations and recently presented in New York at the General Assembly, concerning what is effectively one of the largest murder investigations going on in the world—the use of drone warfare in Pakistan, Afghanistan, Somalia, Yemen, and Gaza. I want to start, however, with a scene from research on a much earlier trial, one of the first in which forensic architecture as a practice dealing with histories of violence was performed.

NEGATIVE POSITIVISM

The new millennium began with a bizarre legal battle. The David Irving trial, which unfolded at the English High Court of Justice between January and April 2000, involved one of the most aggressive cross-examinations of architectural evidence—drawings, models, aerial and ground-level photographs—ever undertaken in a legal context. The case unfolded around a libel suit filed by David Irving against an American writer and her publisher, Penguin Books, for calling him "the most dangerous of all holocaust deniers and a falsifier of history."[5] Awkwardly, the process forced the veracity of claims on both sides to be put on trial, and crucially not by means of historical narration, but by subjecting the accusations to legal rules of evidence. On the tenth and eleventh days of the trial, January 26 and 27, the legal debate revolved around the architecture of one of the gas chambers—an underground structure that was part of Crematorium II in Auschwitz-Birkenau. One detail emerged as central to this debate. Irving, representing himself, focused his cross-examination of the expert witness facing him—architectural historian and Auschwitz expert Robert Jan van Pelt—on four small holes in the ceiling of the concrete roof of the structure.[6] According to the few surviving witnesses—both victims and perpetrators—it was through these holes that the cyanide poison coming out of canisters labeled "Zyklon-B" would enter a room packed with thousands of people.

Robert Jan van Pelt pointing to the ruins of Crematorium II in Auschwitz-Birkenau (the largest existing ruin of a gas chamber, most others having been completely destroyed and removed); the gas chamber is on top and the arrows point to the probable locations of the holes in the ceiling

Van Pelt's expert report, submitted to the court before the session began, conceded that "these four small holes...cannot be observed in the ruined remains of the concrete slab," but explained that verification was impossible due to the state of the roof. The roof slab broke, twisted, and folded in on itself in the explosion that was meant to eliminate its use as evidence, and has only disintegrated in the fifty-six years since. Traces of the holes were discovered a few years later,[7] but in 2000, the court heard the following exchange:

> IRVING: And you do accept, do you not, that if you were to go to Auschwitz the day after tomorrow with a trowel and clean away the gravel and find a reinforced concrete hole where we anticipate it would be from your drawings, this would make an open and shut case and I would happily abandon my action immediately?

> VAN PELT: I cannot comment on this. I am an expert on Auschwitz and not on the way you want to run your case.

> IRVING: There is my offer. I would say that that would drive such a hole through my case that I would have no possible chance of defending it any further.[8]

Irving's line of argument proposed that without these holes, the cyanide poison could not have been introduced into the room, and the room thus could not have functioned as a gas chamber. If the structure was not a gas chamber, then indeed Auschwitz could not have been a death camp. Without Auschwitz as the functional and symbolic center of the extermination process, the Holocaust, as a premeditated policy of industrialized, racially motivated killing, could never have happened. "No holes no holocaust," as another negationist already proposed; and if it didn't happen, Irving could not be accused to be the falsifier of history—*quod erat demonstrandum!*[9]

The use of material evidence to contradict survivors' testimony had already been an established method used by Holocaust deniers. Witness testimony, they claimed, produced "too much metaphysics, not enough materialism."[10] However, it was not simple positivism that led deniers to insist on materiality, but rather a desire to preclude the very ability of witnesses to speak to history at all. By posing matter against memory, they demanded a history without subject and beyond language. In Irving's legal strategy, the fact that the holes could not be found became "negative evidence" against the process of extermination. Negative evidence is an oxymoronic term that legal scholars use in order to refer to an absence of material evidence that they want to be considered as evidence in itself.* It is what defense teams mobilize to disrupt prosecution cases: No body, no gun, no holes. In legal terms, it is a kind of antibody that comes to disrupt and dismantle complex epistemological assemblages of networked evidence. Furthermore, given that a hole is not matter, but a gap within material continuity, the issue at stake was not a simple absence but a certain "absence of an absence." Throughout the trial, Irving also seemed obsessed by the metaphorical power of holes: "I am going to keep on driving holes in this case until your Lordship appreciates the significance of the holes, or their absence."[11]

*For van Pelt, this "negative evidence" demonstrated the opposite—that the Nazis were covering their own traces; they were the first deniers, he explained. He stated that none of the drawings of the gas chamber showed the holes, because the architects were not allowed to draw in these pieces of incriminating evidence. In any case, the absence of evidence was certainly not evidence of an absence.

Harun Farocki's 1988 film *Images of the World and the Inscription of War* presented an inadvertent prequel to this story. On August 25, 1944, a US reconnaissance mission was sent to photograph a petrochemical factory—Monowitz-Buna—next to the Auschwitz-Birkenau extermination camp. The five-by-three miles of territory captured in a single 35mm negative included the roof of Crematorium II, somewhere close to the edge of the frame in the lens' area of parallax distortion. The discovery that this image, along with a few other aerial photographs from the spring and summer of 1944, contained photos of the crematorium took place only in 1978, when they were found by two CIA image analysts named Dino Brugioni and Robert Poirer. When enlarged, Brugioni and Poirer spotted four blurry marks on the roof of the crematorium building and annotated them as "vents."[12]

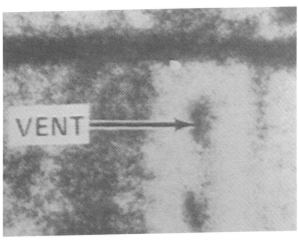

Still from Harun Farocki, *Images of the World and the Inscription of War*, 1989; the film presented blowups of photos in which the blurry marks were annotated by the CIA as "vents" leading to the holes

Irving claimed that the four marks could not be the four holes in the roof. They had a strange interference pattern, he said, and suggested that the negative had been tampered with by the addition of "brush strokes."[13] Already familiar with such arguments from negationist literature, van Pelt presented a report prepared by Nevin Bryant, supervisor of image processing applications at NASA's Jet Propulsion Laboratory in Pasadena and an expert in the analysis of aerial and satellite images. While the CIA analysts were enlarging the negatives with the analog optics available at the end of the 1970s, Bryant used state-of-the-art digital magnification to peer into the "molecular composition of the film." At stake was the way in which concrete elements got recorded by the silver halide crystals, the very chemical composition of a film, with about fifteen thousand feet of atmosphere in between. From this altitude and at the resolution of the specific negative used by the US Air Force, a single grain represented an area of about half a meter squared on the ground.

Bryant suggested that the interference pattern, identified by Irving and other negationists, is a phenomenon that can occur on the level of the grains in the emulsion of the film when single objects on the ground are at, or close to, the size of a single silver salt particle in the film.[14] He first noticed a similar process in a small section of another photograph that was on the same roll of negatives (a reconnaissance plane shoots a fast automatic sequence of photographs along its flight path). This section of the image captured a group of prisoners being marched within the camp. Irving similarly referred to this representation of prisoners as "brush strokes." Responding to the judge's request for clarification, van Pelt repeated Bryant's conclusion: The interference pattern is caused when "the size of a head of a person is the same as the size of a grain in the emulsion of the film, and the result of that was a *moiré effect*, which occurs also in the newspaper when you photograph a picture which has been screened twice."[15]

The size of the hole in the roof of Crematorium II was approximately the size of a person as seen from above. The hole was thus approximately the size of a silver salt grain. When an object photographed approximates the recording ability of a negative, it is in a condition that we can refer to as the *threshold of detectability*. In this condition, the materiality of the object represented (the concrete roof/hole) and the materiality of the surface representing it (the surface of the negative/silver salt grains) should be considered both as *presence* and as *representation*. Each surface must be equally analyzed as an image and as a material reality.

A certain inversion also occurred: The concrete roof was analyzed as a recording device, while the molecular surface of the negative was seen as a material composition of silver crystals.[16] The photograph of the roof was thus a photograph of a photograph.

As the cross-examination went on, it became clear that against the linear argument mobilized by Irving's negative evidence, van Pelt had woven a complex and overwhelmingly convincing network of converging evidence, both for the existence of the holes on the surface of the negative as well as for their existence within the broken concrete surface.*

Irving lost his case, and we need not adjudicate it again here. But the relation between evidence and negation is important, and ours is

*His evidence also included the interpretation of architectural plans drawn from the archive of the Auschwitz Central Construction Office, aerial photography, letters, diaries, logbooks, testimonies, and ground-level photographs.[17]

also a period of negation and denial. Climate change denial, for example—which somehow emerged at the same moment as Holocaust denial, in the middle of the '80s—also busied itself with the existence (or nonexistence) of another hole, the one in the ozone layer. Through that hole, scientists began to explain, lethal radiation would enter the Earth, destroying most forms of life on it. The size of the "chamber" has become the size of the entire planet, and the size of the hole is the size of the continent of the Antarctic. If climate change is genocide in the making, this is certainly an auto-genocide—here, it is the people in the chamber who opened the hole in the protective ceiling above them.

What is it that attracts deniers to holes? Given that a hole is "non-matter," strictly speaking, we are faced with an absence of an absence. But as Henri Bergson noted, a hole is more, not less, information than the matter that surrounds it. This is because the hole is always two things. It is both the materiality of the thing perforated, be it ozone or concrete, *and* its absence. The hole in the ozone layer is different, though: It is not an image of a thing past, like a photograph, but a model of a possible future reality. There's an inversion of time—when speaking of a hole, we speak about the forensics of a damage that has not yet occurred. It's a forensic future.

DRONE WARFARE AT THE THRESHOLD
OF DETECTABILITY

To think more about this forensics of the future (a destruction yet to come), let us jump to the present, and another field that is currently obsessed with future prediction—the calculus of the war on terror, which is being applied now in the context of drone warfare. Indeed, according to the US regulations on how drones and drone operators are allowed to kill, a person can never be targeted for what he or she has done, but rather for what he or she *will have done* in the future. It is not allowed, at least officially, for targeted assassinations to be a punishment—it must be a response to an imminent threat, a response to a crime that has not yet happened. The futurology of contemporary warfare looks for traces that might compose a chain of action to predict that somebody is about to do something. This is both a danger and a challenge as we seek to orient our actions, as architects, toward the future.

I recalled the van Pelt–Irving exchange about holes when asked to undertake, with the Forensic Architecture project, an investigation on drone warfare in Pakistan, Afghanistan, Yemen, Somalia, and Gaza.[18] This was because many of the buildings struck by drones had a specific architectural signature to them—a small hole in their ceiling. The reason for this hole was that drone missiles, such as Hellfire or Spike, are equipped with a delay fuse. The few milliseconds between impact and detonation allow the missiles to penetrate through a roof into the room under it and spray their load of hundreds of lethal steel fragments inside. This blast of small fragments, designed to kill people but to leave the structure intact, is argued by the military to be a humanitarian munitions meant to limit casualties. Like many other techniques and technologies of "lesser evil," this one enabled the proliferation of such strikes, thus causing more casualties.[19] Seen from above, the hole in the roof is the only visible trace that the building was attacked by drones. But this hole, and the violence it evidences, are also at the threshold of detectability. This is because the size of the hole that a missile makes in a roof is smaller than that of a single pixel in the resolution to which publicly available satellite images are degraded.

Until 2014, this resolution was legally kept to 50 cm/ pixel, with a pixel representing half a meter by half a meter of ground.* This resolution was legally determined because it is roughly the size of the human body when seen from above. The pixel resolution is not only a technical product of optics and data-storage capacity, but a "modulor" designed according to the dimensions of the human body. Unlike other architectural modulors (most notably that of Le Corbusier), it was not meant to help organize space, but rather to stamp the human figure out of photographs. The 50 cm resolution is useful because it bypasses risk of privacy infringement when recording people in public spaces, much in the same way that Google Street View blurs the faces of people or car license plates. But the regulation also has a security rationale: It is not only important details of strategic sites that get camouflaged in the 50 cm/pixel resolution, but the consequences of violence and violations as well.* The resolution of satellite images have direct bearing on drone attacks. Although at a resolution of 50 cm the general features of individual buildings can be identified, a hole in a roof—the signature of a drone strike— would appear as nothing more than a slight color variation, a single darker pixel, perhaps, within a pixel composition.

The 50 cm/pixel satellite imagery thus poses a digital

*In 2014, after lobbying by satellite companies, American satellite companies were allowed to provide images in a slightly sharper resolution—about 30 cm/pixel. They successfully argued that private identity would still be masked at this resolution.[20]

*In a further radicalization of the geopolitics of resolution, US satellite image providers make an exception to the 50-cm rule in Israel and the Palestinian territories it occupies. An amendment to the US Land Remote Sensing Policy Act, which sets the permitted resolution of commercial US image satellites, dictates that these areas are shown only in a resolution of 2.5 meters (later effectively eased to 1 meter per pixel) in which a car is made of two pixels and a roof— another common target—is depicted by 6–9 pixels. The snow screen placed over Israel's violation of Palestinian rights in the West Bank and Gaza contributed to Turkey's decision, after the Gaza Flotilla incidents, to send its own image satellite into space and make available 50 cm/pixel images of Palestine/Israel.[21]

Home hit by a shell, killing one man and injuring two others, in Tuffah, northern Gaza, 2009

version of the material problem presented by the silver salt particles in the negatives of the Auschwitz aerial photographs presented in the Irving trial. It masks a hole in a roof—a hole that is similarly related in its dimensions to the human body. In both, the hole in the roof is an indication that the room under it was an assassination chamber. In both, this hole was at the threshold of detectability in the images in which it was captured. My claim is of course not that there is a relation between the Holocaust as an attempt to exterminate an entire people in gas chambers, and a secret and illegal war conducted by the US in densely populated civilian areas, but rather that the forensic-architectural problem that arises forces us to examine the material limit of images.

We do not know the precise optical specifications of drone cameras. Some operators stated publicly (or told us privately) that they could identify people. They claimed that sometimes they could even recognize them. Others said that the resolution was not sharp enough to differentiate children from adults and that they have mistaken spades for guns.[22] All statements confirmed, however, that the human figure is the thing to which drone vision is calibrated, obviously because it is designed to deliver munitions to people and kill them. However, while the human figure is the convergent point of drone vision, it is what satellite images are designed to mask.

The UN, via UNOSAT—its program delivering satellite-image analysis to relief organizations—as well as other research bodies, increasingly monitors violence by purchasing images from the archives of commercially available satellite companies. The analysis is undertaken by studying "before and after" images, which are the most common form of forensic montage designed to frame an event between two spatiotemporal conditions: The "before" setting the benchmark against which the "after" state displays the result of an incident. Because satellite images render people invisible, the focus of the analysis turns to architecture, to the pairing or sequencing of buildings with ruins.

Both the act of military killing and the practice of investigating those killings are image-based practices, afforded through the combination of proximity and remoteness that is the condition of media itself. Drone strikes themselves are performed in a high-resolution designed to show information, but are monitored (by NGOs or the UN) in the poor resolution of satellite photographs designed to hide information. This fact inverts one of the foundational principles of forensics since the nineteenth century, namely, that to resolve a crime the police should be able to see more—in higher resolution, using better optics—than the perpetrator of the crime is able to. This inversion is nested in another, because in the case of drone strikes it is state agencies that are the perpetrators. The difference in vision between remote perpetrator and remote witness is the space of denial—but of a different kind than the denial presented earlier in this essay.

The formulation for denial employed by US agencies is officially sanctioned as the "Glomar response," stating that US state agencies are authorized to "neither confirm nor deny" the existence—or nonexistence—of documents and policies such as a secret war of assassination in Pakistan. To say "this is untrue," or "this did not happen," is an antithesis that requires a counter-narrative. Glomarization is, however, a form of denial that aims to add no information whatsoever. This form of denial has its

Munitions expert Chris Cobb-Smith took this picture standing on the ground floor of the Salha family home in Beit Lahiya, Gaza, 2009

corollary in the visual field through the satellite image's inability to either confirm or deny the existence or nonexistence of holes in roofs that would otherwise constitute evidence of state-sanctioned violence. This form of denial is not simply rhetorical, but rather is made possible by the production of a frontier that has territorial, juridical, and visual characteristics.

Take for example the Waziristan region of Pakistan, since June 2004 one of the focal points for the drone campaign. Waziristan is part of the Federally Administered Tribal Areas (FATA). During the period of the British Raj, FATA was established as an extraterritorial zone of local autonomy. The Pakistani military established checkpoints that filter movement in and out; it also prevented the bringing-in and taking-out of any electronic equipment, including mobile phones, cameras, and navigation equipment.[23] The consequence is an effective media siege in which very few photographs and eyewitness testimonies were allowed to leave these regions. This media blackout enabled drone warfare in these areas. It also helped Pakistani and US sources to deny this campaign ever existed and helped them to misleadingly claim that the casualties of drone strikes died rather in "bomb-making accidents."[24] In masking all signals within it, the pixel is the human-scale equivalent of the territorial-scale media blockage extended over FATA.

A RETURN TO THE WITNESS

I will briefly describe some possibilities of this counter-forensics through two strategies that we have used to bypass those image politics where we can. In the summer of 2012, twenty-two seconds of video footage was smuggled out of Waziristan, passing through six hands before landing in the NBC offices in Islamabad. It was a rare piece of footage, and was broadcasted. Disturbingly, there was also a lot of information in those images, and no attempt to see anything in them. For most people, it's simply a confirmation that something has happened—we see destruction, we see a hole in the roof, we see a building destroyed, and that's it.

We spent six months looking at these twenty-two seconds, frame by frame, and we started seeing things. A first thing to see is not *through* the window, but the window frame itself. The size of the window frame within the photographic frame meant that the person shooting the footage is not at the window but rather inside the room. This person is feeling danger—whether a second U.S. strike or from the Taliban, we don't know. But we know from the size of the frame that this is precious evidence, delivered under perilous circumstances.

We wanted to find the only confirmed target site in Waziristan that we are able to recognize. So the first task is to figure out where this footage is within North Waziristan. The shadow is cast forward, north by northwest—so we are looking northward. We can see that the building from which the photograph was taken is higher than the building destroyed, so we know we have a higher building behind a lower building. We collage the available images together, and get a fuller view of the ruin. We see a bend in the road on the left, and a certain widening of the road on the right. That is initially the typology we're looking for as we scan through the cities of Waziristan—a building that has a high building behind and that kind of arrangement of streets in front.

We find what seems like a match, and start comparing other details. We see fanning on the left, and a tower. There's a higher building, and we can confirm that we see the higher building on the satellite image as well. It's a very laborious process, but over time we become more certain that we've matched the footage to the satellite image. Now we know where the target is. But the problem of pixelation means that we simply cannot know within which pixel the drone rocket has entered and therefore which room. We want to find the room where it happened.

So we look again at the shadows, comparing the length of the shadow to the length of the building, which eventually lets us build a 3-D model of the building that we suspect is the building that was destroyed. We locate it within the extruded map of the city. Now it becomes important to know what time the video was taken, which is very easy with existing architectural

Eyal Weizman

The first stage in understanding what this footage could reveal was to locate the building within the city. The direction of the shadow helped to orient the structure. We determined that the videographer was standing level with the destroyed roof and must therefore have been in a building that was higher than the one that was targeted. Using a collage pieced together from individual frames extracted from the footage, we eventually found the building within a satellite image of Miranshah, with the morphology of the streets as a guide. From Forensic Architecture's "Decoding Video Testimony" project, Miranshah, North Waziristan, March 30, 2012

Behind the missile fragment we noticed a trace on the wall. The room was full of such traces. They seem to be fragmentation patterns from the explosive head of the ammunition. The missile is designed to penetrate through a ceiling, and detonate when inside a room, spraying hundreds of steel fragments and killing everybody in proximity. Each fragment was studied and mapped. Where the distribution of fragments is in lower density, it is likely that something absorbed them. Although we could not be certain, it is possible that the absence of the fragments indicated the places where people died. From Forensic Architecture's "Decoding Video Testimony" project software. That becomes very important, because one piece of evidence is a ray of light entering through the hole in the ceiling, which gives us direction again—meaning that we can use it as a compass by which to locate the room within the building.

Then we begin seeing the finer grain of blast holes—fragments on the roof and on the wall itself. We scan the image and we map all of them to understand what happened with the shrapnel after the missile entered the room. We slowly notice that there are two areas in which there are fewer fragments—which suggests that those areas are where the bodies that absorbed the shrapnel stood. The room's walls thus functioned as something akin to a photograph, exposed to the blast in a similar way to which a negative is exposed to light, just as the remains of bodies created voids in the ash layer over Pompeii, or as a nuclear blast famously etched a "human shadow" onto the steps outside the Sumitomo bank in Hiroshima. Combining pathology and forensic architecture, the traces of dead bodies seem to have become part of the architecture.

Another example comes from the methods we used with a witness who escaped from Waziristan. She had a German passport, which allowed her to come to Europe. Her husband was facing trial in Germany, and she wanted to deliver testimony—but as often happens in traumatic moments, she lost some details of the attack. Our form of assistance was to undertake the very slow process of building a digital model of the house in which she was living. Slowly, through the conjunction of architecture and the details of her stories, the memory came back.

Sitting between her lawyer and an architect acting as a computer modeler, she directed the process in which a detailed model of her house was constructed. The model included all rooms, furniture, and objects the witness could remember. Slowly, as she was sizing the rooms, locating the windows and doors, and placing mundane objects in these spaces, she started recalling and narrating fragments of memory from her life in this house and also from the strike itself. When the digital model was complete, we rendered it and undertook a series of virtual

The witness points to the location of the fan in the model. From Forensic Architecture's "The Architecture of Memory" project, Mir Ali, North Waziristan, October 4, 2010

walk-throughs. "Returning" to the space and time of the strike, the witness could recount her story.[25]

One object in particular was important to the witness. It was a fan. She seemed uneasy about it, repeatedly adjusting its location. At the beginning it had been modeled as a ceiling-mounted ventilator; then the witness placed it as a freestanding fan on a tripod inside a room. A few moments later she took it outside and placed it in a small courtyard that mostly served the women and children. The house was gender-segregated; most of its space was reserved for men, and women were confined to a small part within. This limited the witness optics of the events that unfolded. When "walking" through the model in the digital aftermath of the strike, she recalled finding human flesh on the fan's blades.[26] The fan was a digital object but also a vehicle into her memory. Human memory, architecture, destruction, and digital reconstruction got entangled here in a way that does not surrender to the easy separation of subject and object, testimony and evidence, matter and memory.

None of this is hard evidence. The courts, the UN investigations, and the processes that we have developed aren't simply theoretical, but still, these elements are weak signals, faint memories, speculations, probabilities that exist at the threshold of visibility and also at the threshold of the law. We never know if these investigations have an evidentiary value until they are tested in courts—these things cannot be known *a priori*. The fact that these signals operate beneath the threshold of science and law makes the practice of forensics in excess of both—offering a point of intersection between aesthetics and politics through theory and practice.

This essay is an abridged and altered version of "Matter Against Memory" in *FORENSIS: The Architecture of Public Truth* (Berlin: Sternberg Press, 2014), 361–80. Portions have also been published as "Violence at the Threshold of Detectability," *e-flux journal* 64 (April 2015), www.e-flux.com/journal/violence-at-the-threshold-of-detectability.

1   Sam Kubba, *Architectural Forensics* (New York: McGraw-Hill Professional, 2008). See also www.buildingdesignanalysis.com/forensic.html and Dale Paegelow, *Forensic Architecture: An Introduction* (Patterson: Cromlech Architect, 2001), www.cromlech-architect.com. "Architects who have given their practice over full time to forensic investigations and report writing are few and far between. If I had to hazard a guess, I would say less than five thousand across America. I believe that firms who employ architects for forensic investigation have been around for about 10 to 15 years." Because there are no certification, regulation, or registration bodies, there is no official data about numbers of practitioners.

2   See www.nelsonforensics.com/Architecture.html.

3   These terms are all taken from the terminology of building surveyors.

4   Forensic Aesthetics was the title of a series of seminars I taught with Thomas Keenan and Nikolaus Hirsch at the Städel School in Frankfurt in the academic year 2010–11, www.staedelschule.de/forensic_aesthetics_d.html. Keenan and I developed the concept further in Thomas Keenan and Eyal Weizman, *Mengele's Skull: The Advent of a Forensic Aesthetics* (Berlin: Sternberg Press, 2012).

5   Deborah E. Lipstadt, *Denying the Holocaust: The Growing Assault on Truth and Memory* (New York: Free Press, 1993).

6   An extended version of van Pelt's expert report was republished as Robert Jan van Pelt, *The Case for Auschwitz: Evidence from the Irving Trial* (Bloomington: Indiana University Press, 2002). Van Pelt's work is one of the main inspirations for Forensic Architecture.

7   Van Pelt, *The Case*, 2–3. The holes were since found; see Daniel Keren, Jamie McCarthy, and Harry W. Mazal, "The Ruins of the Gas Chambers: A Forensic Investigation of Crematoriums at Auschwitz I and Auschwitz-Birkenau," *Holocaust and Genocide Studies*, vol. 18, no. 1 (Spring 2004): 68–103. Thanks to Patrick Kroker for this information.

8   *David Irving v. Penguin Books*, day 11.

9   That was Robert Faurisson. Van Pelt, *The Case*, 3ff., 24ff., and 458ff.

10   Keren, McCarthy, and Mazal, "The Ruins of the Gas Chambers."

11   *David Irving v. Penguin Books*, Day 10.

12   Dino A. Brugioni and Robert G. Poirer, "The Holocaust Revisited: A Retrospective Analysis of the Auschwitz-Birkenau Extermination Complex" (Central Intelligence Agency, February 1979), www.cia.gov/library/center-for-the-study-of-intelligence/kent-csi/vol44no4/html/v44i4a06p_0001.htm.

13   Irving was referring to a 1992 study by John C. Ball. See van Pelt, *The Case*, 56.

14   Van Pelt, *The Case*, 84 and 353.

15   *David Irving v. Penguin Books*, Day 11.

16   The relation between the single pixel and the human figure is a constant challenge in aerial and satellite image interpretation. The Tolimir case, one of the last of the Srebrenica cases judged at the International Criminal Tribunal for the former Yugoslavia (decided 2012, currently on appeal), has the following quote in regards to aerial images of the Nova Kasaba soccer field. The Trial Chamber accepted the explanation of the witness in identifying darker pixels as people rather than shadows as claimed by the accused: "THE WITNESS: I have spent numerous and numerous hours analyzing all these pictures and identifying what reference they can have on the ground... It's a football field. There are no bushes in the middle. So these grey zones are not shadows. Though, indeed, a shadow has the same pixel as a group of people on the picture, but if you compare what is officially said on the photograph and the corroboration you can make of what a man represents in terms of a pixel on such a photo, this is why I allow myself to say that the dots that I have marked previously are people." Jean-Rene Ruez, Tolimir case at the ICTY, www.icty.org/x/cases/tolimir/trans/en/100329IT.htm (March 29, 2010), 933.

17   On van Pelt's evidence, see also Debórah Dwork and Robert Jan van Pelt, *Auschwitz, 1270 to the Present: A History* (New York: W.W. Norton & Company, 2002); Robert Jan van Pelt, *Architectural Principles in the Age of Historicism* (New Haven: Yale University Press, 1993); and many other articles and essays.

18   The investigation was undertaken on behalf of various political and legal groups and was presented at the UN General Assembly in 2013 by the UN Special Rapporteur for Counter Terrorism Human Rights, Ben Emerson. The work was also presented in the context of legal action brought about by Pakistani lawyer Shahzad Akhbar in the UK Court of Appeal and in collaboration with the Bureau of Investigative Journalism (BIJ). The team was coordinated by Susan Schuppli (research and coordination), Jacob Burns (research), Steffen Krämer (video compositing and editing), Reiner Beelitz (architectural modeling), Samir Harb (architectural modeling), Zahra Hussain (research assistance), Francesco Sebregondi (research assistance), and Blake Fisher (research assistance). Some cases were undertaken in collaboration with Situ Research. Other partner organizations included the European Center for Constitutional and Human Rights (Andreas Schüller), One World Research (Bridget Prince, Nasser Arrabyee, and Anis Mansour), Al Jazeera English (Ana Naomi de Sousa), Chris Woods (freelance journalist), Edmund Clark (photographer), Chris Cobb-Smith (munitions expert and consultant), and Myra MacDonald (freelance journalist).

19   See my own "665: The Least of All Possible Evils," *e-flux journal* 38 (October 2012); and *The Least of All Possible Evils: Humanitarian Violence from Arendt to Gaza* (New York: Verso Books, 2012).

20   See the United States' 1998 Land Remote Sensing Policy Act, geo.arc.nasa.gov/sge/landsat/15USCch82.html. See also "US lifts restrictions on more detailed satellite images," BBC, June 16, 2014. The European satellite Pléiades, unaffected by the American restrictions, has since the end of 2011 provided 50 cm/pixel images of Palestine/Israel. See also Hito Steyerl's beautiful film *How Not To Be Seen: A Fucking Didactic Educational .MOV File* (2013). The size of the pixel in relation to the size of the body makes camouflage unnecessary.

21   William Fenton, "Why Google Earth Pixelates Israel," *PCMag*, June 14, 2011; Maayan Amir, "Gaza Flotilla," www.forensic-architecture.org/file/gaza-flotilla.

22   Heather Linebaugh, "I worked on the US drone program. The public should know what really goes on," *The Guardian*, December 29, 2013.

23   The Federally Administered Tribal Areas are officially a "Prohibited Area" for which nonresidents require special permission to enter.

24   Jacob Burns, "Persistent Exception: Pakistani Law and the Drone War," in *Forensis: The Architecture of Public Truth*, ed. Forensic Architecture (Berlin: Sternberg Press, 2014).

25   This process of mediation based on embodiment recalled other experiments in "situational awareness" undertaken in the context of US military immersive training environments and post-trauma treatment as captured in Harun Farocki's *Serious Games* (2009–10). A classic predecessor to this practice is narrated in Frances Yates' magnum opus about the Roman and medieval tradition of mnemonic techniques. *The Art of Memory* emphasized the relationship between memory, architecture, and destruction. Frances Yates, *The Art of Memory* (London: Pimlico, 1992).

26   Deborah Brauser, "Novel 'Avatar Therapy' May Silence Voices in Schizophrenia," *Medscape*, July 3, 2014: "Avatar therapy allows patients to choose a digital face (or 'avatar') that best resembles what they picture their phantom 'voice' to look like. A therapist, sitting in a separate room, 'talks' through the animated avatar shown on a computer monitor as it interacts with the patient."

FLASH THEORY
Mark Wigley

It is nice to be with such good friends here today, retreating from the front lines for a few hours to ask ourselves the question, "What are the urgencies of architectural theory?" in 2000+. That is to say, "What are the urgencies for architectural theory in the 21st century?" which is, of course, also the question "What have they been for the last 14 years?" So we are looking back and forward at the same time—flickering. And such a flicker is what interests me here in what are just some notes toward a proto-argument for what might provisionally be called "Flash Theory."

A more or less standard narrative is that there was a "wave" of theory—perhaps the word sounds a bit too Californian, but theory did arrive like a wave and might always take the form of waves, as itself a form of radiation—during the mid-'80s to late-'90s. This wave was dependent on '70s theory but also on a total rejection of the mode of that theory. A space for theory had been constructed in the '70s like any other architectural project—with institutions, programs, curricula, publications, etc., but, most importantly, a set of attitudes—and then a younger generation of thinkers arrived in the '80s, occupied that space, and completely redesigned it. A whole series of questions were asked of architecture that were thought to be improper by our hosts—in terms of philosophy, gender, sexuality, orientation, identity, psychoanalysis, postcoloniality, trans-disciplinarity, etc. The discipline was put on the couch and relentlessly interrogated. The relationship between so-called theory and so-called practice was challenged and complicated. There was quite a lot of blood on the floor—wounded parents and all that. This wave gave way to a 21st-century ecology without so much evident theory, hence the typical question "What happened to theory?" or "What comes after theory?"

These questions were accompanied by the usual hypocrisies of anti-theory theorists, which were in their way quite reassuring. In moments of doubt you can be pretty sure that anti-theory theorists will still be there to keep the music playing, as it were, coming up with less than bright ideas like "post-criticality." Theory is by definition critical, in the sense of opening up to the other. Critical theory just means not being asleep. It's not much more than that. For the advocates of post-criticality, it's hard to imagine a more embarrassing argument to have made. There are always new forms of idiocy being invented, but that's a pretty hard one to beat. All of them ended up running schools of architecture, and I don't think they are interested in any kind of memory project that would remind them of what they were saying earlier since now they are devoted to being awake.

What did happen to theory? It would be tempting to say that theory actually became so widespread that people don't see it—theorists and theories are everywhere you look, so you don't notice them. Or that theory became industrialized. Or that theory triggered such significant transformations of architectural discourse that it became environmental, with theory now embedded within architectural discourse rather than being an alternative or counter-strand of it. Or that new and stealthier modes of theory were developed to continue the theoretical project, as it were. I would argue that all of these are the case, but I don't think that the question is worth answering in that form, because it's based on such a symptomatic misunderstanding about architectural theory.

The conventional sense of architectural theory is that it's a combination of a metaphysical explanation—why architecture? what architecture?—with a physical description or instrumentalization. There's an appeal to some higher-order theory by way of explanation, and an activation and mobilization of that appeal in the instrumental sphere. This leads to the usual idea of architectural theory as a set of statements about what could, should, or should not happen in architecture that are based on a defense of the very idea of architecture. That is to say, architectural theory is a blurring of inscription, description, and prescription.

One might make an argument that this is true of all forms of theory, that inscription, description, and prescription are requirements, as it were, of any kind of theoretical act. But I do think that architects, with a kind of reverse narcissism, spend more time on the metaphysical defense of the idea of architecture than almost any other species of intellectual I know. There is no act of architectural discourse in all of its dimensions—theoretical, practical, curatorial, and otherwise— that doesn't involve a somewhat plaintive defense of the idea of the architect. Plumbers tend not to offer you a theory of the importance of plumbing before they carry out their acts. But no architect, even at the top of the tree, is able to say anything about architecture without pleading for the people they're talking with to agree that architecture is a good idea.

This is particularly the case in the United States, where architecture is clearly not regarded as a good idea, and not by chance was the main home of theory in the '80s and '90s. Hence the remarkably courageous decision of our students not to become plumbers—which would mean being paid, having weekends, having a life, etc. I should note that when this school of architecture was originally formed, it was part of the School of Mines and Sanitary Engineering, and if we had maintained that intimate relationship with plumbing, one might actually be able to make metaphysical arguments and be paid at the same time. The disconnection from sanitary engineering was a mistake on one side and the idea of practice without theory is a mistake on the other side. Much of the work of theory in the '80s was to study the gaps and contradictions between the metaphysical defense and the physical instrumentalization in order to come up with a more nuanced understanding of the discipline.

So theory, in its most typical sense as a series of statements about what could, should, or should not happen, is built simultaneously on a defense of the very idea of architecture and the description of a particular architecture that relates to some kind of future, whether of buildings or cities. It's not a description of a form but of a set of evolving relationships. For example, the question "What is the future of our cities?" is an absolutely urgent one, maybe the most urgent of questions, and certainly massively unclear and therefore inviting answers—the question is driven by the inadequacy of formal descriptions of cities. Urgency might always be related to the inadequacy of a formal description.

Perhaps I can offer some fortune-cookie comments that might further illuminate this intersection of theory and urgency.

The first of such statements would be that the urgencies of theory don't necessarily coincide with the agreed-upon urgencies of the planet or the field. Theory is not about the general concepts organizing contemporary discourse—things like globalization, sustainability, density, the right to the city, access, transparency, surveillance, refugees, human rights—all of these things that are rightfully understood to be urgently important, but neither is it about all the things that are rightfully understood to be urgently important concepts within architecture, like computation, collaboration, regionalism, data, software, new materials, carbon footprints, open source technologies, 3-D printing—all of these motifs around which professional and academic discourse gathers. What's urgent for the world and for architecture is not in any way urgent for theory.

What is urgent for theory, I would argue, is precisely that which is not yet agreed upon, and not yet seen. In this sense, theory is actually not about what might or should or should not happen in the future—it's much more about the very idea of the future as itself a theoretical act. In other words, theory is the act of framing a discourse around a possible future. It's not by chance that "2000+" is the title of John McHale's 1967 special issue of *AD*, which evolved into his *Future of the Future* book in 1969, which was about the history of the future and therefore the possible future of the future. The question for theory, then, is not about the urgent future of today, but more about what's happening with the *idea* of the future.

And the future is always a historical artifact. There is no theory without history, and vice versa. In fact, theory might even be a word for a certain kind of vibration or flickering between a possible past and a possible future, and it might be that history is just another form of this vibration. The starting points might appear radically different, but both history and theory have in common these two sides, as if chasing themselves around a screen in an endless dance. Theory de-emphasizes its dependency on history and history de-emphasizes its dependency on theory—as if they both try to suppress the constant vibration back and forth in order to suppress the strangeness generating that movement. The screen at the heart of the movement, the gap that makes it a vibration, is the present. The present is by definition the least knowable thing of all. Theory and history dance around the present, flickering across it as if the speed of the flicker could absorb it in the way the flickering discontinuous images of a movie produce the effect of continuous movement on a screen that disappears into the effect.

Theory might be a way to deal with the profound strange-ness or otherness of the present. In the case of architecture, theory might be a way of reconciling the absolute strangeness of being in front of or inside of a building, which is never sim-ply about a body and a brain in front of an object or in a space. Our concepts of body and brain are already infused with certain concepts of objects and spaces. A sentence that is seemingly as simple as "I saw the building" would need a whole book to unpack. No description of the experience of an object or space, no matter how long or nuanced, can even start to capture the complexity and strangeness. This is not because experience is of an existential order wholly other than that of words, concepts, and images. On the contrary, this profound strangeness is at the very heart of the mode of thought that generates words like "present," "experience," "object," "body," and "space." There simply would not be the concept of "architecture" without this strangeness. Architecture, that which domesticates by giving a visible order to unseen flows, is completely dependent on the strangeness it represses, a strangeness that energizes theory and history, binding them together in a forever nervous agitation.

So the urgency of architectural theory is equally about the urgencies of history, or more precisely about prehistory—that is to say, the story you're telling about the arrival of the past that would position you in a certain place to make some kind of conjecture about the arrival of a future. What is the platform from which you project or throw that conjecture? That platform could never simply be the infinitely unstable present. So any explicit claim about what could, should, or should not happen always rests on implicit claims about what has happened or even what has just happened, or has just stopped happening. So there's also a kind of memorializing built into the idea of the prehistory. I find myself obsessed with prehistory as a mode of theorizing, or actually as the very mode of theorizing.

Perhaps we could even start to think of theory writing as an occupation, in the double sense of something that you do and also a place that you occupy. Prehistory, it seems to me, is the site of theoretical action. Prehistory opens up a space for possible action, the retroactive view being the engine of forward movement. If you feel the itch to move forward, look backward. Of course, all of this still stays within a pretty conventional understanding of theory—it shouldn't surprise us that prehistories release new potentials, reconfiguring or producing a sense of urgency. So forget what I have been saying. Let's try again, breaking a little bit more into the fortune-cookie.

Theory is implied in all architectural discourse inasmuch as it's architectural discourse. There is no architecture without theory—but theory here is not a description, analysis, explanation, or prescription for architecture. For example, Alberti's *Ten Books on Architecture* might be theory, but it's not all theory, nor is his book any more theoretical than any other document in the field. There's just as much theory in a label, a regulation, a syllabus, a competition, a joke, a protocol, an advertisement, a contract, an instruction, a tomb, an address, an account, a chart, an image, a ticket, or in modes of censorship or prohibition. And wouldn't those last two, censorship and prohibition, be the best possible place for examining the operations of theory as self-conscious attempts to modulate ideas? Shouldn't that be the very place to start looking?

So to describe any one period of architecture as more or less theoretical than another—to think of the '80s and '90s as being more theoretical, for example—is stupid. Theory is not an option. It's not something you're going to have more or less of, since architecture is by definition a theoretical act. Architecture is not by chance philosophy's favorite and even default model of what a theoretical act is. Whenever philosophy wants to say what a theoretical act is, it refers to architecture.

More than that, the very word "architecture," definitely in quotes, is a theoretical act, if not *the* theoretical act—which is why every theoretical statement, from treatises to laundry tickets, must reenact the defense of the idea of architecture, since that's actually the main act. The idea that there *could be architecture* is always more important than the specific kind of architecture or architectural statement.

My main thought here is that architectural theory has a certain effect. It is an opening that releases new potentials. It's a crack that operates as a lens through which to see things differently, and thereby acts as an incubator for different kinds of thought.

Think again about the Classical model of architectural theory. The Parthenon has clearly become the star of this symposium, its freshly face-lifted head rising up again and again and again. It is increasingly a product of a kind of Los Angeles perfection—the chemists are even working on giving it just the right suntan. So one of the world's weirdest architectural objects under permanent reconstruction remains the central paradigm for permanent values in our discipline. Rebuilding it is like rebuilding the evidence that propped up architectural theory. It is as if See Lucia Allais and Mari Lending's discussions of the Parthenon ← p. 33 and ← p. 153 thinking about what is urgent pulls the Parthenon back into the room. The question of urgency is inseparable from that of ancient monuments.

Imagine that Classical architectural theory was correct. Imagine that the Parthenon was sitting up there on the top of the hill and anybody who went up to see it would have an almost orgasmic feeling of being one with the cosmic vibrations of the universe, of literally feeling the mathematical harmonies of the universe passing through their body because they were looking at perfectly proportioned columns. You have to imagine this since it doesn't happen—or at least nobody has ever reported it happening, and the Parthenon is a building about which people don't fail to report their experiences. Architects might camp on the hill for weeks to try to capture the intensity of the place and the mechanism of its effect but people are not collapsing in orgasmic bliss. Quite the opposite. They develop theories, and, in fact, the theory of Classical architecture inserts itself in the place of the very effect that it describes. The Classical theory is that the Parthenon is not an object in this world, but an object halfway between this world, which is a second-order or even third-order Xerox, and the original world, the world of perfect ideas beyond space and time, of the ideal proportions. So in a literal sense, to encounter the Parthenon is to begin to leave the world behind. It is more beautiful than anything else that you can see. It models the very idea of beauty for you.

There is in Classical thinking, then—and I would suggest this thinking remains the default setting of the discipline—a sense that architecture makes the environment visible, whether it be visualizing the invisible harmonic proportions of the cosmos or those of the human body. After all, the human body is not necessarily seen as such until it is figured in columns, which are at once an image of the cosmos beyond and a perfected image of your own body, which is itself a second-order Xerox, one that has to be cleaned up when translated into columns. The column is literally both a mirror image and an image of a distant cosmos. We see ourselves perfected. So the theory of Classical architecture is that columns vibrate between the physical and the metaphysical, and there's a considerable amount of space there, a gap that theory tries to fill or cover over. When modern architects argued for an architecture that visualizes the new orders of industrialization, or when more recent theorists discuss the hidden digital patterns that fill a supposedly post-industrial world, it's the same thing. The function of architecture is to make visible the invisible.

"Making visible" in this sense is not so much revelation or exposure as an opening or a gap that offers a kind of construction site, one that transforms both subject and world. The Classical column is supposed to have the magical singular proportions of the universe, but there is, of course, the issue that if it's a very tall column and it looks shorter at the top, should I adjust it to produce the effect of the truth, or should I tell the truth that might not ring true? Do I follow the rules, or do I lie to produce what they aim at? The principle of *entasis* suggests the latter, that the column is adjusted to me. The image of the perfection of the universe starts to model itself on my own imperfect perceptual relationship to it, hanging there as a kind of interface between the mystery of the universe and the mystery of myself. It's not exposing either myself or the universe, but acting instead as a way of negotiating between them.

With the Classical column, the indeterminacy and other-ness of our own bodies and of the cosmos are given a singular silhouette. The Classical temple represents the possibility of a stable image in the face of multiple instabilities. And there is the final complication. Paradoxically, the Classical idea is so much about the possibility of a stable image that the image itself is actually not required to be stable at all. Famously, the Parthenon breaks almost all the rules that had built up over time with the previous temples, and it's internally inconsistent. In projecting a kind of stability, the building itself is incredibly unstable in its application of those supposedly stable truths.

So the fact that the Parthenon doesn't agree with itself is no problem, because it's still effectively representing the idea of one singular unchanging image. As the theory gang of the '80s remembers well, you can only produce the effect of a stable image with an image that's not stable. You have to play, you have to vibrate to make this possible. It's not only that the column is adjusted for the viewer. There's no systematic alignment of the proportions within one building or between any buildings. And in fact there was no huge discomfort when this whole theory was undone, most famously by Claude Perrault's charts that demonstrated that none of the Classical examples agreed with each other. Perrault may have been radically modern in his way, but there wasn't any sense of trauma, of the death of the Classical, or the death of the stable image. The Parthenon was simply not damaged by that. On the contrary, since it stands as a representation of the *possibility* of a stable image, one doesn't need the stable image itself. It's the possibility of seeing, rather than what you see, that is productive here. What you see is not necessarily that important.

The fact that architecture in the Classical imagination enables us to imagine that we see our world does not mean that architecture itself is seen. This seems to be true of all forms of architecture. It's not safe to assume that anyone saw the Parthenon, ever. Or at least we should ask ourselves the question, "What does it mean to see the Parthenon?" There's no such thing as architecture experienced directly as itself, since architecture is less an object to be seen than an object that offers a way of seeing. In this sense I'm drawn to Marshall McLuhan's 1966 idea of art as anti-environment, what he called a "perceptual probe" that makes the environment visible. It reveals what's in front See panel discussion → p. 294 of you but you didn't see. So the mechanism of seeing, the thing that allows you to see, cannot itself be seen in the moment of allowing you to see. Instead it slips in, enabling something or triggering some kind of response.

One could say then that the role of architecture is to allow you to see your world, and I do think that is the mission of the architect—architects are extraordinarily gifted in allowing people to think that they are seeing their world, and therefore feel a sense of place within that thing that they think they see. Staying with McLuhan's idea of anti-environment, architecture produces a hesitation in the everyday rhythms of perceptual life, a hesitation in which for the first time you see the environment, which is by definition that which is always around you, like water for a fish. Fish only have a concept of water when you pull them out of the water, and they very, very quickly start to theorize.

If architecture is that which allows you to see those things that you cannot see because they're right in front of you all the time, and if architecture necessarily disappears in making the environment visible, then my proposition here is that theory is the thing that makes architecture visible. Theory is a flash that exposes the architectural effect, without which there would be no effect. Without the flash of theory, the Parthenon is not the

Parthenon (as if in saying "the" Parthenon, we're all talking about the same thing). Architectural theory allows architecture to be momentarily seen, which goes back to the Classical roots of word theory, *theora*, "to see." Architectural theory is in this sense not only an architectural act, it is *the* architectural act.

See panel discussion → p. 297

Theory is the flash that allows architecture to be seen as a lingering afterimage. For a moment it's blinding, but there is an afterimage within which there is a sense of what architecture is. Or to say it another way around, for architectural theory, architecture itself is the environment that is to be exposed and thereby potentially transformed. You could say that architectural theory is a kind of anti-environment of the anti-environment—it's an anti-anti-environment that sets off a chain of exposures, as it were. This flash of theory starts with the word "architecture," and I think never really strays away from that word. There is only that word—architecture's version of "In the beginning…"

For theory to be an agent of vision in this sense does not presuppose clarity. Theory doesn't come along and simply illuminate things. On the contrary, to see, or in this case to see seeing, or to see architecture as that which allows you to see, is precisely to respect the blur, the murkiness, the doubling, the vibrations, the contradictions, the instabilities, the space in which an image could appear. The space in which an image could appear has to be a space in which vision is compromised, a kind of proto-visual space. This is not only a space in which the image will appear, but a space from which the image could never detach itself. By the same logic, theory itself is not visible as such. That which enables sight is a blind spot by definition. In the moment of the flash, the eyes tend to close for an instant—the word "flash" is really about what you don't see. But then your eyes open and something appears out of that loss of vision, literally a blinding.

So the historical question, "What happened to theory?" becomes a more theoretical question: What is seen in the moment that theory is not seen? What appears in the immediate after-math of theory? Which is just the question "How does theory happen anyway?" Before we even start talking about what's going on in theoryland, what the hell is theory anyway? How does it work? We've already touched the idea that theory is not very easy to see, that it doesn't occupy a place, that it takes many forms other than books and articles. And the location of architectural theory within an architecture school, which would seem to be a site of theory's making, is never clear. It certainly doesn't live in the so-called theory classes. It's dispersed across studios, lectures, seminars, exhibitions, websites, syllabi, labels, essays, texts, tracts, emails, tweets, and posters.

If we can say that theory is by definition deterritorialized in this sense, that doesn't mean it can't be taught. On the contrary, it might be the only thing we're really trying to teach in a school of architecture. If there is no architecture without theory, and if the architect is by definition a theorist, the thing that we're trying to teach is that theoretical act that allows the use of the word "architecture." In some sense, that's exactly what it is to receive a degree in a professional school of architecture—the right to call yourself an architect, the legal right to use the word "architecture." You do a lot of training here in order to be allowed to speak that one word, that more-than-religious word. Teaching theory isn't so different from teaching design. It's equally inductive. It's equally allergic to methodology. And anyway, "design" is just another word for the aspiration to the theoretical act. In the end, schools of architecture teach you how to talk. Drawing is optional, or it's considered a way of talking. I love the idea that theory classes might be called drawing classes, and vice versa.

See panel discussion ← p. 65

This is the whole point of the cliché about doing theory in the morning and design in the afternoon. It's not about separating those two things, but producing the illusion that the afternoon, which is when the blood sugar level is at its worst, when you're a bit hazy, allows you to be infused with theory from the morning, which you have digested at lunch. Hence, the important role of lunch in any discussion of architectural theory. Theory, we are asked to believe, is meant to percolate downward throughout the day with the real production happening in the deep night when human beings are sleeping. There's actually no evidence that anything significant is produced in schools of architecture after midnight, but it is not possible to be an architecture student without communicating blissed fatigue to fellow architects or to human beings. Locating theory in the morning, giving it a specific name and place, is the means to allow it to infuse everything else. The figure of the designer emerges out of a haze in which theory is no longer distinct. The very concept of design refers to the production of an articulate object, an object that has absorbed theory and could talk.

From the student days onward, the designer is actually an effect of design. It's certainly not the case that a designer designs—a designer *is* designed. Likewise, theory does not presuppose the figure of a theorist or even that of a group of theorists. In reverse, self-identified theory doesn't necessarily have a theoretical effect. In other words, if you do believe there was a hell of a lot of theory going on in the '80s, I wouldn't presuppose from that that there was necessarily a theoretical effect of all that work. The more insistently people refer to themselves as theorists, the likelier it is that they've left the theoretical effect behind.

But while I would argue that the '80s and '90s were no more or less theoretical than the rest of architecture, I do think that period saw a kind of a doubling of theory, or a kind of highlighting of the theory effect. Those decades involved a number of us trying to make theory itself visible by concentrating on the structural role of the blind spots in the discourse—allowing certain things to be discussed that had not been considered architectural up to that point. There was a great concern for any repressions, occlusions, disavowals, blocks, gaps, slippages, repetitions, rifts, faults, cracks, ripples, shearings—these were the symptoms on which theoretical work was carried out.

The work was carried out by a shockingly small number of people. The word "group" hardly even works, because it was a ridiculously small number of people who were nevertheless treated as if they had a deadly virus. This pathetically small group tended to occupy the more or less protected enclaves of Ivy League universities, in which the virus wouldn't present much of a threat to the human species, given the polemical detachment of universities from everyday life. This very small group of people in these very traditional spaces operated with very traditional means—lectures, conferences, essays, journals, exhibition catalogs, and books. Nothing to be upset about, really.

In the current age of the so-called disappearance of theory, one of the symptoms has been that the schools are now run by theorists. So it's a very odd form of disappearance—the theorists engineered openings in the conventional protocols of education to produce new kinds of incubation. That would seem to be theory on steroids, as distinct from theory's disappearance—and perhaps it was a kind of dispersal that was called for by the earlier theoretical work. Again, it's a question of prehistory. I think one could discuss theory in the 21st century by producing a prehistory that understands what came before as a call for dispersal, for infusion—as if the '80s and '90s were the morning and this is the afternoon and today we are discussing what might happen after midnight. The urgencies of theory might be precisely in this dispersal—that is to say, in a continuous relocation and undoing of normative architecture. Believe it or not, running a school of architecture could be treated as a theoretical work. There are today dramatically new horizontal mobilities, new forms of interaction between people that have transformed research, design, construction, analysis, and publication, and that definitely represent a sort of changed territory or set of territories for the theory effect to be considered.

The horizontal is an urgent project. Architectural discourse, I would suggest—and by architectural discourse, I mean it all, the whole thing—is extraordinarily hierarchical. I defy you to find a less hierarchical discipline. Places like the Vatican don't get near architecture for its stratification. Architectural discourse as a kind of organism is mainly and efficiently devoted to nothing happening at all. It's a pyramid, an Egyptian work with a very, very small set of voices competing for attention at the top, the stars, and a vast sea of voices below. There are always more than one million students of architecture on the planet graduating every year—one million, one million, one million. Think about it. And then there are four or five men, maybe a woman here or there, at the top of this pyramid. Beneath them, a series of very precise layers or valves that filter and control the flow, minimizing the upward movement, so each one of the million could dream of being one day at the top of the pyramid—but you would have to fight your way through these filters, which are mainly designed to stop you from moving upward. In reverse, those at the top give very little evidence of having climbed and are infinitely sensitive to how to absorb things from below in a way that ensures nothing changes. They engineer slowness.

One symptom of our field that I am always amazed by and horrified by is how many extraordinarily interesting research projects are carried out by architects and scholars over a long period of time that lead to very interesting exhibitions with associated publications that are in your hand and are then left in hotel rooms because they're a bit too heavy to carry home, or a bit too heavy to absorb. And yet, all those publications left behind are an incredibly serious and interesting body of work that's going on right now across the planet. So if architectural discourse is a pyramid, when you look at the wider parts of the structure there is very, very serious work going on. The only thing that stops a kind of revolution within the discipline is the lack of attention to that work, a refusal to archive it and to allow it to be shared—even gathering it in the form of a simple PDF archive would be a transformation. Digital archives and interfaces for sharing can liberate a quantum leap in collective intelligence and inventiveness, new forms of creativity and criticality.

This is, I think, the beginnings of a possible transformation of the field because these more horizontal models could lead to an inversion. And this inversion could be more a question of survival than revolution. The discipline of architecture could find itself as irrelevant as quickly as happened to newspapers, and why would we imagine otherwise? The university is one of the most likely institutions to go through the newspaper effect of suddenly becoming respectable and honorable while no longer being the source of record. At the very least, the institution of the university will clearly transform radically, and this change needs to be relentlessly engaged and questioned.

Theory has a responsibility in this moment to challenge the institutional protocols that nurture and sustain it, starting with the architecture school, then with the university. Knowledge production, if we can use that language, is evolving very rapidly through models of distributed intelligence, open source networks, and so on. Scholarship itself has been revolutionized more completely than professional practice, and yet we don't discuss that. The ecology of theory is evolving. There are new opportunities and responsibilities, but also already new orthodoxies to question. For example, a description of what is unique and what we love about architectural studios now sounds exactly like scientists' descriptions of the laboratories in which they generate their work, which in turn don't sound any different from the way that cities advertise their "innovation capacity" and their general drive toward creativity. The language is the same. Architectural studios are actually paradigmatic of a set of dominant political-economic narratives. Any idea that the studio is an experimental place from which one could then "change the world," as it were, is somewhat ridiculous, given that the world is increasingly describing itself as an architectural studio. On the contrary, the urgency of theory is to intervene across the whole landscape, producing hesitations in all the routines, opening up our thoughts in a restless subversion of anything regarded as best practice. At the very least, it seems to me that schools, and especially schools of architecture, need to turn themselves inside out, not in order to blend into the market—and I think there is that drive in contemporary universities—but quite the opposite, to take whatever vestiges there are of critical theory out of the refrigerator. In other words, to get that virus out into the world.

See also Arindam Dutta's account of the contemporary university ← p. 78–81

I don't accept the old image of the university as a space of open experimental thinking versus a world of pragmatic activities, harnessed to hegemonic narratives sustaining uneven distribution of resources and so on. Any description of the hegemony of the market is usually a better description of the inside of a university than the outside. Take the recent newspaper articles about how the leading universities now only accept 5 percent of their applicants—things like this are actually symptoms of the imminent demise of the university. These are signs that the university itself is the space *without* question, the space you *must be* in, the space so integrated with its outside that there is an enormous attempt to immigrate to its inside. This is the opposite of distance from the market and from fixed views. It represents the end of the university.

It seems to me that this is a moment of great fragility for the university, but it's also therefore an exciting moment. There is a need to construct a new future for the university, which returns us to the idea of architectural theory's own future—the future of blinding flashes that provoke momentary insight. Architectural theory can take advantage of the new fragility of the institutions that it inhabits. Our task is not to respond to the perceived urgencies and agreed-upon urgencies of the present moment, even those of the university, but to produce new senses of urgency. And if those new urgencies are in some way linked in a series of horizontal exchanges, being at the top of the pyramid could become a singularly uninteresting aspiration.

URGENT MATTERS OF ARCHITECTURE
Mabel O. Wilson

We ask the question "Who builds your architecture?" to provoke a response from architects and other allied fields about how globalization affects labor in architecture. Who Builds Your Architecture? (WBYA?) has organized national and inter-

Who Builds Your Architecture? (WBYA?) is an interdisciplinary advocacy group that works to educate architects and other allied fields on the effects of globalization on architecture labor. WBYA? promotes fair working conditions and sustainable building practices at building sites worldwide. See www.whobuilds.org.

national forums to examine and discuss the recent problems facing migrant construction workers.[1] Over the past two decades, the construction of large-scale architectural and infrastructural projects around the world has proceeded at a dizzying pace. Cities compete for the tallest corporate headquarters, the most luxurious hotel, the biggest mall, the largest museum, or the most cutting-edge, green university campus to solidify their stature as global leaders and guarantee a good return on investment. Yet behind the boosterism touting sustainability and regeneration as desirable outcomes of these new buildings, which are packaged in a range of design aesthetics from traditional to futuristic, human rights reports and investigative journalism have revealed how the thousands of construction workers employed to build these signature projects, other less prominent buildings, and massive infrastructure projects have been ruthlessly and routinely exploited.

Over the course of the past three years, when WBYA? broached the question "Who builds your architecture?" to professional organizations, architectural firms, and architects, it elicited some concern but was also met with silence or polite evasion. For those architects who did respond to our query, they often cited "contractual constraints" as the reason why architects had no power to intervene in the exploitation of construction workers, a rationale that casts the problem outside the purview of the profession. This echoed the response offered by architect Zaha Hadid when *The Guardian* asked the Pritzker Prize–winning designer to comment on the deaths of migrant construction workers on construction sites in Qatar, where she has been commissioned to design a major stadium project for

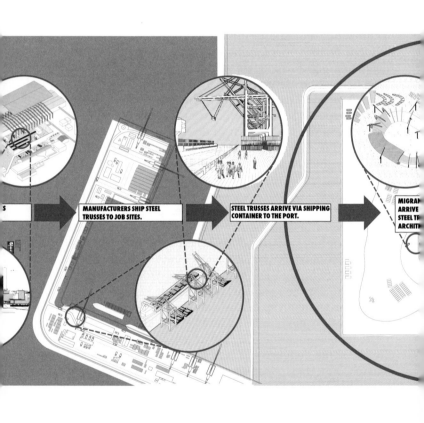

MANUFACTURERS SHIP STEEL
TRUSSES TO JOB SITES.

STEEL TRUSSES ARRIVE VIA SHIPPING
CONTAINER TO THE PORT.

MIGRA
ARRIVE
STEEL TR
ARCHIT

the *Fédération Internationale de Football Association* (FIFA) 2022 World Cup matches. Her response was "I have nothing to do with the workers." She then transferred the resolution of their plight to the authority of the State: "I think that's an issue the government—if there's a problem—should pick up. Hopefully, these things will be resolved." Hadid expressed her deep concern over the deaths in the Iraq conflict but asserted that she could not intervene in that conflict. Architects were not obligated to solve the problems of construction workers, Hadid insisted. "I'm not taking it lightly but I think it's for the government to look to take care of. It's not my duty as an architect to look at it."[2]

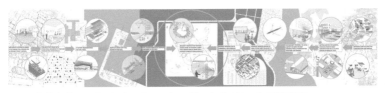

Map of global supply chain of construction industry → gatefold

The need to understand how the global supply chain of the construction industry produces buildings—in other words, how buildings are not only conceived by architects but also how they are materialized by a network that mobilizes architects, construction workers, and a host of other actors—has necessitated an examination that deploys the representational tools and techniques of architecture along with a critical analysis that theorizes architecture's entanglements within geopolitical and economic structures. A resolution to this daunting problem should certainly not rest solely on the shoulders of architects, but as the artists and activists of the collective GulfLabor have demonstrated in their protest to ensure fair treatment of the migrant construction workers who will build the Guggenheim Museum in Abu Dhabi (designed by another Pritzker winner Frank Gehry), this kind of pressure can be one of many actions strategically arrayed to shift the networks that bring together all of the actors and resources to build these large-scale projects.[3]

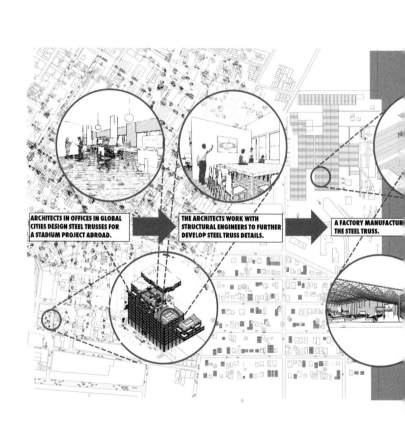

ARCHITECTS IN OFFICES IN GLOBAL
CITIES DESIGN STEEL TRUSSES FOR
A STADIUM PROJECT ABROAD.

THE ARCHITECTS WORK WITH
STRUCTURAL ENGINEERS TO FURTHER
DEVELOP STEEL TRUSS DETAILS.

A FACTORY MANUFACTUR
THE STEEL TRUSS.

WBYA?'s investigations ask: Where is architecture within these circuits, and what various actions might architects take to better the conditions under which workers build?

WHO IS BUILDING

Over the last thirty years, urbanization in various regions around the world has functioned as a lucrative terrain for surplus capital generation, a growth facilitated by the internationalization of finance markets. "The property market," writes David Harvey, has "absorbed a great deal of surplus capital through new construction."[4] With the rise of the industrializing BRICS nations (Brazil, Russia, India, China, South Africa) along with various forms of resource extraction and debt financing providing new sources of capital for both public and private investment, urban development has become a primary vehicle for generating profit and wealth. The construction sector, which is flooded by development financing on the construction end and mortgage financing on the business and consumer end, has become so large and successful that it functions as a leading economic indicator for many national economies. Both the planning of whole cities in African countries by the Chinese government and the construction of factories in Mexico's duty- and tariff-free *maquiladora* zones by US companies typify how large-scale construction projects become the vehicles of cross-border government-brokered economic expansion.[5] Public and private investment has also been channeled into nation-branding enterprises to reshape (and homogenize) the skylines of Astana, Rio, Guangzhou, Doha, Taipei, Miami, Lagos, and many other cities seeking "world-class" status to attract financial partners and tourist dollars. Reinhold Martin takes architectural measure of these transactions when he observes that "architecture and urbanism form one element in a complex network of cultural practices that make financial globalization—and by extension, its crises—not only visible but also imaginable (and therefore possible)."[6]

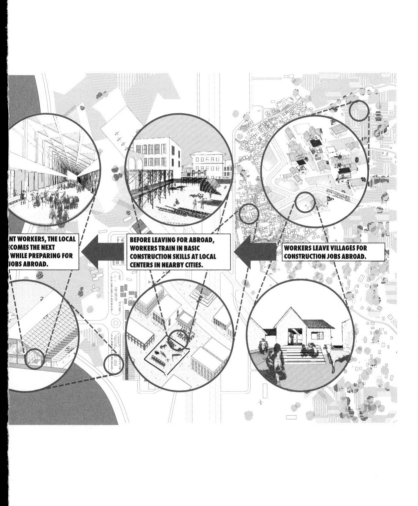

NT WORKERS, THE LOCAL ECOMES THE NEXT WHILE PREPARING FOR JOBS ABROAD.

BEFORE LEAVING FOR ABROAD, WORKERS TRAIN IN BASIC CONSTRUCTION SKILLS AT LOCAL CENTERS IN NEARBY CITIES.

WORKERS LEAVE VILLAGES FOR CONSTRUCTION JOBS ABROAD.

Mabel O. Wilson

In this regard, architecture produces an alluring image of a future in which vertiginous feats of engineering in the form of twisted helices and bulbous pinecones signify the future of business. Massive shopping malls with miles of storefronts purveying global luxury brands and towering atria that enclose water parks represent the future of shopping and entertainment. Top museums compete with one another to erect the most fantastical architectural backdrop for their expanding collections of old masters and cutting-edge art in order to symbolize the future of culture. International campuses built by American universities capitalizing on the rising value of knowledge production worldwide exemplify the future of education. Massively state-financed facilities for private sporting events, such as FIFA and the Olympics, market the future of leisure. Faux Tuscan villas built anywhere from Lagos to Dubai to Mumbai are ironically advertised as the homes of the future. By adapting this set of global architectural branding strategies and tropes, cities demonstrate that they—along with their nations—embrace foreign investment. Such moves to build up and transform their city's physical inventory also allow them to tap into cultural and heritage networks such as the Guggenheim's brand or UNESCO designation to leverage visibility and prestige. However, to erect many of these award-winning projects, thousands of migrant construction workers are recruited. They end up laboring at building sites under exploitative conditions that include withheld pay, poorly regulated labor recruitment practices, lax safety measures, and substandard housing. How these buildings and mega-projects are erected stands in direct contradiction to the aspirations of cultural openness and historical significance these cities and nations wish to project to the world.

For the cycle of capital accumulation to generate additional wealth through large-scale building projects, a substantial workforce employed over the course of several years of the construction process is needed. If the local pool of labor is too small, especially for projects that require an army of workers thousands strong, then private contractors or state authorities draft a labor pool from migrant and immigrant populations who

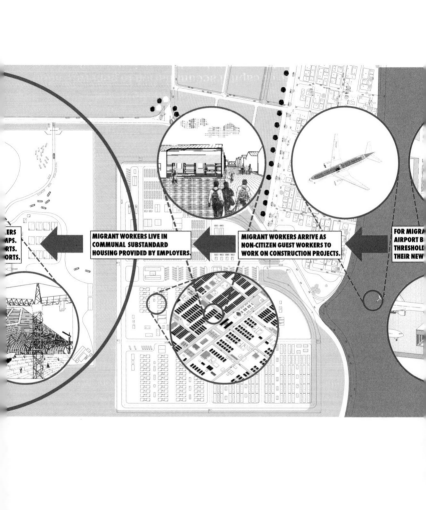

...ERS ...MPS. ...RTS. ...ORTS.

MIGRANT WORKERS LIVE IN COMMUNAL SUBSTANDARD HOUSING PROVIDED BY EMPLOYERS.

MIGRANT WORKERS ARRIVE AS NON-CITIZEN GUEST WORKERS TO WORK ON CONSTRUCTION PROJECTS.

FOR MIGR... AIRPORT B... THRESHOL... THEIR NEW...

live elsewhere.[7] On building sites in places like Saadiyat Island, Abu Dhabi and Doha, for example, construction workers are being recruited from all parts of the Middle East, Southeast Asia, and Northern Africa. According to Amnesty International, there are more than 1.35 million foreign nationals working in Qatar—a country home to approximately 250,000 citizens.[8] Since migrant workers are not citizens of the nations in which they work, they have very few rights. There are very few avenues available for abused workers to protest poor treatment even though many have committed to multiyear labor contracts. Construction workers often face unscrupulous conduct by recruitment firms, subcontractors, and local authorities. Persistent problems with the recruitment process can involve exorbitant fees charged by recruitment firms and false representation of the type of work and compensation offered. Employers confiscate passports to prevent flight or deliberately fail to issue proper identification cards that would allow workers to move freely around the city. Migrant workers are also subject to dangerous and at times deadly conditions on jobsites. In the worst-case scenarios, workers live in poorly maintained, substandard accommodations located in sprawling "workers' camps." Companies construct these camps at the outskirts of the city, far from jobsites and areas where amenities can be easily accessed.[9]

Because of the challenges posed by jurisdictional differences between the nation-states where migrant workers come from and the countries where they work, human rights and international labor organizations have been systematically challenging the legalities of the current recruitment system found in many parts of the world. The law is clearly the primary and critical area in which to intervene and abolish exploitive dimensions of the current system. However, many of the problems migrant construction workers face are also inherently spatial, urban, and architectural in nature. Profiled in Amnesty International's report *The Dark Side of Migration* (2013), the example of how Krantz Engineering mismanaged their workforce on an educational campus project outside of Doha reveals how global circuits of the construction global supply chain move workers, architects, and engineers, capital and debt, building materials and waste to and from building sites—but in very unequal ways.[10] The disjunctive relationship between what Arjun Appadurai has labeled as "ethno-," "media-," "techo-," "finance-," and "ideo-scapes" can all be located within these networks—where we also find the possibility for critical imaginaries that initiate new social movements, not only among the ranks of the disenfranchised construction workers but also in direct relation to the architects who create the drawings that instruct workers in how to build the architecture.[11]

DISCIPLINARY AND PROFESSIONAL PRACTICES

Globalization's multiplication of actors and points of access have affected not only architecture's professional practices—in other words, how buildings are built—but also its disciplinary practices, how buildings are *thought*. The rise of "post-critical" theory sought to reboot the discipline in order to optimize its performance within a field transformed by more complex terrains of production enabled by computing technologies. These theorists argued—with the noble intentions of repositioning the discipline's operative field—that architecture is best served by a move away from the well-worn dialectics of critical theory and toward a projective practice that "does not make a claim for expertise outside of the field of architecture nor does it limit its field of expertise to an absolute definition of architecture."[12] As a critique of the discipline's previous critical practices of autonomy and process, the projective practice operates on a different bandwidth to cast models of "alternative" rather than oppositional modes of disciplinary engagement. Despite these liberating promises, however, what has emerged, according to Daniel Barber's assessment of post-criticality, is a return to "an autonomous architectural formalism" that rallies the wagons to unintentionally re-inscribe architecture's disciplinary boundaries. The post-critical's flaccid deployment of technique to engage the complex networks through which architecture operates fails to "destabilize architecture's disciplinarity."[13] Architecture, as Barber notes, has always been a "radically anti-disciplinary field" that cobbled together its sphere of knowledge from economic, political, cultural, and material domains.[14] One transformation that has been an outcome of the introduction of new technologies of representation and production to architecture, for example, has been to reorganize hierarchies of labor within practice. In his review of the historical transformation of how architects practice from the mid-century to today, scholar Andrew Ross discerns that the most recent incorporation of new technologies into the design and construction process has prompted two divergent reactions from architects. According to Ross, they either become "proponents of a brave new world of design," buoyantly proclaiming that modernizing the field will fully maximize the potential of the "hitherto-underutilized cognitive faculties" of the architect, or they become "forecasters," soothsayers of architecture's demise, envisioning "automation as a de-skilling process."[15]

The focus of architects on algorithmically created form-making and digitally simulated renderings of projects—methods that concentrate creative energies on articulating the surface of architecture rather than its material impact—could be read as symptomatic of how architecture is practiced within a disciplinary cocoon. Perhaps this internalization might also be a result of how the profession is dominated, as are many transactions between individuals and institutions, by an aversion to risk and a desire to diminish liability. It is these contractual obligations and professional liabilities that regulate the types of relationships that get established between all the parties engaged in building architecture. In a typical building project, architects are contractually accountable to the client. The client also enters into a contractual agreement with a contractor, who can apportion segments of the building's construction to other contractors. This procedure transpires across the building supply chain. For construction labor, workers can be sub-sub-subcontracted to provide services during any phase of the building's construction. One outcome of this process is that risk along with accountability is distributed among a legion of contractors in the same manner that securitization distributes risk in the mortgage market. Securitization, as the implosion of the housing market in 2008 demonstrated, did not eliminate risk; rather, it aggregated and spread the vulnerability—precipitating catastrophic outcomes. The connections between architect and construction worker, however, have become so mediated through numerous factors such as legal structures to reduce liability and the increased number of participants in the building process—architects, engineers, contractors, managers, agents, representatives, supervisors, consultants, and more—that it has become an abstract relationship to both groups. Amid this atomization of the various tasks of the building process, architects are nonetheless intimately linked to the workers who construct their project through the knowledge transfer implicit in the central contract document between architect and client: the construction drawing.

If we scrutinize more closely how architects work, Building Information Modeling (BIM) software facilitates collaborative exchanges between architects, engineers, and contractors to make the design, consulting, and construction process more efficient. Similar to how the contracting process subdivides work within the construction process, the design process has also been parcelized into specific domains managed by consultants who specialize in geo-tech engineering, façade design, sustainability, accessibility, food services, and terrorism prevention, to name a few. BIM modeling platforms aid architects in monitoring in real time the ways that changes to their design influence a range of factors such as material selection and cost as well as approximating the phasing of construction and the maintenance schedule of the finished building. For all of BIM's up-to-the-nanosecond/down-to-the-millimeter modeling capability, however, the cost of labor is not yet a factor within the equation. Given that every aspect of the design and construction process can be accounted for through BIM modeling—from conceptual design through demolition—perhaps it is this visualization tool that imparts to the architect a sense of agency in decisions that ultimately do affect how construction workers operate in the field. With new technologies of efficiency and building intelligence reshaping every phase of contemporary practice, architects can coordinate the logistics of assembly for each stage of the building process, thus leaving little outside their purview.

WBYA? contends that this labor issue falls under the purview of the professional ethics of architects. Architects cannot solve the problem alone, but a solution will require legal intervention, economic incentives, and grassroots activism from all participants in order to achieve a fair resolution for the workers. We believe that as a social justice issue, the problem should be treated and acted upon in the same manner as and with the same vigor that environmental concerns have been addressed through the development of sustainability practices and protocols over the past four decades. Human sustainability should be an urgent matter for architecture to consider.

This essay draws from WBYA?'s research projects, public discussions, and workshops that have been led by Jordan Carver, Kadambari Baxi, and Laura Diamond Dixit with the support of Beth Stryker, Tiffany Rattray, and Lindsey Lee.

1   *The Guardian* has published extensive reports on the problems of construction labor exploitation in the Middle East. This reportage relied in part on reports by human rights organizations such as Human Rights Watch, Amnesty International, and the International Trade Union Confederation (ITUC). See Amnesty International, *The Dark Side of Migration: Spotlight on Qatar's Construction Sector Ahead of the World Cup* (London: Amnesty International Publications, 2013); Human Rights Watch, *"Island of Happiness": Exploitation of Migrant Workers on Saadiyat Island, Abu Dhabi* (New York: Human Rights Watch), 2009; and Human Rights Watch, *"Island of Happiness" Revisited* (New York: Human Rights Watch), 2012.

2   James Riach, "Zaha Hadid defends Qatar World Cup role following migrant worker deaths," *The Guardian,* February 25, 2014, www.theguardian.com/world/2014/feb/25/zaha-hadid-qatar-world-cup-migrant-worker-deaths.

3   GulfLabor was formed in October 2013; see gulflabor.org. For a summation of Gehry Partners's statement on treatment of construction workers see Anne Fixson, "What Is Frank Gehry Doing About Labor Conditions in Abu Dhabi?" in *Architectural Record,* September 25, 2014, archrecord.construction.com/news/2014/09/140922-Frank-Gehry-Works-to-Improve-Worker-Conditions-on-Abu-Dhabi-Site.asp.

4   The geographer David Harvey has argued that investments of surplus capital have been funneled into building booms in major cities like Dubai, Moscow, and Johannesburg. See David Harvey, *Rebel Cities: From the Right to the City to the Urban Revolution* (London: Verso, 2013), 12.

5   See Urban China: Chinese Urbanism in Africa, www.gowestproject.com/portfolio/urban-china-chinese-cities-in-africa.

6   Reinhold Martin, "Financial Imaginaries," *Grey Room* 42, (Winter 2011): 66.

7   Harvey, *Rebel Cities,* 5–6.

8   See Amnesty International, *The Dark Side of Migration,* 17.

9   These conditions have been documented in a number of publications including Human Rights Watch, *"Island of Happiness"* and *"Island of Happiness" Revisited.*

10   Amnesty International, *The Dark Side of Migration,* 17–30.

11   Arjun Appadurai, "Disjuncture and Difference in Global Cultural Economy," in *Modernity at Large: Cultural Dimensions of Globalization* (Minneapolis: University of Minnesota Press, 2003), 33.

12   Robert Somol and Sarah Whiting, "Notes Around the Doppler Effect and Other Moods of Modernism," *Perspecta* 33 (2002): 72–122.

13   Daniel Barber, "Militant Architecture: Destabilising Architecture's Disciplinarity," in *Critical Architecture,* ed. Jane Rendell, Jonathan Hill, Murray Fraser, and Mark Dorrian (London: Routledge, 2007), 60.

14   Barber, "Militant Architecture," 64.

15   Andrew Ross, "Foreword," in *Building (in) the Future: Recasting Labor in Architecture,* ed. Peggy Deamer and Phillip Bernstein (New York and New Haven: Princeton Architectural Press and Yale School of Architecture, 2010), 12.

MARK WASIUTA: I'm feeling pretty good about
the Ws right now. [Laughter] Eyal, I'm interested in what seems to be a shift in this
project from your previous work in Mengele's
Skull (2012), the book you wrote with Tom
Keenan, in which you think through the idea
of forensic aesthetics, which is performed
through rhetorics of articulation and theatricality and forms of representation. It seems to
me that this new work isn't an exposure of
forensic aesthetics but an actual enactment
of forensics, which, of course, relies on aesthetics. So there seems to be not only a
shift in modality, let's say, but also something that requires a new theoretical position
around forensics.

And Mark, you mentioned McLuhan's invisible
environment, and his notion that when an advertisement has become so environmental that it
goes unperceived, it's really doing its work.
In your model, theory is environmental in that
sense. But at the same time, it's also incredibly precise, interruptive, and consequential.
So I'm wondering how you reconcile the ubiquity
of theory, the fact of it being everywhere,
with the fact that it's simultaneously so precise that it can operate recursively to expose
architecture's exposing of environment.

EYAL WEIZMAN: In each of the twenty or so
investigations we've done that deal with forensic architecture, the specific case poses the
problem of aesthetics differently. But I would
say that in the shift from Mengele's Skull,
which as you say sees the forensic aesthetic
articulating itself in a sort of theatricality

and presentation, our more recent work sees aesthetic operating firstly in its most traditional sense, in its pre-Kantian mode. In that understanding, aesthetics is that which relates to the senses—not to human senses, initially, but to material aesthetics, a material sensibility that articulates itself both in terms of presence and representation. If the nineteenth century needed silver salt and darkrooms to see surface as image, now we have different technologies.

So the first layer of a forensic aesthetics is the nonhuman or material aesthetics. In order for this aesthetics to function politically, it needs to be interpreted, debated, and presented, and before that can happen, a forum needs to be created. Our sensibility about making objects discursive relates to the term "forensis," the original Latin word, which pertains to the "forum" rather than "forensics," which evokes more of a police operation. The history of forensis, then, necessarily includes the construction of spaces. There's another level to the aesthetics, though, which involves our own politics and our own being-in-the-world. That is to say, it's important to aestheticize ourselves—to be in the world in a way that is sensitive and sensible to whatever happens around us.

WIGLEY: That's so much more interesting than what I'm about to say. [Laughter] One interesting thing about McLuhan's argument is how anti-environment and environment can swap places, and indeed always swap places. It's an echo of Tafuri's thought that an avant-garde is always eventually normalized and absorbed, which for Tafuri meant that an avant-garde is obliged to a kind of restless activity, never assuming that the work is done.

To say it more slowly, maybe there are three levels of theory being identified. One is self-identified theory—the stuff you find in theory class. Then there is the theory that's ubiquitously written into all the elements of the discourse. Then there's what I'm referring to as "flash theory," which is the moment in which you trigger the relationship between those two things. The function of a school is to direct resources to that flash, and to develop a sensitivity to a flash whose consequences are not known.

What's interesting is that this flash effect isn't going to be found more in self-anointed theory than in the ubiquitous kind. The flash is always a challenge to what we think of as theory—it produces a sense of insight, but it's momentary insight. What's funny is that theory did become environmental in the twenty-first century, at the moment that these claims about the demise of theory were being made by theorists, who were generally tenured faculty members. It has to be said, it was funny. [Laughter]

LUCIA ALLAIS: Well, the professors who were carrying this "virus" of theory, as you put it earlier, Mark, were much admired by their students because they were afraid neither of difficulty nor introspection. You could argue that their power lay in the dual fact that they

were not afraid to say things that were difficult to understand, and not afraid to look
at themselves and therefore to internalize critique. Does this internalization fall outside
of the "flash"? I can see how historical work
(or theory as found in a certain kind of
historical work) has taken over the burden of
difficulty. I, for one, am often accused of
saying things that are too difficult for people
to understand. But what about what Eyal is
describing as hyper-awareness? When we ask what
happened to theory, are we talking about the
disappearance of a form of introspection?

WIGLEY: I hope not. My main point is that
if you ask, "What happened to theory?" without
asking yourself, "What is theory, anyway?"
then the answers won't be very interesting. My
answer to that question would be different
today than it was maybe fifteen years ago—it's
always evolving. That's the project for me, to
wonder what architectural theory is. My main
interest is in the architect as a species. From
a distance they resemble humans but close up,
they appear quite differently, in that they're
a species that simultaneously talks and tries
to understand what "talk" is.

For me, one of the pleasures of teaching is
to revisit those things that you most believe
in and to ask yourself, "Does that really still
work?" The dimension of theory that was of
greatest interest to me in the '80s and '90s
was the self-identified theory, that first-order kind of theory. Currently I don't find that
very interesting.

MABEL WILSON: I taught architectural theory for
a number of years and according to the curriculum, one of the courses was labeled Theory,
and the second course was labeled Contemporary
Theory, where we would read you, Mark. [Laugh-
ter] But in the Contemporary Theory class, one
exercise that helped me and the students com-
prehend the role of theory was to review the
precise etymology of the word "theory" and its
connection back to its root word "theater."
The theater is a space of performance, and the
school allows for the performance of knowledge.
The roots of "thea" and "theoria"—to see—is
entirely relevant to the idea of knowing. One
responds "I see" in order to convey "I know and
understand what you mean."

But I want to return to a point Eyal made about
the politics and architecture of negation.
Where claims to citizenship and subjectivity
are refused by the State, there emerges a
condition in which individuals aren't seen and
known—they're not anyone. The idea of the
preemptive strike isn't just that you're eradicating someone at the other end of the missile,
but rather you are eradicating the possibility of even knowing who that someone is—they
don't yet exist. They haven't even committed
any acts, criminal or otherwise. They're just
bodies. I think that's precisely how migrant
workers are perceived—they're bodies that
provide physical energy necessary for the production, mobilization, and movement of global
surplus capital to be converted into buildings. Many of these bodies become expendable
once they have been used for the task of construction. I think this is precisely why there

have been so many deaths of migrant workers. They're not given a subjectivity in the places where they work that entails recognizable forms of rights, human ones or rights of citizenship. This indeterminate status becomes even more complicated because of class and racial divisions.

So if part of the etymology of theory is that it helps us see and know the world, then one of our obligations as architects is to help ourselves see these unknowns. In the case of construction labor, their passports are confiscated and they also don't have residency passes to move freely in cities where they work. The workers literally can't be made visible and therefore cannot protest their poor treatment within the public sphere of the cities of these emerging and supposedly progressive states.

WIGLEY: So in that sense, your project is architectural not because these are workers on building sites but because the exposure of the workers is something that architectural theory can do. That's what makes it architectural.

CATHERINE INGRAHAM: I want to speak to the question of forensic architecture and the idea of the "forum." Eyal, you've been using two concepts that I've also been using in a different context: "representation" and "presence." Alain Badiou talks about how it's possible for something or someone to be represented but not present; and it's also possible to be present and not represented. Looking at the plan of Auschwitz, for example, one might notice how much that plan looks like a housing settlement.

So you could say that architecture or urbanism
of some kind is represented, but in every way
is not present at the scene taking place there.
It is as if a second or third level of translation is required to understand how housing
might also be incarceration and how incarceration might also be a kind of death row.

I'm wondering whether you're finding, in your
analysis, an architectural form that is given
representation but is not present to what is
actually taking place. You're saying there is a
registration of what's happening in the walls,
which could be considered a detectable participation, a presence, of architecture in the
violence that is taking place.

WEIZMAN: Two instances in relation to Auschwitz
are particularly interesting, and in both what
was important in a drawing or in a text was not
what was written or drawn but the ink itself.
David Irving made his name as a rather respectable, if very right wing, historian, and he
wrote a biography of Hitler. When the magazine
Stern bought the "Hitler diaries" for six
million German marks, it was by no means certain
that they were not faked. They needed to be
authenticated, and so Stern invited a cohort
of Hitler historians to look at them. All
of them were looking for authenticity by tuning
in to facts and to the way Hitler's voice was
articulated in the diaries. Finally, and embar-
rassingly for them, they authenticate the
diaries. At the press conference where they
authenticate it, Irving—and this is a few years
before he becomes a negationist—shouts from
the floor, "Check the ink." Nobody bothered to

check the ink, and it came back as being from the postwar period. The ink is what's called "negative evidence." There's no way to bypass that, and it's not about the representation. It's the presence of the ink.

The second moment where ink appears is when Robert Jan van Pelt, a brilliant architectural historian, travels to Auschwitz as the archives are being opened sometimes in the 1980s. And of course the only archive that the Nazis didn't bother—or forgot—to destroy when they retreated in January of '45 was the architectural archive. He starts an analysis of the architectural plans. The two most amazingly incriminating moments that he finds were not in what was drawn but in what was erased from the paper. Van Pelt discovers that by a simple act of shaving blade erasure, a door that was drawn to open towards the inside of the room is erased—just that line and quarter-circle that represents a door. That line and quarter-circle has been redrawn opening towards the outside, but the signs of erasure are beneath it. The shift in the function of this room—a room that was then turned into a gas chamber—to genocide is registered by that erasure and flipping of the door, because when there are dead bodies inside against the door, you can no longer open it inwards.

We do not always know how to interpret information. Interpretation is always very contradictory—there are various claims that can be made with, on behalf of, and through materials. The threshold of detectability is exactly that moment when you do not know whether what you're reading is right, when two things seem to emerge simultaneously. Mark, when you were speaking about theory having almost a desire to disappear, or a kind of optics of theory, I was thinking how in forensics, there is a certain kind of threshold where all of a sudden the entire optical gestalt seems to appear. The moment of failure and the moment where something enters into visibility is also the moment when the apparatus behind it is somehow exposed.

AUDIENCE: Eyal, one of the very powerful things that I took from your presentation is that one can make a case for the relevance of architectural theory by way of insisting on a dialogue with aesthetics. Is there a particular tradition of aesthetic thought with which you find yourself in dialogue? You also make the very powerful observation that the threshold of the visible could in fact be the condition of the possibility of the threshold of law. I wonder if a broader critique of political theory is embedded in that claim. Could you also be suggesting that it's precisely through architecture and aesthetics that one could challenge and further the ongoing debates about the politics of our time?

WEIZMAN: Well, to your first question, I think that aesthetics is not something that is employed. It's a kind of a being-in-the-world on the level of both the object and the subject. Aestheticizing ourselves to politics—having an exposed skin, being open to sense and pain—lets us develop a hyper-sensitive kind of sensorium with the world around us.... Aesthetics possesses us, rather than being a tool in

our hands. But I'd say it's also connected
to the idea of truth, because there's something
also precious about sensing, especially when
one discusses issues of negation. There is
a current and wrongly held belief: Fiction and
lies are constructions, while truth simply
lingers there. Truth is simple. Lies are aesthetic creations.

I think we also need to turn it around and see
the enormous labor that the approximation
of truth requires on the level of material, on
the level of the subject and that of the theater of the forum, and also on the level of the
construction of forums for looking at truth.
To try to tell the truth, you need to construct
forums.

WASIUTA: Maybe we could return here to the
question of architectural labor, which also
builds forums for making certain things visible. We were in Doha recently, where the
Qatari Museum Authority is responsible for
most of that city's hiring of immigrant labor.
Their mandate is to build new citizens through
museums, as a corrective against the past—
the exposure to art is somehow going to enno-
ble you and make a new citizen of you. This
is already a peculiar construction of subjectivity but also an incredible blindness toward
a kind of refused citizenship for those doing
the building.

MARK JARZOMBEK: There's a whole history of
death and disaster and labor in architecture,
all the way back to the slaves who made the
pyramids and the million and a half people who

died making the Chinese walls. There's still no
memorial for those lost souls, and not really
a history either. It seems like your project is
an attempt to start from a core horrific situation and look forward into contemporary
ethical questions within our own culture. How
do we move it further? It seems great to pick
on the AIA, and I think we should, but can we
ask questions about architecture and bodies and
labor that casts it as a fundamental part of
architectural theory, and not the sorts of
legalistic labor relations questions that we
tend to bracket off into some other department?

WILSON: One of the questions at the core of
"Who Builds Your Architecture?" is which bodies
are constituted as those who labor on building
sites. In the familiar cases I presented and
that we have researched, such as Doha and Abu
Dhabi, these workers are typically Pakistanis
and Bangladeshis. Part of what I'm interested
in trying to understand is why those particular bodies are expendable as workers, and other
bodies are not. The American architect's body,
for example, is not expendable.

Within the equation of who matters, there's a
way that these workers remain invisible and
unseen. The manner in which we replicate those
distinctions and hierarchies between workers
and architects continued to surprise us in our
research. When we asked our fellow architects,
"Would you sign a pledge against the exploitation of construction workers?" They would often
respond, "No, we're not contractually obligated to hire the workers so we can't sign the
pledge." Somehow, through the nature of how

contracts are implemented and the profession-
alization of architecture, people constantly
distanced themselves from what was in fact
going on within their own job sites.

So for me, this is not only a critical question that we find in practice, but there's a
similar gap within architectural discourse. One
of my next projects is called "Building Race
and Nation." I'll be studying the formation
of the United States in the post-Enlightenment
era where slave labor was used to build a fair
amount of the civic architecture of Washing-
ton, D.C. So on one hand there is an aesthetic
and a political imaginary of what this new
nation-state could be as a republic dedicated
to freedom and liberty, and who counted as its
ruling body citizens, as self-conscious subjects. But on the other hand there were also
those enslaved laboring bodies who were tasked
with building these institutions that made the
workings of the new republic possible. This
schism appears again in places like Doha. It is
the paradox that Mark identified that the workers are building libraries for citizens of a
new modern Qatar, while the workers themselves
have absolutely no rights. The replay of these
historical conditions is something to which we
should be attentive.

Image Credits

Pp. 13–20 courtesy of GSAPP

Lucia Allais, *Just in Time*

P. 24 courtesy of Lewis Hyde

P. 26 published in Henri Bergson, *Matière et mémoire: essai sur la relation du corps a l'esprit*, 3rd ed. (1896; Paris: Félix Alcan, 1903), 108; 143

P. 28 from the League of Nations Photographic archive

P. 30 published in Richard Boelcsey, *La Première décade de la Société des Nations* (Berlin: Editions du Magazine des nations, Marquardt et Co., 1930)

Pp. 33 and 41 courtesy of the Archive Jules Destrée, Musée Jules Destrée

Pp. 35, 36, and 38 published in Nikolaos Balanos, *Les monuments de l'Acropole*; *relèvement et conservation* (Paris: Charles Massin et Albert Lévy, 1938), plate 90; dépliant 05, fig. 02; and dépliants 08 and 13

Arindam Dutta, *The Political Economy of Theory*

P. 75 courtesy of Hout Architecture

P. 83 courtesy of the Knight Foundation via Creative Commons

John Harwood, *Broadcast Architectures*

P. 101 published in *Journal of the Royal Institution of Great Britain* (November 1831)

P. 103 published in *Electrical Review* (March 6, 1884)

Pp. 107 and 108 published in *American Architect* (June 1935)

P. 109 courtesy of the BBC

Beatriz Colomina, *Privacy and Publicity in the Age of Social Media*

P. 122 © Burt Glinn, courtesy of Magnum Photos

P. 127 © Archigram, courtesy of the Shelley Power Literary Agency

P. 128 photograph by Dennis Crompton, © Archigram, courtesy of the Shelley Power Literary Agency

P. 130 courtesy of Radius-TWC

Mark Jarzombek, *The Rise of the So-Called Pre-Modern*

Pp. 137 and 138 courtesy of Mark Jarzombek

Image Credits

Mari Lending, *The Urgencies of Theoretical Stuff*

P. 150 courtesy of Mari Lending

P. 152 published in *Assemblage* (1991)

P. 153 © Acropolis Restoration Service Archive

P. 155 courtesy of the Trustees of the British Museum

Spyros Papapetros, *Wig[g]le-y Ornamental*

Pp. 166, 167, and 168 published in *Assemblage* (1991)

P. 176 courtesy of Klassik Stiftung Weimar, Museen

P. 178 © 2014 Estate of Gordon Matta-Clark / Artists Rights Society (ARS), New York

Pelin Tan, *Transversal Materialism*

P. 207 courtesy of Emre Hüner

P. 208 courtesy of Emre Hüner and Rodeo, Istanbul

Pp. 209 and 210 courtesy of Anton Vidokle

Bernard Tschumi, *Some Notes on Architectural Theory*

P. 225 courtesy of Bernard Tschumi Architects

P. 226 and 227 © Iwan Baan, courtesy of Bernard Tschumi Architects

Eyal Weizman, *Matter Against Memory*

P. 243 published in Daniel Keren et al., "The Ruins of the Gas Chambers," *Holocaust and Genocide Studies* (Spring 2004)

P. 246 © Harun Farocki GbR

P. 251 © Kent Klich

P. 253 © Chris Cobb-Smith/ Amnesty International

P. 256 top courtesy of Forensic Architecture

Pp. 256 bottom and 258 courtesy of Forensic Architecture and SITU Research

Mabel Wilson, *Urgent Matters of Architecture*

Pp. 284 and 285 courtesy of Who Builds Your Architecture?

Biographies

LUCIA ALLAIS is a historian and theorist who specializes in architecture's intellectual and political history since the Enlightenment, with a focus on international networks and institutions in the twentieth century. She is assistant professor at the Princeton University School of Architecture. Her forthcoming book, Designs of Destruction, traces the rise of a new political aesthetics in mid-twentieth-century international organizations, through the work of experts who were charged with protecting monuments from the combined destructive effects of war, modernism, and modernization. Allais is a member of the Aggregate architectural history collaborative and an editor of Grey Room.

BEATRIZ COLOMINA is professor of history and theory of architecture at Princeton University, where she directs the Ph.D. program as well as the Program in Media and Modernity. Her publications include Privacy and Publicity: Modern Architecture as Mass Media (MIT Press, 1994), Sexuality and Space (Princeton Architectural Press, 1992), and Domesticity at War (ACTAR and MIT Press, 2007), as well as the co-edited volumes Clip/Stamp/Fold: The Radical

Architecture of Little Magazines 196X–197X (ACTAR, 2011) and Cold War Hot Houses: Inventing Postwar Culture from Cockpit to Playboy (Princeton Architectural Press, 2004).

MARK COUSINS is director of histories and theories at the Architectural Association. He is a founding member and senior fellow of the London Consortium, and has been a member of the Arts Council. He has written on the relation of the human sciences and psychoanalysis and his publications include a book on Michel Foucault (with Athar Hussain), the introduction to a translation of Freud's writings on the unconscious, and his famed series of articles on "The Ugly." He has delivered the Friday Afternoon Lectures at the Architectural Association for more than thirty years.

ARINDAM DUTTA is associate professor of architectural history at MIT, where he directs the History, Theory, Criticism Program in Art and Architecture as well as the SMArchS Program. He is the author of The Bureaucracy of Beauty: Design in the Age of Its Global Reproducibility (Routledge, 2007), a wide-ranging work of cultural theory that connects literary studies, post-coloniality, the history of architecture and design, and the history and present of empire. He is also the editor of A Second Modernism: Architecture, MIT, and the "Techno-Social" Moment, on the postwar conjuncture of architectural thought and linguistic/systems theories (MIT Press, 2013).

KELLER EASTERLING is an architect, writer, and professor at Yale. In addition to Extrastatecraft: The Power of Infrastructure Space (Verso, 2014), Easterling is the author of Subtraction (Sternberg, 2014), The Action Is the Form (Strelka Press, 2012), Enduring Innocence: Global Architecture and Its Political Masquerades (MIT, 2005), and Organization Space: Landscapes, Highways, and Houses in America (MIT, 1999). Easterling's essay "Floor" was recently included in the Elements exhibition of the 2014 Venice Biennale.

JAMES GRAHAM is the director of publications at the Columbia University Graduate School of Architecture, Planning and Preservation, where he also teaches and pursues his Ph.D. in architectural history. He is the founding editor of the Avery Review, a journal of critical essays on architecture, as well as

a number of volumes published by GSAPP Books. His dissertation, The Psychotechnical Architect: Perception, Vocation, and the Laboratory Cultures of Modernism, 1914-45, looks at the intersections of architecture and applied psychology in both pedagogy in practice.

JOHN HARWOOD is associate professor of modern and contemporary architectural history in the Department of Art at Oberlin College. He is the author of The Interface: IBM and the Transformation of Corporate Design (University of Minnesota Press, 2011), which received the 2014 Alice Davis Hitchcock Award from the Society of Architectural Historians. He is an editor of Grey Room, a journal of art, architecture, media, and politics published by MIT Press, and a founding member of the architectural history collaborative Aggregate. He is currently writing two books, Architectures of Mass Media: Telephony, Radio, Television and Corporate Architecture, 17th to 20th Centuries.

CATHERINE INGRAHAM is a professor of architecture at Pratt Institute who has helped formulate seminal debates in architecture over the past twenty years. She received her Ph.D. at Johns Hopkins

University. Dr. Ingraham was an editor of Assemblage from 1991 to 1998 and has published numerous books and essays on contemporary architecture and theory. Her books include Architecture, Animal, Human: The Asymmetrical Condition (Routledge, 2006), Architecture and the Burdens of Linearity (Yale University Press, 1998), and Restructuring Architectural Theory (Northwestern University Press, 1989).

MARK JARZOMBEK is professor of the history and theory of architecture at MIT's School of Architecture and Planning. Jarzombek works on a wide range of topics from the twelfth century to the modern era, with a particular focus on the history, theory, and philosophy of architecture. He has published the groundbreaking textbook titled A Global History of Architecture (Wiley Press, 2006) with co-author Vikram Prakash and the noted illustrator Francis D.K. Ching. He is the sole author of Architecture of First Societies: A Global Perspective (Wiley Press, 2013).

MARI LENDING is professor of architectural theory and history at the Oslo School of Architecture and Design, and a senior researcher in the international research projects "The Printed and the Built: Architecture and Public Debate in Modern Europe" and "Place and Displacement: Exhibiting Architecture," run out of OCCAS (the Oslo Center for Critical Architectural Studies) at the school in Oslo. She is currently working on a book on nineteenth-century plaster cast collections, with the working title Monuments in Flux: Plaster Casts as Mass Medium. She recently published, with Mari Hvattum, the book Modeling Time: The Permanent Collection, 1925–2014 (Oslo: Torpedo Press, 2014), drawing on the exhibition "Model as Ruin" at the House of Artists in Oslo.

SPYROS PAPAPETROS is associate professor of architectural theory and historiography, acting co-director of the program in Media and Modernity, and a member of the executive committee of the program in European Cultural Studies at Princeton University. He is the author of On the Animation of the Inorganic: Art, Architecture, and the Extension of Life (The University of Chicago Press, 2012) and the co-editor (with Julian Rose) of Retracing the Expanded Field: A Conference on Art and Architecture (MIT Press, 2014). He is currently

Biographies

completing a second personal book project titled World Ornament, examining nineteenth- and early twentieth-century historiographies of bodily and architectural adornment on a global scale.

FELICITY D. SCOTT is associate professor of architecture, director of the Ph.D. program, and co-director of the program in Critical, Curatorial, and Conceptual Practices in Architecture (CCCP) at Columbia GSAPP. In addition to articles on contemporary art and architecture, she is the author of Architecture or Techno-Utopia: Politics After Modernism (MIT Press, 2007), Living Archive 7: Ant Farm (ACTAR Editorial, 2008), and Outlaw Territories: Environments of Insecurity/Architectures of Counter-Insurgency, forthcoming on Zone Books. She was also a founding co-editor of Grey Room, a quarterly journal about architecture, art, media, and politics published by MIT Press since 2000.

PELIN TAN is a sociologist and art historian. She concluded her Ph.D. on socially engaged art in urban space and her postdoc on the methodology of artistic research at the Art, Culture, and Technology Program of the School of Architecture and Planning, MIT. With artist Anton Vidokle, she co-directed three episodes of a sci-fi film about the future of art. Tan was an associate curator of Adhocracy, the first Istanbul Design Biennial (2012), and co-curator of Adhocracy Athens (2015). Tan is an associate professor and vice-dean of the faculty of architecture of Mardin Artuklu University. She has two forthcoming books, ARAZI (from the Critical Spatial Practices series, Sternberg Press, 2015) and Unconditional Hospitality and Threshold Architecture (dpr-barcelona, 2015).

BERNARD TSCHUMI is professor of architecture at Columbia GSAPP, and is widely known as both an architect and a theorist. His practice has designed a number of seminal projects, including the Parc de la Villette in Paris and the Acropolis Museum in Athens, and his work was recently featured in a solo show at the Centre Pompidou in Paris. His publications include Architecture Concepts: Red Is Not a Color (2012), the four-volume Event-Cities series, Architecture and Disjunction (1994), and The Manhattan Transcripts (1981). He was dean of GSAPP from 1988 to 2003.

EYAL WEIZMAN is an architect, professor of spatial and visual cultures, and director of the Centre for Research Architecture at Goldsmiths, University of London. He is the principal investigator of the Forensic Architecture project, and a founding member of the architectural collective DAAR in Beit Sahour/Palestine. His books include FORENSIS: The Architecture of Public Truth (co-edited with Forensic Architecture, 2014), Mengele's Skull (with Thomas Keenan, 2012), The Least of All Possible Evils (2009), Hollow Land (2007), and A Civilian Occupation (2003). He has worked with a variety of NGOs worldwide and was a member of the B'Tselem board of directors.

MARK WIGLEY served as the dean of the Columbia University Graduate School of Architecture, Planning and Preservation from 2004 to 2014, where he continues to teach as professor of architecture. An accomplished scholar and design teacher, Wigley has written extensively on the theory and practice of architecture. He is the author of Bucky Inc.: Architecture in the Age of Radio (2015), Constant's New Babylon: The Hyper-Architecture of Desire (1998), White Walls, Designer Dresses: The Fashioning of Modern Architecture (1995), and The Architecture of Deconstruction: Derrida's Haunt (1993). He co-edited The Activist Drawing: Retracing Situationist Architectures from Constant's New Babylon to Beyond (2001). Wigley has served as curator for widely attended exhibitions at the Museum of Modern Art, New York; The Drawing Center, New York; Canadian Centre for Architecture, Montreal; and Witte de With Museum, Rotterdam.

As the Nancy and George E. Rupp Professor, MABEL O. WILSON teaches architectural design and history/theory courses at Columbia University's GSAPP and is appointed as a Senior Fellow at the Institute for Research in African American Studies. Her scholarly essays have appeared in numerous journals and books on critical geography, memory studies, art, and architecture. Her book Negro Building: Black Americans in the World of Fairs and Museums (University of California Press, 2012) was the runner-up for the John Hope Franklin Prize (2013). She is a co-founder of Who Builds Your Architecture?, which examines the links between labor, architecture, and the global networks that form around building buildings.

⊠

GSAPP BOOKS
An imprint of The Graduate
School of Architecture,
Planning and Preservation
Columbia University
1172 Amsterdam Ave.
407 Avery Hall
New York, NY 10027

Visit our website at
arch.columbia.edu/books

GSAPP Books distributed by
Columbia University Press
at cup.columbia.edu

This book has been pro-
duced through the Office
of the Dean, Amale
Andraos, and the Office
of Print Publications.
Special thanks to Gavin
Browning and Paul Dallas
for the organization
of the conference.

ISBN 978-1-941332-07-8

SERIES EDITORS
James Graham &
Caitlin Blanchfield

VOLUME EDITOR
James Graham

SERIES DESIGN
Neil Donnelly &
Stefan Thorsteinsson

VOLUME DESIGN
Neil Donnelly &
Sean Yendrys

COPY EDITOR
Ellen Tarlin

PRINTER
Die Keure

LIBRARY OF CONGRESS CATALOGING-
IN-PUBLICATION DATA
2000+ (Conference)
(2014 : Columbia University)
2000+ : the urgencies of
architectural theory /
Convened by Mark Wigley ;
Edited by James Graham.
  pages cm
Includes bibliographical
references.
 ISBN 978-1-941332-07-8
1. Architecture--Philosophy--
Congresses. I. Title.
 NA2500.A15 2014
 720.1--dc23

2015022059